SOCIAL CURRENTS IN NORTH AFRICA

T0386717

OSAMA ABI-MERSHED

(*Editor*)

Social Currents in North Africa

جـامـعـة جـورجـتـاون قـطـر
GEORGETOWN UNIVERSITY QATAR

Center *for* International *and* Regional Studies

HURST & COMPANY, LONDON

Published in collaboration with Center for International and Regional Studies,
Georgetown University—Qatar in 2018 by
C. Hurst & Co. (Publishers) Ltd.,
41 Great Russell Street, London, WC1B 3PL
© Osama Abi-Mershed and the Contributors, 2018
Printed in India

The right of Osama Abi-Mershed and the Contributors to be identified as
the authors of this publication is asserted by them in accordance with the
Copyright, Designs and Patents Act, 1988.

A Cataloguing-in-Publication data record for this book
is available from the British Library.

ISBN: 9781849048279

This book is printed using paper from registered sustainable
and managed sources.

www.hurstpublishers.com

CONTENTS

v

ACKNOWLEDGMENTS

I am deeply indebted to the many colleagues and friends who supported this book project from its inception, and made its publication possible. Mehran Kamrava, Director of the Center for International and Regional Studies at Georgetown University in Qatar (CIRS), and Zahra Babar, Associate Director for Research, were the driving force and inspiration in its conceptualization. I thank them for their professionalism, collegiality, and trust throughout the process, for their rewarding efforts in convening our distinguished group of contributing scholars, and for their generous mentoring of our working group discussions under the auspices of the CIRS.

I am equally grateful to Suzi Mirgani, Managing Editor of CIRS Publications, for her meticulous and substantive review of the enclosed chapters, and for her invaluable editorial advice and input. I also thank Jackie Starbird, Vicki Valosik, Thayer Hastings, and Jason Cardinali for their very careful reading of the chapters, and for their instrumental revisions, analyses, and summaries of the content.

Through the different stages of this project book, I benefited immensely from the advice of Lahouari Addi, Mahfoud Amara, and Loubna Skalli Hanna, and from the incomparable assistance of Haya Al Noaimi, Elizabeth Wanucha, Valbona Zenku, Barb Gillis, Dwaa Osman, Islam Hassan, Jackie Starbird, and Misba Bhatti. I also offer my genuine appreciation to the Qatar Foundation for its support of research and other scholarly endeavors, to the anonymous reviewers for their constructive feedback, and to Michael Dwyer, Jon de Peyer, Daisy Leitch, Camilla Wyatt, and Jack McGinn for their editorial input and support.

Finally, I am extremely grateful for the commitments of our contributors to the project, and for the investments in time and effort. While the Arab upris-

ACKNOWLEDGMENTS

ings are a recent historical development in the region, their academic attention to the political, socio-cultural, and economic affairs of North Africa is longstanding, and their contributions to this volume are the product of many years of research and reflection. I thank them for sharing their individual findings in our collective volume, and for their exemplary patience as we brought the long process of publication to its completion.

CONTRIBUTORS

Osama Abi-Mershed is Associate Professor of History and former Director of the Center for Contemporary Arab Studies at Georgetown University. His academic research focuses on the ideologies and practices of colonial modernization in nineteenth-century Algeria, and on processes of state- and nation-making in France and North Africa. His most recent publications include the introductory chapter in *Perspectives on Western Sahara: Myths, Nationalisms, and Geopolitics* (Rowman & Littlefield, 2014), the book *Apostles of Modernity: Saint-Simonians and the French Civilizing Mission in Algeria* (Stanford University Press, 2010), and the edited book, *Trajectories of Education in the Arab World: Legacies and Challenges* (Routledge, 2010).

Aomar Boum is Associate Professor of Anthropology at the University of California, Los Angeles. His research interests revolve around the Middle East as well as North, West, and Sub-Saharan Africa. His main research explores how generations of Moroccan Muslims remember, picture, and construct Moroccan Jews, Jewishness, and Judaism. His most recent publications include *Memories of Absence: How Muslims Remember Jews in Morocco* (Stanford University Press, 2013). He is currently finishing a co-authored manuscript on the monarchy, Jews and Holocaust politics in Morocco; and a single authored book on the Baha'i Question in Morocco.

Charis Boutieri is Assistant Professor in the Social Anthropology of the Middle East at King's College London. Her research addresses knowledge production and dissemination in North Africa (Morocco and Tunisia), the imbrication of colonial, nationalist, and international development agendas in the structure and experience of education, language and power, lived democracy and democratization, and youth. Her recent publications include

Learning in Morocco: Language Politics and the Abandoned Educational Dream (Indiana University Press, 2016), a contribution in *Wired Citizenship: Youth Learning and Activism in the Middle East* (Routledge, 2014), and articles in the *Anthropology and Education Quarterly* (2013), and the *International Journal for Middle East Studies* (2012). She has also written opinion pieces for the online publications *Jadaliyya* and *Open Democracy* and is co-founder of the Maghreb Academic Network, the first academic forum focused on the Maghreb region in the UK.

Matt Buehler is a 2017 fellow at Harvard University's Middle East Initiative at the Belfer Center for Science and International Affairs within the John F. Kennedy School of Government. He is an assistant professor of political science at the University of Tennessee, and is also a global security fellow at the Howard H. Baker Center for Public Policy. Previously, he was a post-doctoral fellow at the Center for International and Regional Studies, Georgetown University in Qatar. His research area is comparative politics with expertise in the Middle East, and his interests include democratization, authoritarianism, the Arab uprisings, public opinion research, Islamist movements, and North African politics. His book, *Why Alliances Fail: Opposition Coalitions between Islamists and Leftists in North Africa*, is under review with Syracuse University Press. Other recent publications include: "The Autocrat's Advisors: Opening the Black Box or Ruling Coalitions in Tunisia's Authoritarian Regime" (2017) and "Do You Have 'Connections' at the Courthouse? An Original Survey on Informal Influence and Judicial Rulings in Morocco" (2016), both published in *Political Research Quarterly*. Most recently, he has completed public opinion polls in North Africa on diverse topics such as migration, nuclear nonproliferation, and legal reform.

Francesco Cavatorta is Associate Professor in the Department of Political Science at Université Laval in Quebec, Canada. He previously served as Senior Lecturer in International Relations and Middle East Politics at the School of Law and Government at Dublin City University in Ireland. His research focuses on democratization and authoritarianism in the Arab world, the role of Islamist parties and movements, and the dynamics of civil society. His most recent publications include articles in *Middle East Law and Governance, Mediterranean Politics, Democratization, Middle Eastern Studies*, and the *Journal of Political Ideologies*. With Fabio Merone he co-edited *Salafism after the Arab Awakening: Contending with People's Power* (Hurst, 2016). He is co-author of the textbook *Politics and Governance in the Middle*

East (Palgrave, 2015) and co-editor of *Civil Society Activism in Syria and Iran* (Lynne Rienner, 2013).

Nouri Gana is Associate Professor of Comparative Literature and Near Eastern Languages and Cultures at the University of California, Los Angeles. He has published articles and chapters on the literatures and cultures of the Arab world and its diasporas in such scholarly venues as *Comparative Literature Studies*, *PMLA*, *Public Culture*, and *Social Text*. He also contributed op-eds to *The Guardian*, *El Pais*, *Electronic Intifada*, *Jadaliyya*, and *CounterPunch*. He is the author of *Signifying Loss: Toward a Poetics of Narrative Mourning* (Bucknell University Press, 2011), and the editor of *The Making of the Tunisian Revolution: Contexts, Architects, Prospects* and *The Edinburgh Companion to the Arab Novel in English* (Edinburgh University Press, 2013). He is currently completing a book manuscript on the politics of melancholia in the Arab world and another on the history of cultural dissent in colonial and postcolonial Tunisia.

Ricardo René Larémont is professor of political science and sociology at SUNY Binghamton and an Atlantic Council Senior Scholar. His principal books include: *Al-tasawuf al-maghrebi: qadaya muasira* (Moroccan Cultural Studies Centre, 2017) with Khalid Bekkaoui; *Pursuing Security and Shared Development in Euro-Mediterranean Migrations* (Aracne, 2017) with Emanuela Claudia del Re; *Revolution, Revolt, and Reform in North Africa* (Routledge, 2013); *Al-rabia al-arabi: al-intifada w'al islah w'al-thawra* (Al-Maaref, 2013) with Youssef Sawani; *Islamic Law and Politics in Northern Nigeria* (Africa World Press, 2011); *Borders, Nationalism, and the African State* (Lynne Rienner, 2005); *The Causes of War and the Consequences of Peacekeeping in Africa* (Heinemann, 2002); and, *Islam and the Politics of Resistance in Algeria, 1783–1992* (Africa World Press, 2000). His research has been supported by the Carnegie Corporation, the Ford Foundation, the Rockefeller Foundation, the United States Institute of Peace, the Office of Naval Research, and the United States Department of Education.

Fabio Merone is a post-doctoral fellow at Ghent University. His research focuses on the evolution of Islamism in Tunisian democratic transition. He has been based in Tunisia for over twelve years and is currently working on a project titled, "Tunisia as a secure state: Salafism and post-revolutionary politics in the aftermath of Arab authoritarianism." He has published articles in *Democratization*, *Middle East Policy*, the *British Journal of Middle Eastern Studies*, *Middle East Law and Governance* and the *Journal of Political*

Ideologies. He is also co-editor of the volume *Salafism after the Awakening: Contending with People's Power* (Hurst, 2016).

Zekeria Ould Ahmed Salem is Associate Professor in the Department of Political Science at Northwestern University in Chicago. Previously, he was Professor of Political Science at the University of Nouakchott in Mauritania. He was a visiting Fulbright Scholar at the University of Florida from 2010–2011, and served subsequently as a Senior Visiting Fellow at the Institute for Advanced Study in Paris (2012) and Nantes (2013). His most recent book is titled *Prêcher dans le Désert: Islam politique et changement social en Mauritanie* (Karthala, 2013). Other publications include a case-study chapter on Mauritania in *Islamist Radicalization in North Africa: Politics and Process* (Routledge, 2011), a chapter on the transformations in the Haratin movement in Mauritania in *Movers and Shakers: Social Movements in Africa* (Brill, 2009), and a chapter in *Islam and Muslim Politics in Africa* (Palgrave Macmillan, 2007). He has also published articles in the *Canadian Journal of African Studies* (2010) and *The Journal of North African Studies* (2005).

Paul A. Silverstein is Professor of Anthropology at Reed College. He is the author of *Algeria in France* and co-editor of *Memory and Violence in the Middle East and North Africa* (Indiana University Press, 2004, 2006). His recent research on Amazigh activism, racial politics, migration, and territorial development in southeastern Morocco has appeared in *The Journal of North African Studies*, *Material Religion*, *Nations and Nationalism*, *The Brown Journal of World Affairs*, and the *Middle East Report*, as well as in a number of edited volumes. He is co-editor of the book series "Public Cultures of the Middle East and North Africa" with Indiana University Press, and chair of the board of directors of the Middle East Research and Information Project (MERIP).

Alice Wilson is Lecturer in Social Anthropology at the University of Sussex, UK. Her research interests include state power, sovereignty, citizenship, taxation, and forced migration, with a geographical focus on the Middle East and North Africa. Her book *Sovereignty in Exile: A Saharan Liberation Movement Governs* (University of Pennsylvania Press, 2016) examines revolutionary power in the government-in-exile led by the liberation movement from Western Sahara. *Sovereignty in Exile* won Honorable Mention in the 2017 book prize for the Middle East Section of the American Anthropological Association. Wilson is co-editor of the special issue *Understanding Legitimacy: Perspectives from Anomalous Geopolitical Spaces* in *Geoforum*.

1

SOCIAL CURRENTS IN NORTH AFRICA

Osama Abi-Mershed

The contributions to this volume are the outcome of two research workshops on "Social Currents in the Maghreb" organized by the Center for International and Regional Studies (CIRS) at Georgetown University at Qatar in January and June 2014. Scholars in the field of North African or Maghrebi studies were invited to reflect upon their specialized disciplinary or methodological approaches to the region, and comment on the overall validity of North Africa as a cohesive geo-historical unit for social scientific analysis. Such critical reassessments of the disciplinary contours of North African studies have become all the more desirable in light of the momentous and unforeseen socio-political upheavals, known as the Arab uprisings, that started in Tunisia in December 2010. The "territory-crossing" reach and substantive implications of the uprisings have compelled North Africanists to review some of the paradigmatic and procedural assumptions in their field of studies, and to don fresh conceptual and methodological lenses when reading Arab societies more broadly. To this end, participants in the CIRS workshops were encouraged to contemplate the following academic questions: have the Arab uprisings exposed heretofore under-estimated regional commonalities for historians and social scientists to explain? Can post-uprising research promote greater analytic rigor and disciplinary synergies in North African studies, to the benefit of more varied trans-regional and comparative perspectives on national developments?

In a recent assessment of the field of North African studies, James MacDougall and Robert Parks noted that it remains fragmented and polarized between the structural and general methods favored by political scientists and economists, and the more localized and particular lenses of sociologists and cultural anthropologists.[1] This "multi-scalar dilemma," or the forced correlation between macro- and micro-level phenomena and considerations, is best illustrated by the proclivity among North Africanists to confine the historical unity of the Maghreb to its "formative" colonial past, while affording the territorial nation-state undue primacy in post-colonial case studies. The tendency, according to MacDougall and Parks, "has restricted possible research agendas and the insights that might be gained from combining different levels of analysis in different locations across political frontiers."[2] With this and similar verdicts in mind,[3] the CIRS workshops sought, first, to consider the regional implications of the popular protests of 2010–2011, and second, to test the capacity of individual case studies to suggest a unifying analytical and conceptual understanding of the region as a whole.

With regard to the first concern, the contributors to this volume— renowned scholars in the disciplines of political science, history, sociology, anthropology, and media studies—have engaged deeply and critically with the latest social scientific literature on the Maghreb. Separately, their theoretical and empirical approaches to the subject matter aim to situate the distinct structural properties of North African societies, and their individual historical and material specificities, within the broad context of regional and international developments. Taken as a whole, their individual findings confirm that the scientific legibility of North Africa is not fully captured in fixed political divisions and periodizations, or by state- and elite-centered processes alone. Rather, their chapters refine the geo-historical unity of the Maghreb by accounting for social connectivities and flows within the nation-state and across political boundaries. Accordingly, the chapters collected within this volume demonstrate that non-institutional phenomena across time and space—in this case, the congealing of individual ideals and experiences into group practices and social mobilizations—are equally formative to the ongoing project of post-colonial sovereignty, to social construction and deployments of state power, and to local outlooks on social equity, economic prospects, and cultural identity.

Second, the workshop participants were called upon to engage with the overarching theme of "social currents", defined here as the manifestation in collective social practices and actions of the experiences and values held in common by members of a given society, and which are essential to their individual identification with larger social groupings. In attempting to historicize the impulses that motivated the Arab uprisings, the organizers of the workshops aimed to shed light on the weight of collective identifications in mobilizing socio-political action across North Africa and the Middle East. Social currents were to serve as the prism through which to take meaningful stock of the multiple individual principles, dispositions, and pursuits that merged into the collective and transnational protests of 2010–2011.

Here, the insights of Émile Durkheim (1858–1917) concerning the connections between the moral norms that govern a given society and the collective actions of its individual members may offer an instructive vantage point for historical and sociological analyses of the Arab uprisings, and perhaps provide the common conceptual and empirical thread linking the various contributions to this volume.[4] Durkheim starts from the principle that social groups are as bound together by material relations and factual contracts as they are by the normative beliefs, moral consensus, and rules of conduct that undergird the stability and perpetuation of any social order in a particular time and place. He devised the notion of a "collective consciousness" to describe the mental processes by which individual beings come to identify with larger social groups and structures. The collective consciousness exercises an internal regulative effect on autonomous social actors. It entrenches a collective moral discipline that sanctions or prohibits the decisions and practices of individual actors. Yet, according to Durkheim, the common beliefs and dispositions of individual actors are also externally visible to the extent that they are integral to the established socio-political order. They are legible "social facts" because they are products of, and subject to, various routinized forms of social control:

> Society is not simply an aggregate of individuals, but is a being which has existed prior to those who today compose it, and which will survive them; which influences (acts upon) them more than they influence it, and which has its own life, consciousness, its own interests and destiny.[5]

Durkheim's social facts, in other words, are historically and sociologically observable in their propensity to induce individual members to act according to group filiation, shared values, cultural standards, and collective patterns or social currents rather than personal preference.[6] To this effect, the

3

volume's contributors have considered a range of formal or internal social facts in North Africa in an effort to determine their role in priming the mobilizations of 2010–2011, as well as detect their resonance in subsequent socio-political developments.

Several chapters underscore the salience of normative beliefs and rules of conduct in maintaining (or challenging) the established socio-political order. They consider a range of official and popular projects to redefine the moral contract between North African states and societies, whether undertaken by governments, labor associations, Islamist parties, educational reformers, grassroots activists, or producers of cultural signifiers. Some contributors have situated their understanding of social currents within the formal politico-legal institutions of governance and their socio-historical effects on systemic political alignments, distributions of wealth, and group affiliations. Others have focused more intently on the ideological mediations by which North Africans are reproduced as subjects of state power: educational systems, mass media communications and representations, cultural and artistic productions, etc. Their combined approaches to social currents in North Africa compel us to reflect more profoundly on the institutional structures and ideological stimuli that have informed recent group behavior and political mobilizations in the Maghreb, and to articulate more theoretical understandings of the social factors that caused the collective needs of North Africans to pressure or outpace the existing regulatory order, establish new social solidarities, and in many cases, trigger a mass social movement.

Indeed, by exposing the differential, often coercive, power of collective affiliations and beliefs upon the individual negotiations with the social environment, several contributors raise critical questions concerning the long-term historical consequences of the tumultuous events of 2010–2011, from the workings of religious beliefs in the public sphere to the moral economies of language instruction and cultural production. Their analyses of the institutional and cultural parameters of social currents in the Maghreb leave little doubt that while the uprisings may turn out to be transitory and evanescent, their legacies will endure in the material and mental transformations that have been bequeathed to future generations of North Africans.[7] More significantly, their distinct assessments of the renegotiated fields of political action in the wake of 2011 introduce conceptual paradigms with which to account for the new social facts that have recently empowered North Africans to act collectively. Together, the following chapters deliver critical comments on the genealogies of behavioral and ideological norms in contemporary North Africa, offer insightful perspectives on the new rationalities of governance after 2011, and raise important conceptual interpretations for the field of North Africa studies to consider.

In their review of the Islamist currents in Morocco and Tunisia, Francesco Cavatorta and Fabio Merone investigate the socio-political decisions and maneuvers taken by the Justice and Development Party (PJD) and the Nahda Movement (Ennahda), respectively, to gain access to state power in the aftermath of the 2011 uprisings. Their findings challenge directly the notion of a "post-Islamist" phase in Arab politics, and raise critical observations regarding the political compatibility of Islamist principles with democratic governance. More significantly, their study of the electoral strategies of Ennahda and the PJD exposes the increasing diversity in the socio-political discourses and practices of the two parties since 2011. According to Cavatorta and Merone, formal institutional realities and the imperatives of electoral success compelled Ennahda and the PJD to behave like institutionalized parties in their respective political systems. They negotiated their entry into coalition governments by modulating their political platforms and compromising on core Islamist aims, such as the establishment of an "Islamic State" and the application of *shari'ah* law. These political compromises were not without risks to the Islamist credentials of the PJD and Ennahda, as disaffected constituents may turn to informal communal or familial avenues to attain the desired societal transformations. Thus, according to Cavatorta and Merone, the advances gained by the PJD and Ennahda since 2011 have not only introduced a more refined Islamist identity and agenda into state politics, but have also stimulated important social transformations in the private sphere.

In a similar vein, Ricardo René Larémont reviews the uneasy and turbulent historical relationship between North African governments from Morocco to Egypt and their resident Sufi and Salafi organizations. Echoing the comments of Cavatorta and Merone, Larémont's analysis suggests that the widening range in the political practices of Islamist parties is also producing different conceptual interpretations of foundational Islamist, in this case Salafist, notions and models. He breaks down the broad networks of Salafi or Sufi associations, active since the nineteenth century, to underline the existence of distinct sub-currents within each, and presents the post-2011 context as a critical historical juncture in the evolving interactions within the State-Salafi-Sufi triad. In the aftermath of the Arab uprisings, resurgent Salafi organizations, notably the Muslim Brotherhood in Egypt, the Ennahda Movement in Tunisia, the Justice and Construction Party in Libya, and the Justice and

Development Party in Morocco, achieved important socio-political gains. While their successes were stimulated mainly by social injustice and poor living conditions, the parties also gained traction for their ideological criticism of secular politics. However, North African authorities since 2011 have played upon the important variations within Salafi organizations across North Africa, and have promoted Sufi brotherhoods and institutional Salafi parties to counter the sway of jihadi Salafi groups that are more prone to advocate violent tactics against the state and more likely to affiliate with the Al-Qaeda network. The strategy has been particularly effective in Morocco, where the PJD party has led recent coalition governments, and a member of the Sufi Qadiriyya-Boutchichiyya Brotherhood has served as Minister of Awqaf (religious endowments) and Islamic Affairs.

Shifting from Islamist politics to labor activism, Matt Buehler contrasts the development of labor unions in Morocco with their Tunisian and Egyptian counterparts, especially as a means to illustrate the effects of the 2010–2011 uprisings on labor organization and activism. He specifically follows the fluctuating fortunes of Moroccan labor unions since the 1950s, especially in terms of their relations with the ruling monarchy. The influence of organized labor on government policies waned significantly in the 1970s, and by the 1990s, labor activism was limited almost exclusively to the public sector in the wake of the government's policies of economic privatization and political marginalization. In 2011, however, Moroccan labor unions capitalized on the gains made by sister organizations in post-revolution Tunisia and Egypt, and exploited the monarchy's fears over spreading civil unrest and public disorder to exact fundamental concessions from the government. During this campaign, which preceded the political protests organized by the 20 February Movement, different groups and sectors within organized labor coordinated their demands into a unified platform, and their manpower eventually amplified the ranks of opposition groups like 20 February. According to Buehler, while labor unions in Morocco have yet to realize all their demands from 2011, his findings point to the significant development of synergies between organized labor and other opposition movements calling for broader political and socio-economic reform.

Like Buehler, Paul Silverstein also considers the impact of the 1990s on socio-political activism in North Africa; in this case, the movement for the recognition of Amazigh cultural rights. Silverstein outlines the evolution of Amazigh activism from its origins as a movement of dissent against the hegemonizing Arabization of Maghrebi culture and education, to the increasing legitimization of Amazigh rights and traits following the political shift to "neoliberal governance" in the 1990s. With neoliberal governance, Silverstein claims, Amazigh identity and culture assumed a popular aesthetic appeal through commodification, and activism shifted its focus from cultural and linguistic recognition to issues of social and economic justice. The "mainstreaming" of Amazigh activism, its growing legitimacy and professionalization, was attained at the cost of closer alignments with governmental bodies. To this extent, the specific struggles of the Amazigh movement may be taken as a yardstick with which to gauge larger shifts in the political and social landscapes of North Africa. Indeed, for Silverstein, the transnational dimensions of Amazigh identity and the "horizontalism" in Amazigh decision making provide openings for scholars to examine state-society relations independently of national frameworks.

Silverstein's study of Amazigh politics finds many echoes in Charis Boutieri's ethnographic study of the politics of language instruction in Morocco. The starting point for her analysis is the amended Constitution of 1 July 2011, which among other purported reforms, reinstated Arabic *fusha* as the official language of the Kingdom, recognized *amazighiyya* as its second official language, and called for the preservation of *hassaniyya* (a variety of Maghrebi Arabic). The constitutional amendments pertaining to the plural linguistic identities of Morocco have been interpreted as the culmination of the shift, beginning in the 1990s, away from the state's monocultural focus on *fusha*. Moreover, in the post-2011 context of popular mobilization and defiance, they have embodied one of the government's myriad accommodating responses to pro-democracy pressures. Boutieri, however, challenges the very "universality" of neoliberal principles, especially in their implications for national educational policies, and homes in on the pressures exerted upon the latter by the labor demands of global capitalism. She shows how the assumed universalism of liberal democratization and multilingualism in effect privileges the structural and cultural hierarchies of the global market, and at the same time, ensures the supremacy and efficiency of the ideology of global capitalism. To this extent, the institutionalization of multilingualism by the Constitution of 2011 enshrined the socio-linguistic hierarchies that satisfy the exigencies of global markets. The kingdom's bifurcated private and public educational systems continue to prioritize globalized languages, while limiting opportunities for non-English or non-French speakers and marginalizing "minority" indigenous languages. *Darija* (spoken Arabic) is still the common means of expression among Moroccans, who despite the inclusion of *amazighiyya* in the Constitution of 2011, remain generally skeptical about its standardization and integration into the public school system.

Currents in social and political activism are also at the heart of the individual chapters by Zekeria Ould Ahmed Salem and Alice Wilson. Ould Ahmed Salem examines mobilizations led by Haratin activists—associated mainly with the El-Hor Movement—against the enduring practices of slavery in Mauritania, while Wilson looks at the efforts by pro-Polisario militants to diversify the movement's international base of aid and support. Ould Ahmed Salem's exposition of the legacies of slavery, which endure in such practices as domestic servitude, serfdom, and debt bondage, is a sobering reminder of the deep historical roots of Mauritania's "peculiar institution". While Mauritanian authorities have recently rejoined local and international calls to abolish such forms of enslavement, the rulings of the special criminal court to prosecute trials against purveyors of slavery are rarely enforced, and manumitted Haratin often remain economically dependent on their former masters. Moreover, socio-cultural prejudices discriminate against the Haratin, and preclude them from equal economic and educational opportunities and access to basic services. Despite this reality, Ould Ahmed Salem notes that anti-slavery views have been increasingly adopted in public discourse, and main-stream political parties are vying for popularity by adding abolitionist rhetoric to their electoral platforms. As a result, through their anti-slavery activism, the Haratin have emerged as a distinct "social group", and increased public aware-ness of their cause has become the site for negotiating identity and formal politics in Mauritania. To this extent, Ould Ahmed Salem sees potential links between abolitionist struggles in Mauritania and the 2010–2011 uprisings.

Wilson revisits the history of the Polisario Front through her analysis of the movement's changing base of support. From its origins in the early 1970s as a "classic" Third World liberation movement, closely aligned with the regional Cold War proxies, the Polisario developed into a social movement with mul-tiple sources of financial and political backing, including critical support from non-state actors, such as multilateral organizations, international solidarity and aid association, and the Sahrawi diaspora. In her chapter, Wilson surveys multiple Sahrawi advocacy organizations and capitalizes on extensive field-work in refugee camps to reveal the Front's effectiveness in diversifying its sources of support, while balancing contradictory interests among its various sponsors. To this extent, she delivers a useful corrective to conventional assess-ments of the Polisario Front as a static organization, and of the conflict in Western Sahara as a political stalemate. Nor does she present the movement as the exclusive client of the Algerian government. She asserts rather that the active diversification of its support base has opened the Polisario Front to broader international influences, and especially to the values and discourses of diasporic and European-based groups. This growing influence explains partially the movement's recent embrace of human rights standards. According to Wilson, this conversion, although it occurred "on the eve" or "on the margins" of the events of 2010–2011, still invites comparisons between the Polisario and other social movements.

In his approach to cultural dissent in Tunisia, Nouri Gana studies the texts of five films to clarify how they gradually cultivated a sensitivity for public dissidence among Tunisian viewers. Gana explains that with the overthrow of Zine El Abidine Ben Ali in January 2011, all evidence or suggestion of association between "producers of culture", film directors and actors among them, and the fallen regime became grounds for public scrutiny and social censure. Yet, Gana is interested in gauging the revolutionary credentials of artistic and cultural productions, and he examines Tunisian films mainly for their capacity to challenge normative socio-political realities—the patriarchal order, for example—and thus to empower calls for social reform by sharpening the critical political focus of their viewers. He selects five films that he finds central to encouraging critical public dissonance with the normative ideologies of the Tunisian state, and credits them with having amplified public appeals for social justice, and thus paving the road to popular protests. To this effect, Gana traces historical cycles and continuities between the current post-revolutionary context and the early decades of post-colonial independence. In both contexts, cinema served as the forum for shaping the collective public condemnation of extant socio-political conditions. When the heightened expectations of national liberation and political enfranchisement were unmet, Tunisian cultural productions and films functioned increasingly as a site for contesting socio-political norms. Their former denunciations of colonial injustice were reoriented to address the inequities and abuses of the post-colonial state.

Aomar Boum, finally, examines the revival of interest in the Jewish heritage of Morocco and Tunisia following the signing of the Oslo Declaration of Principles in 1993. While "unofficial" exchanges between the North African states and Israel had commenced in the 1960s—for the promotion of tourism in the case of Tunisia, and for agricultural and military cooperation in the case of Morocco—Boum argues that the public discourse on the preservation of North Africa's Jewish heritage has been a critical and overlooked factor in modulating the triangular relationship between the authorities of Morocco and Tunisia, their resident and native Jewish communities, and the State of Israel. In the 1980s, such arrangements persisted, although they focused increasingly on "Jewish Heritage Tourism," which was appreciated as a boon for the local economies. Paradoxically, the triangular relationship entered a particularly ambivalent phase after Oslo, as now permissible official diplomatic relations with Israel had to be cultivated discreetly in the face of growing popular affinity for the Palestinian cause following the First Intifada (1987–1993). Tunisian and Moroccan authorities continued to promote Jewish Heritage Tourism in the context of growing local anti-normalization activism. Thus, Boum historicizes the efforts to conserve the Jewish cultural legacy of Tunisia and Morocco, and the strength of his study resides in his detailed examination of the tensions between the historical recognition of North Africa's Jewish heritage—exemplified here by public attempts to educate Tunisians and Moroccans about the histories of their country's enduring Jewish communities—and local anti-Israeli sentiments. The tensions have resulted in what Boum labels the "museumification", or the visible commodification, of North African "Jewishness" in spaces where Jewish life had been rendered invisible in practice.

The contributors to this volume, through their varied individual disciplinary approaches and perspectives, have sought to identify and explore a range of emerging conceptual and practical questions in the field of North African studies following the events of 2010–2011. Their rigorous analyses of the ongoing consequences of the Arab uprisings add a much needed supplement to the existing literature on the Middle East and North Africa. Hopefully, they will also encourage further scholarship on the structural and ideological mobilizations behind "social currents" in North Africa and the broader Arab world.

2

ISLAMIST PARTIES AND TRANSFORMATION IN TUNISIA AND MOROCCO

Francesco Cavatorta and *Fabio Merone*

The arrival to power of Islamist parties in Tunisia, Morocco, and Egypt in 2011, following the events of the "Arab Awakening," has led to renewed scholarly interest in Islamist politics.[1] Prior to the Awakening, Islamist parties and movements had nearly faded into insignificance within the scholarship of the Middle East and North Africa, as they seemed to no longer be the most relevant political actors in the region. Two factors contributed to this misperception. First, the thesis of "upgraded Arab authoritarianism" suggested that authoritarian rule in the region would endure unchallenged for the foreseeable future because it had been capable of renewing itself through the 1990s and 2000s. Accordingly, specialists concluded that it was more productive to look at the mechanisms that ensured authoritarian survival rather than to examine long-standing opposition movements.[2] Second, other social actors, namely grassroots movements and liberal groups with a seemingly non-political agenda, were regarded as the new protagonists of Arab civil societies.[3] In addition, Islamism seemed to have moved away from its focus on political power

11

and towards non-political activities.[4] As a result, scholars focused increasingly on either "post-Islamism" or armed Islamist groups, and thus abandoned to a certain extent the study of what could be termed "Orthodox Islamism."[5] The "thesis of post-Islamism," which finds its roots in the works of Asef Bayat and Olivier Roy,[6] holds that politically engaged Islamism, having failed to effect macro-political change by establishing the Islamic state, was progressively disappearing as a political project in favor of more private practices of religiosity. Concurrently, as the "public" engagement of Islamists degenerated throughout the 2000s into acts of violence committed by myriad armed groups operating within and beyond the region, scholars began to pay greater attention to the phenomenon of jihadism.

Thus, with few exceptions among scholars,[7] Islamist parties were gradually neglected as objects of study. This has been particularly true with respect to the Maghreb, where it was deemed that Islamist actors had apparently given up their vision of radical transformation and "disappeared" in the face of modernity, so often touted by authoritarian leaders in the region.[8] In North Africa, Islamism had been contained by cooptation in the political process,[9] by repression,[10] or by self-exclusion.[11] Inevitably then, many policy and academic circles were taken by surprise by the rise of Islamist parties in 2011. Once the general shock subsided, a number of research agendas were developed in order to account for the landslide victory of the Muslim Brotherhood in Egypt, the revival of Ennahda's fortunes in Tunisia, and the impressive results of the Party for Justice and Development (PJD) in the Moroccan legislative elections. At the same time, the thesis of post-Islamism came under severe criticism in the face of concrete evidence that the political project of Islamist parties was not just alive, but was succeeding at the polls.

This chapter surveys the most important debates generated by these research agendas, and argues that, despite some impressive contributions, their focus remains generally limited to certain aspects of Islamist politics. Specifically, post-2011 research agendas continue to dismiss the relevance of party politics due to the longstanding belief—quite justified in most cases— that parties in the Middle East and particularly in North Africa are insignificant political actors. In light of the events of 2011, however, it is necessary to examine party politics more closely, especially the ideologically driven Islamist parties that often hold the key to the success or failure of regime change in the region. Scrutinizing Islamist parties can reveal critical social, political, generational, and ideological factors affecting Islamism as a whole, including the Salafi trend. More specifically, scholars must overcome their tendency to overlook the profound diversity, fragmentation, and tensions that exist within Islamism proper, as noted by Francois Burgat.[12] Such diversity plays a role not only in the political institutional arena (i.e., electoral competition between different Islamist parties), but also in social domains, where there are heated ideological debates and diverse instances and forms of activism within the Islamist sphere that many observers have yet to fully grasp and analyze. Finally, the chapter points to the seeming paradox of the thesis of post-Islamism, which in some ways has been confirmed rather than challenged by the arrival of the Moroccan PJD and the Tunisian Ennahda to power.

Scholarly debates after the Awakening

The prominent role of Islamist parties in the aftermath of the Arab Awakening has led to renewed interest in Islamist politics, with numerous scholars seeking to analyze different aspects of the re-emergence of Islamism. At least six distinct research agendas have emerged from this intellectual re-engagement.

The first agenda regurgitated the debate about the full compatibility,[13] incompatibility,[14] or partial compatibility of Islam with democracy.[15] This research line of inquiry, long deemed a rather sterile and pointless debate, was re-ignited as soon as Islamist parties started to win elections in the region, as highlighted in the works of Brumberg and later by Masoud.[16] Thus, the scholarly community endured a rehash of many arguments claiming that Islam—wrongly conflated with Islamist parties—was not consistent in any meaningful way with democracy. Islamist parties were therefore condemned *a priori* as undemocratic and illiberal. The debate naturally intensified after the Muslim Brotherhood in Egypt was ousted from power by a military coup in July 2013.

The second agenda consisted of reassessing the thesis of political "moderation through inclusion." This thesis, designed to explain the progressive loss of radicality of communist and socialist parties in Western Europe as they became integrated in liberal-democratic political structures, postulates that involving highly ideological parties in plural institutional politics generates a moderating effect on the parties themselves. This means that they recognize the benefits of "playing" the game and its associated constraints such as the need for compromise so as to broaden their appeal. In short, they have to moderate their most radical stances in order to participate and be successful. In a 2011 article, Schwedler analyzed in great detail the validity of the moderation thesis as it pertains to Islamist parties,[17] but no Islamist party in the Arab world had, by that point, been able to compete in fully free and fair elections. Following the

Arab Awakening however, scholars could not only test the moderation thesis in practice in Egypt, Tunisia, Libya and, to a lesser extent, Morocco, but also could do so with the knowledge that Islamist parties would be crucial contributors to building ostensibly pluralistic political systems. Thus, scholars used a number of different methodologies to test the moderating effect of institutional inclusion and participation on Islamist parties.[18]

The third agenda aimed to observe the performance of Islamist parties in power. This line of inquiry attempted to evaluate how Islamist parties fared in government, how they managed to deal with the imperatives of complex governance, how they interacted with other political movements and institutional actors, and what kinds of policies they promoted. This evaluative effort concentrated mostly on Ennahda in Tunisia and on the Egyptian Muslim Brotherhood until it was ousted from power. It attempted mainly to understand the ways in which these parties navigated between their ideological tenets, the realities of daily politicking, and the pressures coming from the streets, where expectations of change were significant.[19]

The fourth agenda embarked on what may be labelled a scholarship of "rediscovery," whereby its main objective consisted of revisiting the reasons why Islamism, as both a social and political force, was neglected in academic and policy circles. This scholarship attempted to explain how Islamism managed to survive and then thrive once political liberalization occurred. This strand is particularly interested in the Tunisian case, where Islamism had seemingly disappeared in the later years of the Ben Ali regime, but made a significant comeback following his downfall.[20]

The fifth agenda comprised more policy-oriented studies that looked at the implications of the failures of the government of Morsi, and its eventual removal by military coup.[21] The focus here is on the repercussions that the outlawing of the Muslim Brotherhood might have on Islamist politics more broadly and, in particular, on the potential move towards armed extremism given the way in which it was ejected from power despite its adherence to democratic mechanisms. In addition, there is a concern as to what the military coup might mean for Western powers and the United States more specifically, due to the way the United States implicitly welcomed the news that the Egyptian military had decided to take over political power.

The final trend in scholarship has involved renewing former interest in Salafism in response to its arrival on the political scene, with its inroads in Egypt standing out. Salafism had been a neglected topic insofar as it was discussed mainly in the context of Islamist armed violence, but the Arab

Awakening demonstrated that there is much more to it.[22] It follows that Salafism in all its different declinations—scientific, political and armed—is currently central to discussions about the social and political forces that the Arab Awakening liberated, although it is usually perceived to be a significant obstacle to the prospects of democratization in the region.[23]

Some of these research trends are certainly important and need to be explored further, especially since the openness that exists in most North African societies today provides the opportunity to examine Islamist parties in greater detail. Areas in particular need of research are the relationship between the Islamism of the Brotherhood and that of the Salafi groups, and the way Islamist parties function once they gain power and the consequences of their policies. At the same time, there are debates and discussions that do not advance our knowledge of Islamism, including the "compatibility" argument, which has been settled for some time, as well as trying to "chase" the news by delving into potential scenarios of what might happen in the future.

It is to encourage scholarship on Islamism following the changes the Awakening brought about that Stein,[24] for instance, and the academics around the project "Rethinking Islamist Politics"[25] call for a renewed effort at understanding Islamist ideas and groups. The political and social transformations of the Arab Awakening have engendered a number of pressing research themes regarding Islamist activism, as it is broadly understood.

Islamist parties in Tunisia and Morocco

In examining the impact of the Arab Awakening on Islamist parties, North Africa is particularly interesting since Islamist parties won legislative elections in both Tunisia and Morocco, leading them to power in coalition governments. The two cases present substantial differences because the Moroccan Islamists operate in a system where real policymaking power still resides largely with the monarchy. It should be noted that the institutional constraints the Moroccan PJD has had to contend with—such as the executive powers and religious legitimacy of the monarch as the principal political actor in the country—are very significant when compared to the democratizing environment the Tunisian Islamists operate in. However, both cases point to interesting ideological innovations and policy prescriptions that may better contribute to the understanding of their development than does the traditional "moderation through inclusion" thesis.[26] In addition, as Buehler convincingly argues, the PJD was able to use "the unrest to increase its bargaining

15

power, sideline its rivals, and win its policy demands,"[27] suggesting that their threat to become less moderate in order to achieve their political objectives was reasonably successful. The most interesting aspect of both Ennahda and the PJD's rise to power is that it does not necessarily feel like an Islamist success story. In fact, based on the linkages and cooperative agreements they had with liberal, leftist, and secular political movements, and on their experience and the policies they promoted in government, one may ask just how Islamist these two parties are. Though perhaps the questions revolve around the extent to which the ideological project of political Islam has been exhausted in light of post-Arab Awakening developments and whether these are cases of full-fledged post-Islamism. For some time, a number of scholars have believed that the Islamist political project regarding contemporary politics and, crucially, modern state-making, had lost relevance by the 1990s.[28] This was especially true in North Africa, where the modernizing secular policies most notably in Tunisia, but also in Morocco and Algeria, seemed to have introduced notions of governance—loosely based on *laicité*—that not only contradicted the Islamist project, but also were believed to be shared by the majority of the population as well as by the majority of the political and economic elites. The reality, at least electorally, has proven to be very different, with Islamist parties performing well in both Tunisia and Morocco. The electoral weight of Islamist parties should not, however, obscure the reality of the compromises they have had to make in order to be legitimately included in the political system. Thus, while the notion of post-Islamism—understood as the failure of Islamist politics and its retreat to the private sphere—might not entirely correspond to reality, it is nevertheless striking to note that the compromises made have been related to what are believed to be the distinctive, core objectives of Islamism, namely the creation of an Islamic state and the introduction of shari'ah law as the source of all legislation.[29] The relevance of this compromise is particularly clear in Tunisia. The Ennahda party, and its leader Rachid Ghannouchi, had moderated their political stances at least two decades previously when the party came out in support of democratic mechanisms and fundamental liberties.[30] Nonetheless, it was still surprising for many to see them move away from any notion of an Islamic state and instead embrace the idea of a civil state. In addition, they backed away from a confrontation with other parties and accepted that references to shari'ah law should not appear in the Constitution. In Morocco, the PJD has also accepted profound ideological and political constraints in order to enter the institutional game, and has, on a number of significant issues that are salient to its conservative constituency, adopted very pragmatic positions. There are three reasons that can explain such compromises. The first is the constraints placed upon them by the authoritarian regime, particularly in the case of the PJD. While there has been a significant step towards liberalization with the promulgation of a new constitution following large-scale protests in the country, the Moroccan political system remains in the hands of the monarchy, which retains crucial executive powers.[31] The second is the impact of coalition politics. In both Tunisia and Morocco, the Islamist parties did not win a majority of seats and therefore cannot govern alone. Both Ennahda and the PJD have had to form coalitions with political parties ideologically distant from Islamism; this awkward alliance has provided a means to keep the Islamists in check. Thus, it could be argued that the compromises are, in part, the product of coalition governments and that despite the skepticism of some, these coalition pacts have largely held.[32] Finally, both Tunisia and Morocco are home to lively and active secular civil society groups that have mobilized extensively, and often preemptively, to ensure that the aspects and policies of the Islamists deemed most deleterious would not be transformed into legislation. For example, the remarkable effort Tunisian civil society has made to defend personal status legislation (for example, women's rights) and to prevent the inclusion of references to shari'ah in the draft constitution have been effective in convincing Ennahda to accept the idea of a civil state.

Irrespective of the reasons behind the decision of Islamist parties to accept compromises and behave as pragmatic political actors, such decisions must be justified both internally and externally. As with any other political movement, Islamist parties have internal constituencies that need to be both materially and ideologically satisfied. The ascent to power has certainly allowed many within the Islamist movement to take advantage of the perks of government, both in terms of the status it confers and, to an extent, the ability to implement their policy preferences. This is particularly important for an older generation of Islamist activists who have spent considerable time in jail, in exile, or at the margins of the political system. As mentioned, however, the most significant ideological objectives of Islamism have had to be sacrificed. And this "sacrifice" is not temporary, as the conditions that prevent the creation of a genuine Islamic state are structural rather than mutable. This means that Islamist parties in Tunisia and Morocco have had to justify their pragmatist turn in ideological terms, particularly when confronting combative, secular parts of society. The Tunisian case is illustrative in this sense. There are two ways in which ideological innovations to justify political pragmatism can be seen at work when it comes to Ennahda.

First is the attempt to refer to the intellectual discourse of scholars and thinkers who do not necessarily share the views, interpretations, or strategies of the Muslim Brotherhood, which is perceived to be more rigid and ideological, and therefore less capable of accepting the necessity of political compromise, even in the renewed effort to build an effective post-colonial state. Whether this is actually true is somewhat irrelevant since there is a perception within the leadership of the party that Tunisia is a case *sui generis* where the political behavior of the Brotherhood would not be simply inefficient, but also wrong. Ghannouchi had largely departed from the ideological positions of the Brotherhood some time ago, but within the party this position was not widely shared, nor is it still. In any case, the current imperative to underline differences in the situation with which the Egyptian Muslim Brotherhood must contend in order to justify its political pacts with secular, center-left and leftist parties and its support for the new constitution has meant revisiting the work of a number of North African scholars who, in the past, argued for an approach to politics that was different from that of the Brotherhood. Chief among them is Malek Bennabi, an Algerian scholar who rose to prominence in the mid twentieth century for his writings on colonialism, Islam, democracy, and pluralism.[33] While he can be considered an Islamist, he adopted a positive view of democracy very early on. His interest was not so much in the procedures and mechanisms of democratic government as in the fact that democracy was a state of mind and a national spirit that needed to be developed, since this respect for the plurality of society was intrinsic to Islam. Crucial to his fame also was his polemic against Sayyid Qutb. While Bennabi admired Qutb's moral stance against authoritarianism and defended his right to voice his opinions on violent political change, he profoundly disagreed with his interpretation of the state of the modern Arab world. According to Bennabi, more democracy and more pluralism were far more necessary than a simple call to implement the shari'ah and suggested that accountable political structures were more important than the implementation of religious law per se. Bennabi's views were not very popular among Islamists across the Arab world who, at the time, had no interest in a positive take on democratic governance, although his work on—and against—colonialism remained important. Ghannouchi and Ennahda have often implicitly referred back to Bennabi's work to argue that democracy and pluralism are necessary and functional to the defense and promotion of Islam and the Arab-Muslim identity.[34] Bennabi's work must, of course, be considered within a wider context in which other scholars close to the "Andalusian" experience have mobilized to support the uniqueness of the Tunisian Islamist landscape, which has always been tolerant of plural identities. It might be a coincidence, but after the military coup in Egypt against the Brotherhood's elected president in the summer of 2013, Ennahda accelerated the work of the Constituent Assembly, and the Tunisian constitution was swiftly approved with the party accepting a consensual document and refraining from confronting its political rivals. In a personal interview with Ghannouchi, it became quite clear that he considered Bennabi an intellectual inspiration and claimed that he had spent time studying with him. Bennabi's work is integrated into the Tunisian context with references to Tunisian intellectual religious scholars of the nineteenth and twentieth centuries, such as Mohamed Tahar Ben Achour and his son Mohamed Fadhel Ben Achour. The latter was a modernist religious figure and a principled nationalist. Through the rediscovery of such figures, Ennahda is attempting to distance itself from the rigidity of what Ghannouchi also called "eastern" interpretations of the relationship between politics and religion. In doing so, it is nationalizing an essentially internationalist project. While most scholars accept that Islamist parties across the region operate and behave through national opportunities, constraints, and environments, the Islamist project always retains an internationalist aspect with its emphasis on a common transnational Arab-Muslim heritage that it believes should, at some point, find a common home under the same political authority. In preferring to distance itself from the ideological godfathers of Islamism and looking locally for sources of ideological legitimization, Ennahda is controversially repositioning its Islamist credentials within a very specific national and nationalist framework, emphasizing the uniqueness of the Tunisian Islamist tradition and its compatibility with the modernism of democracy, pluralism, and human rights. This is extremely important in so far as it is a pattern that might eventually be repeated elsewhere and suggests that at the ideological level there might be a shift towards accepting the current constraints of the modern nation-state as structural, and therefore unchangeable. While the Tunisian Ennahda has gone the farthest, it should be highlighted that the banned al-Adl wal-Ihsan in Morocco has also been reliant on "local" interpretations of Islamism and cannot, therefore, be easily categorized in terms of its ideological principles and sources of inspiration.[35] In some ways, this ideological debate reprises the one that had characterized the Algerian FIS in the late 1980s and early 1990s when FIS was attempting to reconcile its two dominant factions that were divided between Islamist Algerian nationalists and fully-fledged *Ikhwan*-inspired Islamists.[36] At the time, this ideological debate, which ended with the 1992 military coup, did not seem especially relevant, but it appears now that it was actually quite significant as an ideological attempt to shape Islamism according to local experiences and conditions. It is even more relevant when one thinks of the internationalist project and its emphasis on the elimination of borders that other Islamist actors, such as the al Baghdadi-led Islamic State, promote.

A second noticeable change is the arrival to positions of influence of a small, but powerful cohort of Islamist intellectuals, whose scholarly and political output might be labelled "Islamo-liberalism." Such a cohort is present in the two Islamist parties analyzed here and seems to be increasingly influential in guiding the party's strategy and shaping policy preferences. Again, this is most notable in Tunisia as its political environment allows for an easier public detection of such trends, but it is also a phenomenon that touches the Party for Justice and Development. These intellectual activists attempt to maintain a degree of coherence between Islamism, now broadly understood as a general reference term for the values inspiring the party, and the necessity of embracing a type of politics that abandons the categories of religion. In this respect, they try to combine the best of tradition with the best of modernity in order to court widespread appeal. The imperative of having to be a catch-all party is a significant problem for Islamist parties because they must appeal to multiple social constituencies that have often conflicting interests. Both Ennahda and the PJD, and previously the Algerian FIS, are reasonably popular among most sectors of society because they remain vague on socio-economic issues. Thus the work of this new generation of intellectual activists is to make sure that the program of the party and its behavior are accepted and acceptable to the other political formations (by toning down the religious rhetoric) but also sufficiently distinguishable in terms of its values to make it broadly appealing to a conservative electorate. Religion enters the picture on the issue of trust and honesty. Much is usually made of the fact that the Islamists' work in providing social services is crucial to their electoral success, but this might be overemphasized. In the Tunisian case, for example, Ennahda did extremely well in the 2011 elections without relying on an extensive or well-established network of charities. Part of the explanation for its appeal might be that voters tend to trust avowedly religious candidates more than they trust non-religious ones (or at least the ones who do not chose to display their religiosity and personal piety at every turn). Thus, Islamist parties in Tunisia and Morocco have candidates who not only possess professional experience and degrees, but also who are known to be pious. This is not done necessarily to impose a religious agenda on politics, but rather to signal that if the candidate is pious, he is inherently trustworthy and honest.

In short, the new ideological developments seem to point to the partial validity of the post-Islamism thesis when it comes to issues such as the Islamic state and shari'ah law,[37] but, at the same time, they prove post-Islamism partially incorrect in so far as the religious references remain intact and religiosity wins votes. To support this, it would be necessary to dig deeper into the convergence between the values of voters and what the parties offer, but there is a lack of reliable data or measures that could tell us what parties actually stand for and what voters perceive to be salient issues. There is plenty of anecdotal and ad hoc empirical evidence—often instrumentalized for political purposes—about the policy preferences and weight of ideology within Islamist parties just as there is anecdotal evidence about the issues that genuinely matter to voters, both at the individual and aggregate level, and how these reflect their social values. However, we do not have systematic data on any of this. There are, of course, numerous opinion polls and surveys that have been conducted to capture this sort of information, but they are not necessarily reliable and, as in the case of the Tunisian elections of October 2011, have proven far from the mark in predicting party support. A comprehensive analysis of the party's policy positions on a number of issues, including the economy, social policy, and foreign policy, would be needed in order to verify the ways in which Islamist parties position themselves on the ideological map of the country and to validate the effectiveness of this ideological repositioning—or lack thereof. The same exercise could be repeated with all political parties within the same environment. This would provide data to suggest where Islamist parties stand in relation to the other parties in the same system on a range of issues crucial to the country in question, and would permit data-based discussions as to why they might be where they are and how they do or do not differ from other parties. Such comprehensive studies have been carried out in other regions of the world through research programs, such as the "party manifestos project" or the "experts survey project" to map out parties' policy positions and their relationship to one another.[38]

As mentioned, the beliefs and choices of the electorate should also be further explored to examine the degree of convergence or divergence that exists between these beliefs and the propositions made by political parties. This is already done through instruments like the World Values Survey or the Arab-Barometer, but the data provided could be better targeted to access how the values of citizens reflect what political parties promise to deliver.

The loss of radicalité

What emerges quite clearly from the discussion above is that institutionalized Islamist political parties in Tunisia and Morocco have lost what one might call their radical edge. Before assuming power—whether isolated in opposition, as is the case of the PJD, or completely banned from political life, as with Ennahda—these parties put forth a radical image of themselves, more so in relation to the sweeping social, economic, and political changes they would undertake than in terms of the role religious precepts would play if they came to power. In these examples, their Islamist solutions were not simply religiously sanctioned, but were revolutionary because they aimed to transform society. In this sense "radicalism" should not be equated to political violence, but rather to an agenda for change that would be genuinely transformative of the social relations, institutional mechanisms, and national identity of the country. All this would be grounded and embedded in a discourse and practice of religiosity that would be the moral and ideological justification for launching such changes. The *radicalité* of the project comes therefore not so much from the tools that would be employed to generate such transformation as from the exclusivity and rigidity of the sources legitimizing it. This radicalism is lost today, as both parties emphasize pragmatism, tolerance, negotiation, incremental change, and, above all, the primacy of democratic mechanisms and social pluralism. Thus, the necessity of compromise and the imperative to ideologically justify pragmatism have had a profound impact on the party and on the wider Islamic constituency, freeing up in some ways the space previously occupied by Islamists to multiple competitors with very different ideas as to how live, promote, and implement Islamism. Specifically, there are three trends that can be identified that relate even more particularly to the younger generation, one of them having to do with changes within the party and two of them involving changes occurring outside of the party and often in conflict with it.

First, there is a generational divide within Islamist parties that inevitably influences their political direction. Much has been written about the participation of the younger members of the Muslim Brotherhood in the demonstrations against the Mubarak regime that involved almost open conflict with the formal structures of the organization, which, for days, had actually discouraged its members from protesting in the streets. The Moroccan PJD adopted a similar attitude when the 20 February Movement began organizing demonstrations across the country, demanding sweeping political changes. While younger and seemingly more "revolutionary" members of the party pushed for participation in such demonstrations, the party opposed it in the name of safeguarding the stability of the monarchy (and therefore self-preservation in the political system, using "un-moderation" simply as a tool to increase its bargaining power with the other actors in the system). In Tunisia the electoral campaign for the Constituent Assembly had mobilized a significant number of younger members of the party who believed that it was finally the Islamists' turn to run the country as they saw fit. The leadership of the party tended to reprimand such shows of enthusiasm, arguing that Ennahda would not be governing on its own and that the Tunisian social structure and identity did not in any case allow for the Islamization of state and society. While the trajectories of the younger generation of party activists differed according to the national environment and the internal politics of individual parties, the literature tends to agree that the younger generation was less ideological, more ready to build bridges across partisan divides, and much more attuned to cosmopolitan values. This made it less inclined to be involved in what has been termed daily "politicking:" the grind of negotiations, compromises and backroom deals that politics requires. However, this may be only partially true. In both Egypt and Morocco, young Islamist activists found common ground with activists of different ideological persuasions reasonably quickly. To a certain extent, this has been the case in Algeria as well, particularly on specific issues such as the case of those whom the security forces and/or armed groups made disappear during the civil war of the 1990s, a file that the regime is not very keen to revisit. However, this generational divide pitting the young idealistic members who are open to compromise and keen to build cross-ideological alliances against the older generation that is either clinging to power or trying to become part of the "system", should not be over-emphasized because there are other developments taking place that make this simplistic assumption of a generational divide problematic. One key development worth exploring is the impact and influence of international democratization programs that have developed in Tunisia (in particular) and in Morocco following the Arab Awakening. Over the last decade there has been an increasing amount of literature on the impact that the international dimension has on processes of regime change and democratization. Since the Arab Awakening, democracies, international nongovernmental organizations, and, crucially, the foundations of political parties have all built a presence in both countries. A large part of their remit is to devise pro-democracy policies that aim to strengthen these new institutions. At the same time, there is a significant focus on youth as the engine of social, political, and economic change. At the intersection of these two concerns—strengthening democratic institutions and engaging the youth in institutionalized politics—there are programs that aim specifically to train a younger generation of political activists in the ways of democracy, pluralism, and multi-party politics. In this context, young party activists from Islamist parties are trained in the functions that they will exercise as future political leaders. They are in a sense, groomed to replace the current leadership, which has accepted and even embraced the game of democracy and pluralism. For example, in 2013 young party activists at one of the leading Tunisian universities, including the leader of Ennahda, were invited to the United States for two weeks to take part in workshops and meetings to witness firsthand how democracy is and should be practiced. The purpose in mentioning these international programs is neither to provide a normative assessment of such programs nor to evaluate their effectiveness, which may vary considerably. The purpose is to note that the generational divide can be both wide and narrow at the same time, with many younger activists abandoning party politics in disillusionment at the loss of revolutionary fervor, with others looking instead to be formally integrated into the changing Islamist parties. Youth have become a favorite topic of research following the uprisings, but much of the analyses focus on young people involved in extremist politics or in mainstream civil society activism, while little is known about young party members. Thus, while it is important to analyze the generational divide as a function of diverging interests, ideological references, and behavior, one should also keep in mind that there might be a significant degree of convergence as well. All this has important implications for how Islamist parties will deal with the external push to further integrate into pluralistic or semi-pluralistic political systems and consequently how they will address the electoral challenges that they will inevitably face once they are perceived to be fully part of the "new" establishment.

The progressive loss of a radical edge has led to a further important consequence for Islamism, namely the diffusion of the meaning of "Islamist." One of the main assumptions of the post-Islamism thesis is that "increases in levels of piety in the Muslim world have been accompanied by a parallel retreat of religiosity in the private domain. In other words, Muslims may be more religious, but they are increasingly disinterested in Islamizing society."[39] As already discussed above, this might be true to a certain extent, and Islamist political parties in Tunisia, and Morocco (and coincidentally in Algeria as well) tend to underscore this reality of having moved away from the effort of top-down Islamization, but there is another phenomenon at play that should be highlighted: de-politicization. The loss of the radical edge, which precedes the Arab Awakening to a large extent, has favored the retreat of many supporters, sympathizers, and former party members into civil society activism. Again this is a phenomenon that has been occurring for quite some time in so far as civil society activism seemed to be the locus of Islamization in places where it was permissible to shape Islamist politics. Today it is also the locus of the creation of alternative types of Islamism that have very little to do with Islamist parties per se.

Traditionally, civil society activism was important to Islamists because they were precluded from entering the political scene as autonomous actors, and therefore found within civil society the necessary space to continue their political work. State power was not attainable and the focus was on attempting to Islamize society through a network of charities and organizations that could eventually be mobilized if and when the political space opened up. Currently, at least in Tunisia and Morocco, this civil society space is only marginally connected with established Islamist political parties. There are organizations that are linked to the PJD, for instance, and that have an overlapping membership as well as integrated objectives (the human rights organization Karama for example), but increasingly the trend is towards distancing civil society activism from party politics. As mentioned above, this is in part the outcome of a process of de-politicization, whereby politics—understood as participation in established institutions and mechanisms—is perceived to be irrelevant, inefficient and corrupt.

The poor performance of Islamist parties in power, in terms of delivering on promises of radical and swift changes, has further undermined the trust of many ordinary citizens who find refuge and ethical satisfaction in performing daily acts of Islamism away from hierarchical party structures. In this realm of Islamist civil society activism, we find a new and innovative declination of what it means to be an Islamist, and it has very little to do with political discussions about what the state should or should not be doing. Instead, we have the growth of associations and groups that find in their distance from politics and "politicking" a reason for their success. In this respect the example of Qur'anic schools in Tunisia is paradigmatic. At the tail end of the Ben Ali years, a few Qur'anic schools began to appear in rather well-off areas of Tunis.[40] These associations were like book clubs in which individuals would meet under the guidance of a religious scholar—usually a non-controversial figure—to learn how to properly read the Qur'an and study its meaning.

Given the suspicions that religious associations historically aroused in Tunisia, security forces kept close watch on them. However, it was determined within the Ministry of Interior that such groups did not constitute a political challenge, as they were solidly quietist and therefore only interested in doctrinal matters, shying away from political issues. In fact, the regime looked almost favourably upon their presence and activism for two reasons. First, they provided a degree of legitimacy to the regime because they made it appear open to non-state-driven religious activities at a time when Ben Ali was attempting to shore up the religious legitimacy of the regime by allowing for religious TV channels and radios to broadcast a very specific brand of Tunisian Islam. Second, they also allowed for the increasing religiosity of ordinary Tunisians to be expressed in non-political and non-controversial settings. These book clubs eventually began to branch out and offer other services, such as after-school activities for children or financing small-scale, charity-oriented projects. More than anything else though, they provided a locus of socialization away from the hustle and bustle of modern life in the capital, where consumerism had become the dominant social value. After the Awakening these Qur'anic schools have increased both in number and in the range of services provided, with an ever-growing cohort of families availing of them. Within secular circles in the country, this is all perceived to be part of a process of Islamization "from below" that is directly linked and coordinated with the electoral success of Ennahda; to the secular circles the correlation represents the perfect storm of the party taking over the state and Islamic associations taking over society. Upon closer look, however, it emerges that Qur'anic schools and similar associations do not have formal and institutionalized links to Ennahda. On the contrary, there is a growing perception in wider Islamist circles that the party is now like all the other political parties in Tunisia— more interested in self-advancement than in providing for society. A similar example can be seen in the associations in Morocco linked to the al-Adl wal-Ihsan that remain separate and in opposition to the choices of the PJD. The everyday Islamism of these associations is far from political preoccupations and is oriented toward the betterment of society as whole, but remains strictly an individual decision. Their relationship with the state, even though it is largely run by an Islamist party, is fraught with tension because there is a para-doxical liberal instinct to put distance between them and the institutions of the state. As the director of one school in Tunis said, "we just want the state to leave us alone to do what we do."[41]

This de-politicization of a natural Islamist constituency is interesting and problematic at the same time. It speaks to a progressive loss of faith in the political system (even in one where Islamists are prominent), a loss of faith in the institutions of the state, which is perceived to be overbearing and over-regulatory, and, more significantly, an absence of interest in the electoral process. The latter sentiment represents a significant obstacle to the consolidation of democracy in Tunisia and in Morocco. It is therefore imperative that more research be conducted in these alternative ways of expressing and performing Islamism, particularly among the younger generation. Patrick Haenni previously examined what he termed "market Islamism,"[42] which he perceived as an expansion of the meaning of Islamist, the way in which Islamists conducted themselves, and how they expressed their religiosity and even their political beliefs through the espousal of market economics. More recently, this "market Islamism" seems to have been questioned within Islamist circles that favour the adoption of more pious behavior in a modernizing and westernizing social context, while remaining distant from the institutions of the state, even though these are run today by Islamist parties.

The third consequence of the loss of the radical edge is the phenomenon of youth radicalization. Although Salafism was attractive across the entire Middle East and North Africa before the Arab Awakening, and its rise is not always linked to the "moderation" of mainstream Islamist parties, its sudden appearance in Tunisia and Morocco is part of the loss of faith in traditional Islamism. The enthusiasm with which many young people joined Ennahda soon after its legalization and participated in the victorious elections of October 2011 now seems like a distant memory. There are few younger people that trust the party or the political system in general. Those who wish to be politically engaged are left to choose a form of jihadi Salafism. A similar pattern has developed in Morocco, although the perceived intensity of the threat to the political system is far less present in Morocco than in Tunisia. The PJD won the elections and seemed intent on introducing some radical changes. This this did not happen and the party was progressively drawn into the Makhzenian network controlled by the monarch, which prevents all political actors from taking bold and deeply transformative policy initiatives. The PJD did not even generate the same level of enthusiasm as enjoyed by Ennahda, at least initially, making it no surprise that the younger Islamist-leaning generation is also de-politicizing or radicalizing.

In this context, it is also not surprising that Salafism has become the outlet for many young people who believe religion should play a more central and even unique role in both state-building and policymaking. If one were to draw a conclusion from the Arab Awakening in terms of winners and losers,

Salafism can certainly be counted a winner in the changes that have taken place. Salafist movements have been traditionally divided into three broad categories: scientific or scripturalist Salafists, jihadi Salafists, and political Salafis. The scientific or scripturalist Salafists, also known as quietists, do not engage in politics, accept the legitimacy of current rulers, and focus their attention on doctrinal matters, making them therefore preoccupied with religious education. The jihadi Salafists have been at the center of scholarly and policymaking attention for over a decade and are engaged in armed violence to bring about an Islamic state where shari'ah would finally be institutionalized. The political Salafis are a small minority of political activists who believe that engaging in politics is necessary in order for Salafism to remain relevant to Muslims. Following the Arab Awakening, these categories need to be scrutinized more thoroughly, although not abandoned.

The rise of Salafism in North Africa, and its appeal to young people, points to an increasing divergence on the interpretation of the purpose of politics between mainstream Islamism (such as that inspired by the Muslim Brotherhood) and Salafis. In countries where a revolution that realizes political institutions took place, such as Tunisia, Salafism arrived on the scene as a way to continue the revolutionary movement. The rapid integration of Ennahda into the political system and its support for a civil state rather than for an Islamic state that would institutionalize shari'ah aggravated many of the young people in disenfranchised urban and rural areas who had been the protagonists of the revolution. Their feeling of being left out is not necessarily due to the unwillingness of Ennahda to pursue religious objectives and policies. Rather it has to do with the "hijacking" of the revolution on the part of an aging and discredited middle-class and in part with the realization within Ennahda that compromise and coalition-building is the only solution to Tunisia's problems.[43]

The anger over the absence of genuinely radical change that they viewed as connected to wealth redistribution, material improvements, and their own social acceptance has mobilized a segment of the youth away from the political system and into religious channels. For example, embracing Salafism allows young people to subvert the traditional deference due to elders in conservative societies,[44] and therefore permits the continuation of revolutionary behavior. It is interesting that the majority of young people turning to Salafism adopt the jihad version of Salafism, but paradoxically reject violence against the Tunisian state. Thus we have a movement (the now-banned Ansar al-Sharia or AST) with jihadi ideology, symbolism, and discourse, but that does not wish to employ violent armed struggle to achieve its political objectives. There are other forms of Salafism present in Tunisia as well, but they do not attract nearly as many followers as AST. The predominance of jihadi Salafism within the wider Salafi *mouvance* is also due to the international situation and, notably, the Syrian civil war, which has become the centre of attention for many young Tunisians for its sectarian revolutionary nature. Salafism has always had, and still has, a very strong sectarian component and the Syrian civil war fits within this predilection of viewing relationships through the lens of sectarianism.

The case of AST is important not only because it presents researchers with the dilemma of how to categorize new Salafi movements arising from the Arab Awakening, but also because it provides an opportunity to examine more closely the ideological and strategic innovations that such movements offer. For example, references (at the ideological level) are often made to the work of the Jordanian Salafi al-Maqdisi, whose work has been the focus of Joas Wagemakers' analysis for some time.[45] Other scholars emerging in North Africa who are becoming influential in jihadi Salafis circles include the Tunisian Khatib al-Idrissi and Abdallah al-Tunsi. At the strategic level, there is also increasing politicization among some Moroccan Salafis as well as Tunisian Salafis who wish to establish or are already establishing political parties to compete with the traditional rivals of the Brotherhood and the secular sectors of society.

In societies where political reforms have taken place but that have failed to genuinely democratize, such as Morocco, Salafism is also on the rise, but it is "moderating" and moving away from jihadism. This is due in part to the loss of faith in the PJD, whose governing record is far from impressive, and therefore leads to a tendency toward the adoption of a more radical religious discourse, which according to some Moroccan Salafis, should have a political audience. However, the growth of Salafism has, in part, been stimulated by the monarchy to counter the real Islamist enemy—al-Adl wal-Ihsan. Salafis who attempted to subvert the Moroccan political system through violence in the mid-2000s have now turned quietist and therefore can be used as support for the monarchy.[46] The problem is that young Salafi militants who are unhappy supporting the monarchy find international causes to join, expressing their radicalism outside the country. A similar process of state encouragement of both Sufism and quietist Salafism to counter Salafi-jihadism has taken place in Algeria.[47]

In short, the rise of Salafism, including its more traditional jihadi version in Libya, is a phenomenon deserving of increased attention because it sheds light on several issues. First, it suggests that there might be a more general shift within Salafism towards a form of politicization or "proto-politicization," as Roel Meijer puts it.[48] This politicization may have significant consequences for the stability of the Tunisian and Moroccan political systems, which find themselves pushed and pulled between the establishment of democratic institutions and the survival of authoritarianism. Second, it indicates that there are ideological developments not only within established Islamist parties, but also on the fringes where the competition for ideological supremacy is crucial to the outcome of political battles. Third, it confirms the significance of transnational links, with organizations such as AST having links with Ansar al-Sharia in Libya, in addition to the linkages that exist between ideologues and scholars of different persuasions thanks to social media. Salafism has a strong transnational dimension and further exploration is needed to account for the ways in which different strands operate.

Conclusion

The Arab world has experienced both tremendous transformations and significant continuity after the Arab Awakening, Islamism has been both the protagonist and the victim of these processes. On one hand, post-Islamism has captured the changes that notable Islamist parties like Ennahda and the PJD have undergone, as well as the reduction of their political objectives. On the other, Islamists, through the adoption of different ideological references, have remained central to politics and to the construction of new political arrangements. They have also remained central within society, although new social currents seem to be increasingly moving away from institutional and formal links to Islamist parties and toward a more autonomous, diverse, and splintered way of understanding and practicing Islamism. Finally, the attempt to rediscover a "nationalized" Islamism through intellectuals who are distinctively North African, the rise of Salafism, and the problematization of its traditional categories all suggest the beginning of a change in the direction of the flow of both ideas and political strategies. Traditionally, the ideological core of both Islamism and Salafism has been in the Mashriq and in the Gulf with scholars examining the influence of the "East" on North African societies. However, the ideological innovations and political behavior of North African Islamists and Salafis could, at this moment in time, instead have an impact on the "East," particularly when taking into account that state structures in Libya, Syria, Yemen, Iraq, and Lebanon have either collapsed or have been severely weakened in comparison to the relative stability of Tunisia, Morocco, and Algeria.

3

SUFISM AND SALAFISM IN THE MAGHREB

POLITICAL IMPLICATIONS

Ricardo René Larémont

During much of the twentieth century, practitioners of Sufism faced extensive criticism from both the jihadist and the anti-colonial Salafi communities, who claimed that Sufi beliefs and practices were heterodox, if not heretical. Even though Sufism had been an indigenous and popular form of religious expression within the region for years, their consistent and heated denunciations of Sufism eventually led to the decline in its practice in the Maghreb. Following this decline, at the end of the twentieth century, political leaders (particularly in Morocco and Algeria) attempted to revive Sufism as a pacifist alternative to jihadi-Salafi beliefs and practices, which they believed encouraged political militancy and threatened the state. This chapter examines societal and state efforts first to discourage Sufism and encourage Salafism during most of the twentieth century, and then to reverse course and try to revive Sufism during the twenty-first century, as an attempt to counter the threat of jihadi Salafism.

31

Salafism: A Taxonomic Clarification

Before discussing Sufism and Salafism in North Africa, we should define Salafism and provide a taxonomy for the various forms of Salafism. For our purposes in this chapter we define a Salafi as a person who, in the social and religious spheres, wishes to adhere to the religious demands of the Qur'an and the Sunna and who, in the political sphere, seeks a system of governance in which the shari'ah, or Islamic law, provides the principal guide for governmental organization and jurisprudence. As part of this intellectual conversation, I provide a system of classification for Salafis that is similar yet also different in at least two significant aspects from the approach taken by my colleague Francesco Cavatorta in Chapter 2 of this volume. Not all Salafis have the same political objectives or tactics, as Table 3.1 attempts to explain. I claim that there are four types of Salafis: anti-colonial Salafis, jihadi Salafis, political Salafis (Merone and Cavatorta prefer to call this category "Islamists"), and institutional rejectionist Salafis (Merone and Cavatorta call this category "scientific" or "scripturalist").[1]

The primary point of disagreement between myself and Cavatorta is that he would define the Freedom and Justice Party/Ikhwan (Egypt), Ennahda (Tunisia), and the Justice and Development Party (Morocco) as "Islamist" because they have renounced or modified their demand that shari'ah be central to the formation of political institutions and jurisprudence. I prefer to categorize the Freedom and Justice Party/Ikhwan and Ennahda as "Political Salafist" because both parties, despite their public declarations, have engaged in "double-speak" on this issue, with their leaders sometimes ascribing to the rejection of the centrality and exclusivity of shari'ah and endorsing ideological pluralism. At other times they have fully endorsed shari'ah and rejected ideological pluralism through their public declarations or political acts. It is because of this inconsistency and continued ambiguity that I use the term "Political Salafist" rather than "Islamist." I am willing to concede that the Justice and Development Party in Morocco seems more consistent with regard to the issue of ideological pluralism and the tolerance of divergent views within politics.

The second disagreement with Cavatorta is that he describes Salafists who decline to participate in government as "scientific" or "scripturalist." I prefer the term "Institutional Rejectionist" because it appears to me more descriptive.

Table 3.1: Taxonomy of Salafists

Category	Examples	Shari'ah as Basis of Governance	Resort to Violence to Attain Objective	Willingness to form Political Party
Anti-Colonial	Abdu, Rida, Al-Kawakibi, Ben Badis, Al-Fasi, Al-Tha'alibi	Yes	Depends upon author	Often
Jihadi	Qutb, Bin Laden	Yes	Yes	No
Political	Al-Banna, Mawdudi	More often than not	No	Yes
Institutional Rejectionist	Various Salafis who reject the need to form political parties (hizbiyya) or to participate in formal politics	Yes	No	No

A Brief Introduction to Sufism in the Maghreb

Like other world religions, Islam manifests a tension between the inner or mystical practice of religion (esoteric belief and practice) and the outward expression of religious belief (exoteric practice). The inward-looking, mystical tradition is prevalent in most world religions, including Buddhism, Judaism, and Christianity, in addition to Islam. The practitioner of the mystical path (including those who practice Sufism) pursues spiritual discipline or spiritual ecstasy (or both) as a means to greater enlightenment. Besides the search for spiritual enlightenment, there are clear social benefits to belonging to a Sufi order. The participant becomes a member of a religious or spiritual community that fosters bonds of solidarity among members. These bonds are beneficial in dealing with social and economic adversity and help explain both the stability of membership and longevity of many Sufi orders.

In contrast to those who pursue the esoteric mystical path, devotees of exoteric religious practice prefer to focus more upon the correct performance of religious ritual, personal or state conformity with religious law, and for those who espouse

33

jihadi Salafism, the creation of political states in which religious law is either the predominant or the exclusive source of adjudication or legislation.

The practice of Sufism has a long history in the Maghreb, which for the purposes of this chapter include the former al-Andalus (southern Spain). During the Almoravid or Al-Murabitun Empire (1040–1147 CE), al-Andalus was part of the Maghreb and, for the purposes of this discussion, should be included in the analysis.[2] Important practitioners and theorists of Sufism in al-Andalus included, among others, Ibn Bajjah, Ibn Tufail, and Ibn Rushd. We can also include Musa ibn Maimun (or Maimonides) within this mystical tradition because, though Jewish, he practiced mysticism and expressed admiration for the Muslim philosophers and mystics al-Farabi, Ibn Sina, and Ibn Rushd in his famous *Guide for the Perplexed*.[3] Indeed, his *Guide* was written in Arabic rather than Hebrew, reflecting the degree to which he had been immersed in Arab culture.

Until the emergence of anti-colonial Salafism and other forms of Salafism in North Africa during the twentieth century, most Muslims in North Africa did not see an inherent contradiction between traditional Islamic belief and Sufi practices. The emergence of the contradiction between traditional faith and Sufism arose only after the propagation of various types of Salafism.[4] Indeed until the emergence of Salafism, Sufi sheikhs rather than members of the *'ulama'* had been foremost among North Africa's social and political leaders. They were at the forefront of movements that demanded social justice, which in their view demanded both the creation of an Islamic state and resistance to colonialism. Examples of Sufi resistance leaders in North Africa included the Emir Abdel Qadir, the leader of the Qadiriyya in Algeria, and Muhammad bin Ahmed al-Moqrani of the Rahmaniyya, both of whom resisted French colonialism in Algeria; Muhammad bin Ali al-Sanusi who led the charge against Italian colonialism in Libya; Muhammad Bu Dali, the leader of the Darqawiyya order in Algeria, who led a revolt against Ottoman rulers; and Muhammad al-Sharardi who challenged the authority of the sultan in nineteenth-century Morocco.[5] In West Africa, Uthman dan Fodio created an Islamic state in what is now northern Nigeria, and Al-Hajj Umar Tall led a revolt to do the same in Futa Jallon and Futa Toro (in contemporary Guinea and Senegal). All these resistance leaders were Sufis.

While there are many Sufi orders in North Africa, this chapter focuses on the larger and more influential orders, including the Shadhiliyya, the Shadhiliyya-Jazuliyya, the Shadhiliyya-Darqawiyya, the Qadiriyya, the Tijaniyya, the Sanusiyya, and the Qadiriyya-Boutchichiyya orders.

The Shadhiliyya

The Shadhiliyya order gave birth to a substantial number of others, not only in North Africa but throughout the rest of the world. The Shadhiliyya was founded by Abul Hasan al-Shadhili (d. 1258) who was born in the Ghumara region of northern Morocco (which lies between Ceuta and Tangier) sometime between 1185 and 1197 CE.[6] Although founded in Morocco, the Shadhiliyya became even more prominent in Egypt because al-Shadhili and his disciples moved there and developed the order in a substantial way. Besides Morocco and Egypt, the Shadhiliyya has a considerable presence in Sudan, Turkey, Syria, Yemen, Bulgaria, Romania, Kosovo, Macedonia, Sri Lanka, and China.

After studying in Fez and Baghdad, al-Shadhili returned to Morocco where he met Abd al-Salam ibn Mashish, an ascetic from the Jbala region of northern Morocco who instructed him to settle in Shadhila, a village that existed at that time in Tunisia. Al-Shadhili went there and established the Shadhiliyya.[7] After having established the order at Shadhila, al-Shadhili then shifted it to Tunis where he would have better opportunities to attract followers.[8] He became substantially popular in Tunis, which led him to be exiled by Sultan Abu Zakariya soon after Abu Zakariya had named himself the new sultan of the Almohad dynasty. Abu Zakariya believed al-Shadhili a potential political rival and demanded his exile. Al-Shadhili left Tunis for Alexandria in 1244/1245 CE, and in Egypt his order grew, especially under the leadership of two of his disciples, Abu al-Abbas al-Mursi and Taj al-Din Ahmad ibn Ata Allah.

In the Maghreb, the Shadhiliyya was reconstructed by Abd al-Rahman al Jazuli (d. 1465) who was initiated into the order in Fez. Under his leadership the order eventually became known as the Shadhiliyya-Jazuliyya. Al-Jazuli wrote an important Sufi text called *Dalail al-Khayrat* (Signs of the Prophet's Benefactions) that would have long-lasting influence within the Sufi community. Also, soon after 1521 CE, when the Sadi dynasty was established in Fez, membership in the Shadhiliyya-Jazuliyya order blossomed as the new dynasty, which needed to solidify its religious legitimacy, established ties with members of the order to do so.[9]

The Shadhiliyya-Darqawiyya order also emerged from the Shadhiliyya order and was founded in the region of Bani Zarwal (north of Fez) by Abu Hamid al-Arbi al-Darqawi (1760–1823). The Darqawiyya differed in political orientation from many other Sufi orders because it advanced a social critique focused on ameliorating the conditions of the poor. Their stance towards poverty and improving social conditions was rather uncompromising, which caused the order to enjoy considerable popularity not only in Morocco but also in Algeria and Tunisia. Because their support came from the poor, their social critique and politics brought them under the surveillance of the authorities and threat of punishment from the sultan. The Darqawiyya nevertheless pursued their social agenda, triggering a large-scale Darqawiyya-led insurrection against Ottoman rule in Oran and Tlemçen between 1783 and 1805. The Darqawiyya insurgents were quite successful and won several pitched battles against Ottoman forces, which caused the rebels to attempt to establish a formal political alliance with Sultan Moulay Suleiman. The sultan rejected their offer because he feared that establishing such an alliance would provoke the wrath of the Ottoman authorities. After his decision, the Darqawiyya insurrection subsequently floundered.

Al-Darqawi's successor, Mohammed al-Harraq, eventually took the Darqawiyya in a less militant direction, while seeking a rapprochement with the monarchy and the bourgeoisie within Fez. He modified the Darqawiyya political critique while reintroducing the use of ritual music and chanting. Because of his efforts, the Darqawiyya regained the favor of Sultan Moulay Suleiman. The once radical Sufi brotherhood became more acceptable to the bourgeoisie and royalty, especially during the nineteenth century. By then, the order had expanded beyond the boundaries of Morocco into Algeria, Tunisia, Libya, Egypt, Palestine, Syria, Lebanon, and as far as Sri Lanka.

The Qadiriyya and Tijaniyya

The Qadiriyya and Tijaniyya are discussed jointly because these two orders still have trans-regional significance and large numbers of adherents. Furthermore, they are trans-Saharan in operation. This trans-regional significance is important for our analysis: the Qadiriyya and Tijaniyya are found in North Africa, West Africa, and the Sahel and, because of the existence of their trans-regional networks, they have the latent potential to play significant roles in society, economics, and politics. The members of the Qadiriyya and the Tijaniyya regularly travel across the regions of North Africa, West Africa, and the Sahel for religious pilgrimage, social interchange, and commerce. By doing so, they have built a barely perceived ambulatory network of social, economic, and political actors with whom they can exchange views and information and participate in commercial transactions. The members of these orders keep a low profile, which leads to less visibility. Nevertheless, they remain extremely important because their largely unnoticed webs of social and economic interchanges can have political implications.

Of these two orders, the Qadiriyya is older than the Tijaniyya. It was founded by Abd al-Qadir al-Jilani (d. 1166) in Baghdad. The Qadiriyya was introduced into Morocco by Abu Midyan al-Ghawth (d. 1198) who met Abd el-Qadir al-Jilani in Baghdad while al-Jilani had been sojourning there.[10] Al-Jilani was born in Nayf in what was then Persia and emigrated to Baghdad when he was eighteen years old. He undertook theology studies at a *madrasa* in Baghdad, and when its leader, al-Muharrami, died without a male heir, al-Jilani became the head of the *madrasa* and founded his order there. One of his followers, Abd al-Razzaq, developed the order in Baghdad after al-Jilani's death.

The second order, the Tijaniyya, was founded by Ahmad al-Tijani (1737–1815) who was born in Aïn Mahdi in western Algeria.[11] Al-Tijani moved to Fez between 1757 and 1758. While in Fez he joined three orders: the Qadiriyya, the Nasiriyya, and a smaller order led by Ahmad al-Habin bin Muhammad. He then moved to Al-Abyad in the Algerian desert where he studied for five years with Abdel Qadir bin Muhammad, a well-known Sufi. For the next few years he journeyed, first to Egypt and then Mecca, then back to Egypt where he was appointed as a *khalifa* in the Khalwatiyya-Bakriyya order by Mahmud al-Kurdi.[12]

After traveling to Fez and Tuat, he then settled at the oasis of Abu Samghun where he announced between 1781–2 that the Prophet Muhammad had come to him in a dream and commanded him to set up his own order. He then broke links with the Khalwatiyya-Bakriyya order and returned to Fez where he intended to build his new order. While in Fez he came under the royal patronage of Sultan Moulay Suleiman (1792–1822), which caused his order to grow considerably. According to Mohamed El-Mansour, al-Tijani received the sultan's generous patronage because by supporting the Tijaniyya he could counterbalance the social, economic, and political influence of the Shadhiliyya-Jazuliyya order, which had the potential to threaten his rule.[13]

Al-Tijani had many followers and students, including Muhammad bin Fuwaydir al-Abdallawi (d. circa 1821), who introduced the Tijaniyya order into the Tunisian and Algerian Jarid districts, and Muhammad al-Hafiz (d. circa 1830), who introduced his order to Mauritania.[14] Among his more illustrious followers was Sidi Ibrahim al-Riahi (1767–1849) who introduced the Tijaniyya into Tunis proper. Al-Riahi had studied shari'ah, *faqih*, the Qur'an, and the Sunna at al-Zeitouna University in Tunis before traveling to Fez in 1804 where he studied with al-Tijani.[15] Upon returning to Tunis from Fez, he was appointed chief mufti in 1828 and eventually became the imam of al-Zeitouna Mosque and University in 1839—the only person to be appointed to both positions at the same time.[16] Al-Riahi was probably the most influential religious figure of his time in Tunisia, partly because of this leadership position at al-Zeitouna and partly because of his administration of the Tijaniyya and Shadhiliyya Sufi orders. He wrote important works on Arabic language and grammar along with sermons and essays on theology that were compiled by his grandson in a book entitled *Fragrant Emanations from the Life of Sidi Ibrahim al-Riahi*.

Another al-Tijani disciple, Muhammad al-Hafiz, introduced the Tijaniyya to Mauritania.[17] From Mauritania the order eventually spread southwards through much of West Africa. The order's spread into West Africa occurred because of the proselytizing work undertaken by Mawlud Fal (1774–1818). Fal initiated al-Hajj Umar Tall and al-Hajj Malik Sy into the order, and both became important religious and political leaders in West Africa. Tall established an important Islamic state in West Africa that included various regions in what is now Mali, Ghana, Senegal, and Niger. His state lasted from 1848 until 1863. Al-Hajj Malik Sy became an important leader of the Tijaniyya in Senegal and to some extent in Mauritania, and was an important political figure as well.

The Tijaniyya is one of the largest Sufi orders in the world. In North and West Africa, the Tijaniyya have *zawiyas* in Morocco, Algeria, Tunisia, Senegal, Mauritania, Mali, Guinea, Nigeria, Niger, Sierra Leone, Gambia, and Liberia. Beyond North and West Africa, the Tijaniyya can be found in Egypt, Sudan, Palestine, Syria, Iraq, Saudi Arabia, Indonesia, Europe, and the United States. The Tijanis are a formidable social force, their followers being estimated at between 300 and 370 million.[18]

The Sanusiyya

The Sanusiyya was founded in Mecca but rose to prominence in Libya. Its founder, Muhammad bin Ali Al-Sanusi, was born in al-Wasita, a small village to the east of Mostaghanem in western Algeria, in 1787.[19] In 1808 or 1809 he went to Fez, where he quickly joined the Nasiriyya, Tayibiyya, and Darqawiyya orders, all of which had emerged from the Shadhiliyya order. Between 1816 and 1826, Al-Sanusi frequently traveled between Mecca, Fez, and Cairo before eventually settling in Cairo in 1826 after meeting a spiritual guide named Ahmed bin Idris.[20] In 1827 or 1828 bin Idris moved to Yemen, but al-Sanusi and bin Idris stayed in contact. Al-Sanusi claimed that bin Idris had appointed him as the *khalifa* of their Sufi order in Mecca, but after bin Khalifa's death, al-Sanusi's leadership of the order was challenged by a rival named Muhammd bin Uthman al-Marghini. Their rivalry was unresolved leading to the formation of the Marghiniyya order, separate from the Sanusiyya order.[21] The Marghiniyya settled in northeast Sudan and the Sanusiyya operated principally in the Ottoman province of Cyrenaica, which would eventually become part of Libya.

The Sanusiyya thrived in Cyrenaica and established networks of *zawiyas*—a cross between a hostel, a school, and a hospital—that provided rest and comfort for travelers, as well as a critical base for economic and social organization. These *zawiyas*, which became numerous, especially in rural Cyrenaica, enabled the Sanusiyya to strengthen social relations with the residents of the region.[22] Thanks to this societal base, and the well-organized management of the network of *zawiyas*, the Sanusiyya were able to gain considerable social and political autonomy from the Ottoman Empire. With the Sanusiyya effectively governing rural areas, the Ottomans mostly preoccupied themselves with the city of Benghazi, and to some extent the village of Ajdabiyya.[23] The Ottomans ceded control of the countryside to the Sanusiyya because they were effective administrators and because they thought that rural Cyrenaica was of little economic value. So long as rural Cyrenaicans paid their annual tribute to the Ottoman sultan, the Sanusiyya were left alone.[24]

When challenged by Italian invasions and colonization, first from 1911 to 1917 and then again from 1923 to 1942, the Sanusiyya provided a foundation of political and military unity enabling the separate Cyrenaican tribes to organize their resistance. In this process, the Sanusiyya further transformed themselves from a religious order into a form of government that represented the interests of tribes against the Italian state, prompting an Italian attempt to destroy them.[25] As most residents of rural Cyrenaica and the Sanusiyya were nomadic, however, it was very difficult for the Italians—despite extensive repressive measures that included mass murder and concentration camps—to establish effective surveillance and policing of these populations. After their military loss to the Allies in World War II, the Italians were ejected from Cyrenaica and Tripolitania. With their departure, the Sanusiyya and their leader, Sayyid Idris, became the most powerful indigenous political force in the new state of Libya.

The Qadiriyya-Boutchichiyya

The Qadiriyya-Boutchichiyya is the largest and most popular Sufi order in Morocco, with its influence and appeal reaching as far as Europe. It was founded near the city of Berkane during the early twentieth century. When the French captured the city of Oujda in 1907, a local leader of Sufis named Mukhtar bin Hajj Muhyi al-Din led the indigenous resistance movement. He would eventually be captured and incarcerated. Muhyi al-Din died in 1917, and was succeeded by Bou Madyan bin La Mnaour (1873–1955) who is today considered the founder of the Boutchichiyya. La Mnaour would then be succeeded by Hajj Abbas, who died in 1972. From 1972 until now, the order has been led by Sheikh Hajj Hamza.

The Qadiriyya-Boutchichiyya is of religious and political importance because it has taken a stance against political violence and because it has been successful in obtaining a considerable number of adherents, particularly among youth.[26] The order is popular among the youth because it has developed a multi-dimensional approach to promoting Sufism that involves education (particularly by use of its summer seminars on religion, Islamic law, and spirituality); by linkages with the Moroccan monarchy, which provides it with financial support; and by promotion of ecumenism through the Fez Festival of Sacred Music and Fez Festival of Sufi Culture. These activities are supplemented via materials available online, with the order maintaining websites in Arabic, French, and English.

The order's educational project has been guided primarily by the philosopher Taha Abderrahman. His publications include *Usul al-Hiwar* (Principles of Dialogue), *Fiqh al-Falsafa* (Laws of Philosophy), and his influential *Al-Amal al-Dini wa Tajdid al-Aql* (The Work of Religion and the Renewal of Reason) where he argues for "rational" Sufism. His intellectual contributions have attracted large numbers of university students to the order.

The second source of the order's strength comes from its linkages to the Moroccan monarchy. Ahmed Toufiq, the Kingdom's Minister of Religious Affairs, is a member of the Qadiriyya-Boutchichiyya. Toufiq, with the king's and the government's encouragement, has used his role as Minister of Religious Affairs to encourage Sufism as an alternative to jihadist Salafism in Morocco.

The third element that has enhanced the order's popularity has been its direct involvement in two music festivals, the Fez Sacred Music Festival and the Fez Festival of Sufi Culture. Both are directed by Fawzi Skalli, a member of the Qadiriyya-Boutchichiyya. The order has used these festivals to demonstrate that it endorses a modernist approach to life, engaged in piety and spirituality on the one hand, and in ecumenism on the other. This three-pronged, sophisticated approach to proselytization that utilizes education and seminars, linkages to the monarchy, and cultural outreach through music festivals has had quantifiable success.

The Twentieth-Century Salafist Critique of Sufism

Anti-colonial Salafism

While many Salafis claim that the origins of Salafism date back to the founding of Islam during the seventh century CE and the rigorous practices of the time, the contemporary version of Salafism in North Africa that emerged during the late nineteenth century and early twentieth century originally had an anti-colonial expression and orientation. It was primarily articulated by Mohammed Abduh and Rashid Rida, who, through their writings, argued that Muslims needed to understand their religion correctly and live in accordance with its teachings so as to create great nations and successfully resist European colonialism. Abduh and Rida argued that Muslims should engage in cultural resistance against colonialism by re-embracing a more rigorous practice of Islam while at the same time adopting European scientific methods because of their technological advantages. Abduh and Rida also mounted a vigorous criticism of Sufism and especially their ecstatic rituals. They both believed that followers of Sufism tended to focus on the afterlife rather than the present life and that their reliance upon belief in the intervention of saints and the guidance of spiritual masters inhibited them from taking personal responsibility for their lives.[27] Rida, even more than Abduh, became extremely critical of Sufism, drawing himself closer to the more conservative exoteric teachings of Ibn Taymiyyah and the Wahhabis, traditionally hostile towards Sufism.[28] Both Rida's and Abduh's intellectual projects focused upon resuscitating the exoteric practice of Islam while expressing considerable animus towards ecstatic Sufism, which they felt was obscurantist. If they were to accept Sufism at all, Abduh and Rida would tolerate only a meditational, non-ecstatic Sufism, which they would have considered more reasonable.[29] Further, Abduh and Rida alleged that considerable numbers of Sufi leaders had collaborated with European colonialists, which made the followers of Sufism even more worthy of disregard.

After Abduh and Rida's introduction of the anti-Sufi critique, clerics and political leaders in North Africa during the colonial period seized upon their initial efforts to continue to criticize and marginalize Sufism. In Algeria,

Sufism's most vocal critic was Abdelhamid Ben Badis who founded the Association of the Ulema (*Jam'ayyat al-ulema al-muslimin al-aljaza'iriyyin*). The Association had an important influence upon the trajectory of Algerian nationalist history, playing an essential role in propagating Islam and Arabic as the foundations of Algerian identity. By 1954, it was running approximately 200 schools in Algeria, all of which espoused Salafism and had an anti-Sufi orientation. The Association schools played a role in the larger societal anchoring of Islam and Arabic as the keys to constructing an independent Algerian identity; at the same time, they inculcated anti-Sufi perspectives among their students.[30] The Association's magazine *al-Shihab* (The Meteor) singled out the Tijaniyya order with charges of heresy.[31]

In Morocco, the stance of the *ulama* with regard to Sufism was considerably more nuanced. Sufis and Sufism had been long prevalent in the country and had episodically been allied with the monarchy to provide legitimacy for its rule. When anti-Sufism did arise in Morocco it emerged in an anti-colonial context, especially after the French established their "protectorate" in Morocco. Muhammad bin Abd al-Karim led the resistance against the French in northern Morocco and was notably anti-Sufi, particularly with regard to the Darqawiyya order. After Abd al-Karim's revolt was suppressed by the French, a group of Salafi scholars in Fez organized the Hizb al-Islah that roundly criticized the Tijaniyya and the Tayibiyya Sufis for their allegedly heretical practices. Abu Shuaib al-Dukkali, Mohammed bel-Arabi al-Alaou, and Abdessalam Serghini were particularly prominent within this group of critical clerics.[32] Yet another critic of Sufism during the colonial era was Allal al-Fasi, a Salafi-influenced nationalist who helped establish the Istiqlal (Independence) party. In his *al-Harakat al-Istiqlaliyyah fi al-Magrhib al-Arabi* and in his *al-Naqd al-Dhati*, he endorsed a "rational Salafist" approach to politics that was unremittingly critical of Sufism and its leaders.[33]

Still, by contrast, anti-Sufism in Morocco was less virulent than in Algeria. The explanation for this contrast lies in the fact that a particularly brutal form of French colonialism had lasted for 132 years in Algeria (from 1830 until 1962) while a less damaging form was put in place in Morocco and lasted for only forty-four years (from 1912 until 1956). The extremely racist nature of the French colonial regime in Algeria created a juridical, political, and social structure in which indigenous Algerians were considered detestable and were treated as third-class residents within their own country. In this context of systematic oppression and marginalization, Algerian identity became rooted in the use of the Arabic language and the practice of a Salafi (as opposed to Sufi) Islam as the foundation for cultural and political resistance; the roots of this resistance were tied directly to the Association of the Ulema schools, which insisted that Arabic and Salafi Islam were inseparable from Algerian identity.

With French colonialism in Morocco so relatively short-lived, they did not have enough time to inflict serious psychological or cultural damage. The French colonial regime was a "protectorate" and Morocco had not been fully merged into France's government to the extent that Algeria had been. Additionally, Algeria was ruled directly as a *département* of France while General Lyautey in Morocco chose to rule indirectly by maintaining the King of Morocco as the titular head of state while making sure that the French had control of all political, administrative, and fiscal structures.

In Tunisia, the most notable commentator on Sufi and Salafi affairs was Abd al-Aziz al-Tha'albi. He belonged to Muhammad Abduh's school of rational Salafism and was a critic of Sufism, especially of those practitioners more inclined toward the ecstatic rather than the meditational forms of its practice.

In Libya, the Sanusiyya had been the most influential order with King Idris, the leader of the Sanusiyya, serving as the country's king. With Qaddafi's seizure of power in 1969, the significance of the Sanusiyya declined. During his forty-two-year regime, Qaddafi attempted to attenuate most forms of civil society, and the Sanusiyya were impaired from operating or proselytizing.

Jihadist Salafism

After anti-colonial Salafism, a second strain of Salafism emerged in the Muslim world during the second half of the twentieth century, known as jihadist Salafism. Some of the leading theorists of jihadist Salafism in the larger Muslim world were Sayyid Qutb, Abdullah Azzam, Ayman al-Zawahiri, and Osama Bin Laden.

Sayyid Qutb was an Egyptian political thinker who, in his *Ma'alim fil-tariq* (*Milestones*), argued that the realization of a just Islamic society would only be possible with the restoration of the exoteric and charitable practices of the Islamic religion to their original form and with the creation of an Islamic state that exclusively applied shari'ah or Islamic law within its executive, legislative, and judicial branches. Qutb's themes focused upon reversion to the original practice of Islam without the adulteration of religious traditions and upon the creation of an Islamic state exclusively rooted in shari'ah. His views of *jahiliyya*, or ignorance, led him eventually to be critical of Sufism, whose heterodox practices he considered *bid'ah* (innovation, or heresy). His hard-line views, which demanded a return to the "purity" of Islam, were developed intellectually by Abdullah Youssef Azzam, Ayman al-Zawahiri, and Osama Bin Laden, among others. This group of authors played a considerable role in casting Sufism in a negative light during much of the latter half of the twentieth century.

State Strategies in Morocco and Algeria: Reviving Sufism as an Alternative to Jihadist Salafism

As jihadist Salafism became more influential and an increased political threat to the state, two leaders in North Africa—King Mohamed VI of Morocco and President Abdelaziz Bouteflika of Algeria—undertook efforts to encourage a pacifist-oriented form of Sufism as an alternative to jihadist Salafism.

In Morocco, King Hassan II and then his successor, King Mohamed VI, eventually developed a cultural strategy to encourage Sufism to serve as a counterweight to jihadist Salafism and to shore up their regimes. The Moroccan strategy arguably began in 1985 when the monarchy held a conference to offer a public defense of the Tijaniyya brotherhood, which until that moment had often been the subject of pointed criticism by Salafis.[34] When King Mohamed VI ascended to the throne, he accelerated the kingdom's endorsement of Sufi Islam, especially after the 2003 Casablanca bombings that killed forty-five people. Mohamed VI began a "policy of 'restructuring the religious field' that involved particular emphasis upon Sufism."[35] His policy involved encouraging the practice of Sufism (especially through the monarchy's patronage and endorsement of the Qadiriyya-Boutchichiyya Sufi order), governmental monitoring of all imams, and ecumenical religious outreach in the context of cultural and religious festivals. The government tried to assure that all imams, whether Sufi or Salafi, were not espousing a militant anti-government agenda.

The first element of the monarchy's strategy to encourage Sufism has been to frame it as an institution that is positive for the country. In the royal administration's official discourse, Sufism has been promoted as a legitimate Islamic tradition that emphasizes tolerance and dialogue and that ensures social unity, cultural cohesion, and political stability.[36] The king has openly recommended Sufism as a form of Islam that "advocates co-operation and joint action to support fellow humans, to show them love, fraternity and compassion."[37] King Mohamed VI has amplified his father's strategy of encouraging Sufism as a pacifist alternative to jihadist Salafism by aligning with the Qadiriyya-Boutchichiyya order, which has supported the regime for an extended period of time. The present leader of the order, Sheikh Hadj Hamza, is characterized by the regime as tolerant, progressive, and modernist.

Second, Mohamed VI appointed Ahmed Toufiq, a member of the Qadiriyya-Boutchichiyya, as the government's Minister of Religious Affairs, a position he has held since 2007. From his position as Minister of Religious Affairs, Toufiq, in coordination with the king, has encouraged the growth of Sufism not only in Morocco but throughout West Africa and the Sahel. This has positioned the kingdom as a defender and propagator of a more peaceful form of Islam within these regions.

The third element of the monarchy's strategy to encourage Sufism has involved his promotion of international musical festivals, especially the Fez World Sacred Music Festival, which has been in operation since 1994, and the Fez Festival of Sufi Culture since 2006. As mentioned, the Qadiriyya-Boutchichiyya have been involved with both festivals. These events, which involve international performers and an international audience, are broadcast via television and the internet in an astute effort to promote the notion that Islam, and especially Sufi Islam, is a religion that is oriented towards tolerant ecumenism.

While the Moroccan government maintains good relations with the Qadiriyya-Boutchichiyya order, it has had more troubled relations with another grassroots Sufi organization: *Jama'at al-adl wal-ihsan* or Justice and Benevolence Association. In contrast to the Qadiriyya-Boutchichiyya, which has never been openly critical of the monarchy, the founder of the Justice and Benevolence Association, Sheikh Abdessalam Yassine, openly reprimanded King Hassan II in his famous missive, *al-Islam aw al-Tufan* (Islam or the Deluge). After publishing this work, Sheikh Yassine was first imprisoned and then committed to extended house arrest. Ever since then, the monarchy and the government have kept the Justice and Benevolence Association under close watch.

In Algeria the Bouteflika regime attempted to reanimate Sufism as an alternative to jihadist Salafism but with less success. In a 2012 public opinion study conducted among youth in Algeria, it was found that the respondents viewed the government's encouragement of Sufism as cynical and instrumental rather than as a sincere effort to encourage religiosity or piety.[38] President Bouteflika's effort to reanimate Sufism in Algeria was considerably hampered because during the post-independence era, and particularly during the long period that

President Houari Boumédiène was in power, Boumédiène, despite his pursuit of socialism, was closer to the Salafists than to Sufis, whom he believed had collaborated with the French colonial regime. In the wake of Bouteflika's new attempt to encourage Sufism, however, the Tijaniyya has grown, and they have been notably uncritical of President Bouteflika's government. Indeed, because of its quiescence, it has received financial support from the state and is experiencing a very modest revival. The present leader of the Tijaniyya in Algeria, Sheikh Muhammad al-Eid al-Tijani, has played a mediating role in reconciling differences between the leaders of the Tamassin and Aïn Mahdi branches of the Tijaniyya in Algeria while also serving as a liaison to the Tijaniyya *zawiiya* in Fez, Morocco.

Salafism in the Wake of the 2011 Arab Spring Revolts

In the wake of the 2011 Arab Spring revolts, three forms of Salafism—institutional rejectionist Salafism, political Salafism, and jihadist Salafism—have been operating in North Africa. The institutional rejectionist Salafis focus on *dawa* (proselytization) and *tarbiyya* (instruction) and are disinclined to participate in violence, and the political Salafists focus on political participation and electoral contests. In contrast, the jihadist Salafists focus on militant action to effect political change.[39]

One of the significant outcomes of the 2011 Arab Spring revolts was the emergence of political Salafists that successfully formed political parties. These newly-emerged political Salafists then participated in post-revolt elections, winning outright majorities (in Egypt) or pluralities (in Tunisia and Morocco), or finishing second (in Libya). In Egypt, the Muslim Brotherhood's party (the Freedom and Justice Party), along with the separate Salafist al-Nour party, won absolute majorities in the legislative and political elections. In Tunisia, Ennahda won a plurality of the vote and formed a coalition government with secular parties. The Party for Justice and Development (PJD) in Morocco did the same. In Libya, the Justice and Construction party finished second with 17 per cent of the vote, while the non-Islamist National Forces Alliance finished first with 39 per cent of the vote. In Tunisia and Morocco, both Ennahda and the PJD, respectively, have thus far survived various challenges since 2011 to rule in collaboration with secular parties. The Muslim Brotherhood government in Egypt was not given the opportunity to survive; it was ousted by a military coup d'état in August 2013.

Concerning the present discussion of jihadist Salafist trends in North Africa, the best known Salafi-jihadi group in North Africa prior to the 2011

Arab Spring revolts was Al-Qaeda in the Islamic Maghreb (AQIM), which emerged in 2007 from a pre-existing Salafi-jihadi group known as the Group for Preaching and Combat (GSPC). AQIM's objective had been to topple the Algerian government by armed force, but this was thwarted by counterterrorism efforts. Stymied by the government in many regions of the country, AQIM then shifted its operations towards the Kabylie region that lies just east of Algiers, and then to southern Algeria and northern Mali. The Kabylie is mountainous while southern Algeria and northern Mali is vast and remote, making policing and surveillance of these areas very difficult. Therefore, in these regions AQIM has geographical advantages that enable its forces to avoid detection. In addition, in southern Algeria and northern Mali AQIM has made alliances with local Tuareg tribes and collaborates with irredentist Tuareg rebels and other Salafi-jihadi groups, including Ansar al-Din (often based close to Timbuktu and Kidal) and the Movement for Oneness and Jihad in West Africa (MUJAO), located in and near Gao. In 2012, in collaboration with Ansar al-Din and MUJAO, AQIM seized the large northern cities of Kidal, Timbuktu, and Gao before attempting to move further south to Mopti and, eventually, to Bamako, the capital of Mali. Their effort was later reversed by a military intervention sponsored by France and ECOWAS. Besides these Mali-based groups, AQIM has also had episodic contact and conducted training activities with Boko Haram, another Salafi-jihadi group that operates in northern Nigeria and southern Niger.

In the post-Arab Spring revolt era, other Salafi-jihadi groups have emerged in North Africa that are separate but are likely to be ideologically inclined to cooperate with AQIM. These new Salafi-jihadi groups, which operate in Mali, Tunisia, and Libya, often adopt the moniker of Ansar al-Sharia.

The group in Tunisia known as Ansar al-Sharia emerged in the aftermath of the fall of the Ben Ali regime. Some analysts have dated Ansar al-Sharia's official founding to the meeting of its first congress, which was held in a town called Soukra, near Tunis, during April 2011.[40] Its alleged founder was Seifallah Ben Hassine who is known locally as Abu Ayadh. He is reported to have fought in Afghanistan and to have been close to Abu Qatada, an important ideologue within the larger al-Qaeda movement. Abu Ayadh was arrested in Turkey in 2003 and then extradited to Tunisia where he was sentenced by the Ben Ali regime to forty-three years in prison. He was released under the terms of amnesty for political prisoners after Ben Ali's fall. Although Ansar al-Sharia is the most potent Salafi-jihadi group in Tunisia, it is not the only one. Other groups to be counted among the jihadist Salafis include Rahma, led by Said Jaziri (a former member of Ennahda); Asala, led by Mouldi Ali; the Jabhat al-Islah (Reform Front), led by Mohamed Khouja; and Hizb al-Tahrir (Liberation Party).[41]

Within this continuum of Salafi-jihadi groups, Ennahda, which is characterized as a political, rather than a jihadist, Salafi group, has been put in the difficult position of having to try to assuage some of the demands of these jihadist Salafis (such as their desire to create a state exclusively based upon shari'ah law) while at the same time attempting to work with the numerous secular Tunisians who desire a legal system that does not specifically refer to religious law for adjudication. This is an extremely difficult balancing act, given the ideological antagonism among these various political proponents in Tunisia. Time will tell whether Ennahda can effectively function as a broker in such an ideologically adverse environment.

In Libya, the current Salafi-jihadi groups have mostly emerged from the Libyan Islamic Fighting Group (LIFG), which was organized in 1990 to oppose the Qaddafi regime. The LIFG led an insurgency in eastern Libya that lasted from 1995 until 1998 and ended in failure. Beginning in 2005, and through the mediation of Qaddafi's son, Seif al-Islam Qaddafi, the LIFG began a dialogue with the regime. At the end of 2010 and as a result of this dialogue, the LIFG published its *Corrective Studies in Understandings of Jihad, Enforcement of Morality, and Judgment of People*, in which it forbade armed insurgency against the Libyan state and advocated tolerance of other ideologies and religions. In turn, in March 2010, Seif al-Islam Qaddafi announced the release of the LIFG commanders.

In contrast to the Islamists who initially failed to participate in the 2011 Tunisian and Egyptian revolts, the Libyan Islamists, and especially the Libyan jihadist Salafis, were quite involved with the Libyan resistance from the outset. The jihadist Salafis, and the LIFG in particular, played a significant role in the ouster of the Qaddafi regime.[42] The LIFG's role was critical to the success of the Libyan revolt because many LIFG members had experience in combat, having been involved in armed conflicts in Afghanistan, Algeria, and/or Chechnya. At the beginning of the revolt, on 15 January 2011, the LIFG changed its name to the Libyan Islamic Movement for Change (LIMC). In addition to the LIFG/LIMC there was a much smaller Salafi-jihadi group called the Shuhadaa (Martyrs) operating principally in Benghazi.[43]

Not all Islamists in Libya belong to the LIMC or the Martyrs, nor do they all espouse jihadist Salafism. For example, the Islamic Brotherhood in Libya formed the Justice and Construction Party on 3 March 2011, which, like

Ennahda and the Freedom and Justice Party in Tunisia, can be categorized as political Salafists. The Justice and Construction Party was intended to be "a national civil party with an Islamic reference… [having both] Islamists and nationalists" and sought to differentiate itself from the jihadist Islamists.[44] Morocco has undertaken a different path to deal with jihadist Islamists. As mentioned earlier, after the 2003 Casablanca bombings that killed forty-five people, the government and monarchy undertook a program of "restructuring the religious field" that involved encouraging Sufism, especially the Qadiriyya-Boutchichiyya branch of Sufism, as a pacifist alternative to jihadist Salafism. While encouraging Sufism, the government also imprisoned thousands of jihadists, including Mohamed Fizazi and Abdelkarim Chadli, whom the state alleged were linked to the Casablanca killings and AQIM. In 2014, in a complete turnaround and public act of reconciliation, King Mohamed VI visited Mohamed Fizazi, who has since been pardoned by the king at his mosque in Tangiers on 28 March 2014.[45] The monarchy's policy has been to both encourage Sufism as a pacifist alternative and to punish and then pardon any jihadist Salafis who choose to abandon the path of *jihad al-kharij*, or the exterior jihad.[46] Furthermore, in Morocco it is now more difficult for jihadist Salafis to encourage violence to pursue their political objectives when a political Salafi party, the PJD or Justice and Development Party, is the leading party in a coalition government. Because a political Salafi party now holds the reins of government, jihadist Salafists find it more difficult to espouse violence as a means of obtaining their political objectives.

Remaining Reasons for the Continuing Rise of Jihadist Salafism

Jihadist Salafism may continue to be a viable social and political movement during the twenty-first century because it is fueled by continued local acceptance of its primary tenets: that jihadist Salafism can accomplish its goals of social justice and the legitimation of Islamic states through its militant insistence that shari'ah law should be used in both jurisprudence and governance. The continued propagation of this idea of shari'ah rule will be possible, in part, because of the continued transfer of these ideas from the Arabian peninsula, where they have been prominent and even encouraged and supported by the financial largess of the Saudi, Qatari, and other Gulf states. It is also largely accepted at the local level that the "liberal, colonialist, and capitalist" West either tolerated or supported brutal authoritarian regimes in North Africa for an extended period of time, and that provides all the more justification for a return to a legitimate shari'ah-based state that will provide social justice. Western support of authoritarian governments in North Africa, the Middle East, and much of the rest of the Muslim world has often reified local sentiment that liberal democracy has been a cruel, illegitimate import. The writings and popularity of Sayyid Qutb, Muhammad Abd Al-Salam Faraj, Abdullah Azzam, Osama bin Laden, and Ayman al-Zawahiri advanced the notion of the justifiability of jihadist Salafism and the immediate restoration of shari'ah in the face of injustice and oppression.

These reasons may not be all that explains the continued rise of jihadist Salafism. The failure of North African authoritarian governments to bridge the gap between the rich and the poor and their failure to address the question of mass youth unemployment provided fertile ground for reformers to launch the 2011 Arab Spring revolts. Secular leaders launched the revolts to address these issues, yet the political Salafists and the jihadist Salafists have reaped the political benefits in many locales. If these Salafists fail to rectify these larger systemic issues, new revolts, whether inspired by secular forces or by other Salafists, will recur.

Finally, the jihadist Salafists have substantially inverted the arguments made by the anti-colonial Salafists in the early twentieth century. Writing at the beginning of that century, Muhammad Abduh and Rashid Rida suggested that Muslims work toward the restoration of the practice of Islam while also borrowing, where appropriate, from the West in both the technological and political spheres. The new jihadist Salafists embrace only Western technology and completely reject Western political ideas because accepting anything more would be "borrowing from the West." This in turn would perpetuate a state of "humiliating servitude."[47] For the jihadist Salafists, the lines of demarcation have been drawn. They do not yet converge.

4

LABOR PROTEST IN MOROCCO

STRIKES, CONCESSIONS, AND THE ARAB SPRING

Matt Buehler

A growing body of evidence suggests that organized labor associations—members, activists, and leaders of unions—played an important, contributing role to many of the popular protests that swept the Arab world beginning in late 2010. Although neither the originators nor instigators of these protests, labor syndicates contributed to demonstrations and enhanced their size and strength. In Tunisia, seasoned unionists of the Union Générale Tunisienne du Travail (UGTT) participated in protests in Sidi Bouzid, Gafsa, and other small towns in the country's interior before demonstrations migrated to Tunis.[1] In Egypt, mobilization of unions occurred before the Arab uprisings, beginning in 2006, especially among textile workers in the city of al-Mahallah al-Kubra. Their strikes and protests continued during the unrest of 2011.[2] While scholars are beginning to produce research that focuses on labor protest in Tunisia and Egypt during the Arab uprisings, little has been published with an empirical focus on Morocco. To this end, this chapter analyzes the nature of labor protest in Morocco in 2010–2011, and relays the sequencing of events that sparked union unrest in the country. It also describes what (if any) labor demands were realized through participation in protests, and seeks to answer the following question: What role did unions play in the mass mobilizations organized by Morocco's youth movement, the 20 February Movement for Change?

To answer this question, this chapter explores the theory of labor aristocracy in the context of state-labor relations in Morocco. First conceived by Marx, and further developed by Hobsbawm,[3] the theory of labor aristocracy posits that workers are not uniform in their assertiveness toward employers, but rather vary in how they press for material demands.[4] The labor aristocracy is comprised of workers with specialized skills who understand their value to industrial production and firm profits. Were these skilled laborers to strike, their stoppage would seriously diminish the profits of owners. Longshoremen, for example, are a classic example of such labor aristocrats. Their strikes reduce profits by disrupting import-export trade, which causes delays in shipping and spoilage of goods. Because employers understand the economic value of these skilled laborers, the latter can use both strikes and threats to strike to elicit concessions from the former. By threating to strike and walk out of wage negotiations, skilled laborers can draw greater benefits from their employers than if they had undertaken these contentious actions directly, without first bargaining in face-to-face talks.

In recent years, a new labor aristocracy of skilled workers has arisen in Morocco: unionized public employees. Employed in the public sector, these unionists include teachers, doctors, nurses, and clerks in ministries, municipalities, and courthouses. They constitute the human machinery of the state, and play a critical role in administering and delivering its services to citizens. Unlike strikes of private sector syndicates that reduce company profits, stoppages in the work of public employees result in losses for the state by deteriorating the quality and consistency of public services (especially those provided by ministries, schools, hospitals, and other public institutions). Such strikes can provoke anger in citizens, becoming a source of instability in authoritarian regimes. Citizens expect consistency in public service delivery—a feature of what Mehran Kamrava calls their "ruling bargain" with regimes; in this bargain, "the provision of economic goods and services" is traded for the "lack of elite accountability."[5]

Leveraging their unique position as the human machinery of the state, Morocco's labor aristocracy of public employees took advantage of the unrest of the Arab uprisings. That is, they used the popular protests that gripped the country in 2011 to advance their material interests, particularly in improvements in daily wages, working environment, and other professional conditions. Indeed, by joining the street protests and threatening to strike, they forced concessions from the authoritarian regime, which had been reticent to respond to their socio-economic grievances in the mid-2000s. What resulted was that the public employees benefited tremendously from the Arab uprisings, even though Morocco neither experienced regime change nor implemented democratizing reforms.

The next logical question concerns the credibility of the public-employee union threats: What made them believable (and dangerous) to the regime? Perhaps the unionists could have been bluffing, without real intention to strike or protest in the streets. To answer this question, one must understand the historical origins of Morocco's regime, its chief allies, and its union opponents. In the initial days following decolonization, Morocco's kings developed a social base from which they established control and built their regime. Specifically, this base was the rural nobility, which consequently received state largesse, protective laws, and other beneficial policies.[6] Urbanites, working through labor unions, faced off against the monarchy and its rural supporters. Representing urban interests that had become marginalized during economic modernization, labor unions went on strike to force benefits from the regime, which was always reluctant to concede. These labor mobilizations, though often beginning peacefully, frequently evolved into violent protests and riots, especially in the 1960s, 1980s, and 1990s. Given this history, the potential for labor-driven urban violence frightens regime elites and forces them to take union threats seriously. Although there was a lull in labor-driven violence in Morocco in the early 2000s, the Arab Spring was a critical juncture: It, according to social movement theorist Sidney Tarrow, rearranged the "political opportunity structure" to empower the unions in ways unseen since the 1980s and 1990s, when urban riots related to structural readjustment rocked major cities.[7] Put another way, the Arab Spring thrust open a window of opportunity that made the renewed threat of labor protest and urban violence credible, forcing the regime to compromise.

Two key points—theoretical and empirical—emerge from this chapter's narration of the political history of state-labor relations during the Arab uprisings. The first point is theoretical: Morocco's unions behaved strategically to secure their material interests. Before the unrest of 2011, Morocco's elected leadership—led by Istiqlal Prime Minister Abbas al-Fassi—did little to assuage the demands of organized labor. But by April 2011, al-Fassi reversed his strategy and granted the public employee unions many of their key mate-rial requests. This change occurred because although labor unions did not start Arab Spring protests, which must be attributed to youth activists, they effectively exploited them to advance their interests. They used the atmos-phere of discontent created by the 20 February Movement for Change to secure a better bargaining position and to win additional material concessions. The unions secured these new benefits from the regime in direct state-labor negotiations, known as the "social dialogue" (*al-hiwaar al-ijtima'ai*), which took place between 5–26 April 2011.

The chapter's second point is empirical. I show that, as in the cases of Tunisia and Egypt, Morocco witnessed a spike in labor unrest in 2010, months before the beginning of the Arab uprisings. In Morocco, labor protests pre-ceded the demonstrations initiated by the 20 February Movement for Change, which climaxed in February, March, and April 2011.[8] What this upsurge in labor unrest means is that brooding socio-economic frustration—especially related to increases in living costs and decreases in real wages—presaged the youth-organized protests that would occur in 2011. Epitomized in the mate-rial demands of workers, socio-economic discontent was one of the many antecedent factors active in Moroccan society before the unrest. This second point contrasts with the analysis of many scholars, notably Marc Lynch, Philip N. Howard, and Muzammil M. Hussain, who interpret the proliferation of social media either as, at most, a cause for sparking protests or, at least, an instrument for facilitating their mass turnout.[9] By showing that labor unrest started before the youth-led mobilizations in Morocco, the chapter unearths the deeper, bedrock socio-economic dissatisfaction upon which youth-led protests were built.

This chapter is divided into four sections that outline the origins of Morocco's labor unions and detail their involvement in the country's uprisings of 2011. First, the chapter surveys the historical foundations of labor unions in Morocco, focusing on the colonial and post-colonial periods. This early history demonstrates that Morocco's unions have a history of inciting violence to advance their agenda, especially in urban areas, which have historically served as centers of opposition to the monarchy. Second, it sets the baseline to show that, like in Tunisia and Egypt, the period preceding the Arab Spring was marked by increased labor unrest in Morocco. Third, it examines union mobilization during the height of popular protests against Morocco's regime, from February 2011 to June 2011. Finally, the chapter closes by discussing what demands the unions secured from their activism and reviews the key implications from the political historical narrative. The empirical record bears out the argument that labor unions used unrest connected to Morocco's "Arab Spring" to realize some of their core material demands.

1940s–2000: The Origins of Labor Protest and Urban Violence in Morocco

The activism of Moroccan labor unions during the Arab Spring built upon years of experience in popular mobilization, both in the colonial, post-colonial, and contemporary periods. During each of these, labor unions used urban unrest—often violent—to press for their demands and advance their interests. This political history of labor-driven urban violence resurfaced as a threat in the atmosphere of the protests of 2011.

Morocco's first labor union—the Confédération Générale du Travail (CGT)—was founded by the French, not the native Moroccans. European settlers, mostly members of the Casablanca branch of the French Communist Party, created this union in 1943 to advance the interests of workers in the manufacturing plants of Morocco's gritty, industrializing economic capital.[10] There were two trends within Morocco's first labor movement: one that advocated excluding Moroccan laborers from membership and another that proposed incorporating these local workers. The forward-thinking founder of the union, Léon Sultan, sided with the latter. He took this stance for two reasons: First, as Moroccan workers would accept lower wages than their French counterparts, he saw it as beneficial to integrate them into the organization, so that the foreign and local workers could unify, standardize, and coordinate their collective wage negotiations. Second, as an Algerian Jew who had gained French citizenship, Sultan opposed (in principle) the exclusion of Moroccan workers from the labor movement. The common class interests of foreign and local laborers, he reasoned, transcended their differences in nationality, race, or religion.[11] In the end, Moroccans were brought into the union, though they established a separate, auxiliary wing to represent their distinct interests.

At first, the chief nationalist party that agitated for independence, the Istiqlal party, opposed Moroccan involvement in the French-led union, deeming it a colonial strategy to co-opt, control, and contain native workers. Soon afterward, however, the nationalists reversed their decision: working through the labor union, Moroccans could use urban violence to assert themselves against France's colonial occupation, expediting the protectorate's demise. By 1946, Moroccan nationalists had infiltrated the CGT and, in March 1955, voted to make themselves independent from the French syndicate. They prepared to use the union, and its power to incite urban violence, against the occupation. The Moroccans' branch of the CGT asserted its autonomy and donned a new name, the Union Marocaine du Travail (UMT). As the forerunner to all unions led exclusively by Moroccan labor organizers for Moroccan workers, the UMT would become a key actor in the post-colonial period.[12]

During Morocco's colonial struggle in the 1950s, two organizations emerged with substantive ties to the population; specifically, a nationalist party (the Istiqlal Party) and a labor union (the UMT). These two groups often collaborated and connected their struggles to advance their common interests. Mohammed V, Morocco's post-colonial monarch who was exiled between 1953 and 1955, emphasized the importance of unions in his landmark 11 April 1947 speech in Tangiers, in which he described these organizations as a "distinguished vanguard" and the "forces of reinforcement" in the struggle against foreign occupation.[13] In its mission to oust the French from Moroccan territory, the Istiqlal mobilized unionists as its foot soldiers in violent urban confrontations with French forces. Unionists were the core participants of the 8 December 1952 riots in Casablanca, one of the most important episodes of resistance to the administration of General Augustin-Leon Guillaume, an uncompromising resident-general installed to repress the nationalist movement. The 1952 riots were organized in response to the assassination of Tunisian unionist Ferhat Hashad by the Red Hand, a settler terrorist group. The Istiqlal mobilized Moroccan unionists and instructed them to "gather weapons and await instructions." The party subsequently ordered them to launch an assault on the colonial police, which resulted in the death of hundreds. Following the riots, residency officials observed that an atmosphere of "lynching and shooting" pervaded Morocco, and they realized that the colonial protectorate had reached its end.[14]

As the struggle for independence escalated, union confrontations with police became more frequent and violent, especially in urban areas where workers resided. In order to force French withdrawal from Morocco, a concession the resident-general did not want to grant, the unions would have to mobilize in the streets. Between 1955, when the UMT was formally founded, and the year of Morocco's independence, 1956, the UMT had engaged in 1,987 different strikes involving 76,486 workers.[15] In the years following independence, the UMT boasted a mass following unparalleled in other North African states. It had over 576,000 unionized members and was far larger than the main unions of Tunisia and Algeria, which featured 150,000 and 200,000 members, respectively.[16] Given the UMT's important contribution to liberating Morocco from foreign rule, what role would post-colonial leaders allow the syndicate to play in establishing, solidifying, and managing the new post-colonial political system?

After independence, socialists within the Istiqlal party—notably Mehdi Ben Barka—aimed to use the union for party activities in the new post-colonial political environment. Ben Barka sought to connect the unions' struggles for greater socio-economic justice with his party's quest for political power in the new state. He explicated the concept of "political unionism" in which Moroccan unions would utilize their mass following to organize and strike on behalf of his party's causes, while his party in turn would use its influence in formal politics to push through policies beneficial to unions.[17] Their struggles were complementary, not competitive. Indeed, when the socialist wing of Istiqlal split off from the nationalist party in 1959 to found its own party, Mehdi Ben Barka turned to unionists to fill the new party's ranks. He gave the union nearly half of the seats on the new leftist party's secretariat general.[18] In several of Morocco's first elections, specifically in 1960 and 1963, the socialists learned that their relationship with the UMT was instrumental to staging mass gatherings, running electoral campaigns, and rallying voters successfully.

Although the leftist party and the UMT parted ways organizationally in late 1963, the socialists created another allied union in 1978, the Confédération Démocratique du Travail (CDT), and a second in 2002, the Fédération Démocratique du Travail (FDT), to fulfil the role the UMT had played. Even though bumps often arose between the socialists and their affiliated labor unions, the former knew that they depended on the latter to maintain a base, to communicate with citizens, and, most importantly, to win elections. Rallying their mass supporters, the unions could also always marshal the ability to incite urban violence, a power the socialists could not wield alone.

Copying the socialists' model, other parties followed suit and founded their own respective unions. The political parties realized that unions possessed an ability to penetrate society and organize the masses in ways they never could. Hence, throughout the 1960s and 1970s, "it became fashionable for political parties, however meagre their membership, to form trade-union appendages," as Clement Henry notes.[19] After losing the UMT's support in 1959, the Istiqlal created a new union, which it named the Union Générale des Travailleurs du Maroc (UGTM). The Islamists founded their own union in 1974, the Union Nationale du Travail au Maroc (UNTM), which predominantly represented teachers. By the late 1970s, an array of different labor unions—both independent and allied with specific political parties—operated freely in Moroccan society. The 1962 Moroccan constitution created a legal environment that protected workers' right to organize, and, as a result, enabled a multitude of unions to flourish.[20]

Table 4.1. lists the five main labor syndicates and displays their French acronyms, years of establishment, party affiliations, and current secretary-generals. The importance of unions declined in the mid-1970s, when the failed military coups of 1971 and 1973 shifted regime attention to security sector reforms to enhance the army's loyalty and purge its ranks of politicized officers.[21]

Table 4.1: Major Moroccan Labor Unions

Union Name	French Name & Acronym	Year Est.	Party Affiliation	Secretary General
National Labor Union of Morocco	UNTM (*Union Nationale du Travail au Maroc*)	1974	Islamist	Mohamed Yatim
Democratic Federation of Labor	FDT (*Fédération Démocratique du Travail*)	2002	Socialist	Abderrahmane Azzouzi
General Union of Workers of Morocco	UGTM (*Union Générale des Travailleurs du Maroc*)	1960	Istiqlal	Hamid Chabat
Democratic Labor Confederation	CDT (*Confédération Démocratique du Travail*)	1978	None	Noubir Amaoui
Moroccan Labor Union	UMT (*Union Marocaine du Travail*)	1955	None	Miloudi Moukharik

In the 1980s, however, unions began reasserting their political role. On 18 June 1981, Casablanca exploded into riots, the most violent since the anti-colonial unrest of 1952. Organized by the UMT and the CDT, the protests began as a nonviolent march through the centre of Casablanca, in which unionists expressed opposition to the simultaneously increasing cost of living and declining food subsidies. Due to government structural adjustment measures that reduced price subsidies, the price of a number of basic goods—

including tea, bread, and cooking oil—increased from 14 to 77 per cent, starting in May 1981.[22] By joining the ranks of the UMT and CDT unions, impoverished residents of the city's inner *medina* were able to join the demonstrations and vocalize their discontent. These "roaming mobs," as John Entelis describes, "attacked symbols of public authority and numerous businesses."[23] The regime stated that the riots with police resulted in 66 police deaths, whereas the unionists counted 635 victims.

In response to the 1981 riots, the regime arrested a third of the CDT's executive committee, nine representatives in its National Bureau, and almost 100 local organizers.[24] The government also punished the CDT's allied political party, the Socialist Party, by arresting its leaders. Seeking to connect the Socialists' struggle for political power with the unions' demands for the reversal of austerity policies, the party withdrew its deputies from parliament in an act of solidarity. While contentious labor-driven protests would repeat in the 1990s and mid-2000s, none would match the 1981 uprising in its violence and destructiveness. In the aftermath of the protests, the regime cancelled many of the price increases, conceding to the unions' demands in order to alleviate social pressure and avoid urban violence. The riots of 1981 showed that unionists had serious socio-economic grievances with the Moroccan system and were not afraid to mobilize in the streets to force policy change.

In the late 1980s and 1990s, union syndicates again asserted themselves to force concessions from Morocco's ruling regime through direct action and popular protests in urban areas. This time, however, public employee unions made their debut as the key orchestrators of urban unrest. Responding to recommendations from the World Bank and the International Monetary Fund, the regime planned a series of new structural adjustment measures. Prescribed by the bank, such changes included ending protective tariffs for manufacturing, liberalizing trade across borders, and privatizing public services in ministries and municipalities, especially water, electricity, health, education, and sanitation.[25] Winners and losers were created from these policy changes. The biggest loser was the private sector, especially manufacturing. There, workers suffered as the factories they worked for produced lower-quality, higher-cost goods compared with the foreign imports flooding domestic markets. Workers in the private sector stopped unionizing for fear that they would be replaced in the tight labor market, where only 200,000 new jobs were created annually while 300,000 additional workers sought employment each year.[26] Workers in the agricultural sector, by contrast, were the biggest winners. With fewer restrictions on cross-border trade, oranges, tomatoes, and other produce left Moroccan farms and filled grocery shelves in France and Spain, leading to a renaissance in agricultural production.

Efforts to privatize the public sector in the 1990s largely failed, however. With the exception of trash collection and water management in some cities, which were contracted out to private (often French) firms like Veolia Environnement, the public employee unions successfully shot down attempts to privatize public institutions. Indeed, during this period, salaries of public employees rose to over half of total expenditures within the state budget.[27] The public employees secured improved wages after a series of protests that climaxed on 14 December 1990, when 20,000 workers swarmed the streets of Fez and Tangier in a 24-hour general strike that evolved into a riot and resulted in thirty-three deaths and $15 million in property damage. The package of reforms, which included a 15 per cent increase in wages, was further protected in a 1996 agreement in which the regime conceded even more to the unions' demands. Although structural adjustment had weakened Morocco's private sector unions, the public sector unions continued to use protests and strikes—and the associated threat of urban violence—to protect and pursue their material interests.

The 2000s: Regime Resistance to Labor Demands

A new chapter in state-labor relations opened in Morocco in 2007 that preceded union mobilization during the Arab Spring. Upon entering office in 2007 with the electoral mandate of that year's parliamentary elections, Prime Minister Abbas al-Fassi from the Istiqlal party pledged to open negotiations—a new social dialogue—with Morocco's five major labor unions, the UMT, FDT, UGTM, UNTM, and CDT. Al-Fassi announced that he would enter into talks over workers' wages, retirement pensions, and other labor issues. Due to the global economic downturn of 2008, however, the negotiations stalled and, by May 2009, had reached a "closed door," according to union officials.[28] The two sides, al-Fassi and the unions, could not agree. The unions' main demand was for higher wages, especially for workers in the public sector. Although the al-Fassi administration had agreed to a 10 per cent increase, distributed gradually over twelve months, the unionists found this raise insufficient because of the soaring cost of living (which amounted to 16 per cent annually). The unions also alleged that the government had not fulfilled promises regarding a plan to increase compensation for public employees working in small communities, and instead had reduced the number of beneficiaries of the program from 60,000 to 30,000. They also sought changes to the promotion system for the advancement of younger workers who held advanced degrees,[29] and for public employees who had not been promoted because of shortfalls in the state's personnel budget. The unions had real material grievances, inherited from a history of socio-economic marginalization in urban areas.

With the onset of the global economic downturn after 2008, however, the al-Fassi administration refused to accede to the unions' demands. Rejecting requests for higher wages, the Minister of Finance responded that public employees were already well compensated: Indeed, he noted that 73 per cent of the budget for local governments, for example, went to financing the salaries of personnel.[30] In July 2009, the unions decided, collectively, to withdraw from social dialogue negotiations and criticized the al-Fassi administration for not addressing their major concerns. Even the UGTM, a union ostensibly allied with the prime minister's Istiqlal party, decided to walk out of the talks in protest at their ineffectiveness. Upon taking this decision, one negotiator from the UMT announced, "It's no longer possible for the union's leadership to continue sitting down with the government in negotiations without an outcome."[31] To secure their material demands, it seemed that the unions would need to take a more confrontational approach with the regime, which remained complacent.

Even though Morocco's unions walked out of wage negotiations in July 2009 and criticized the regime, they were—in many ways—weak organizations compared with the al-Fassi administration. Several of the unions faced internal discord, which *a priori* placed them at a weak bargaining position *vis-à-vis* the regime. The Islamists' union, the UNTM, experienced conflict between its secretary-general, Mohamed Yatim, and the head of its teachers' association, Abdessalam al-Ma'ati. In November 2010, al-Ma'ati called a special congress and led a faction of unionists that wanted to launch a forensic accounting investigation into the syndicate's expenditures, alleging that Yatim, as secretary-general, should not have full access to its bank account. Al-Ma'ati claimed that Yatim—a top leader in Morocco's Islamist party—was using union funds to support party activities outside of those associated with labor organizing. Yatim denied the allegations and emphasized that the law authorized his access to the bank account, as he was the legal chief of the UNTM.

The conflict between the two UNTM leaders became so arduous that, at one point, the bank froze the union's bank account and did not reactivate it until after a court order. When the court sided in favour of Yatim and against al-Ma'ati in the dispute, the latter launched a personal lawsuit against Prime Minister Abbas al-Fassi because he had chosen to recognize Yatim's leadership of the union, not al-Ma'ati's.[32] After the legal row had ended it was clear that the conflict had been an internal power struggle: The "basic issue," as one Islamist union official explained, was that Yatim's faction "had the union, and the other wing didn't have a foothold in it."[33]

Much like the Islamists' union, the socialists' union—the FDT—also encountered factional infighting in 2010. Two groups faced off for control: One faction allied with the union's traditional leadership, whereas the other faction sided with an ambitious politician and member of the Socialist Party's secretariat general, Driss Lachgar. The unionists complained that Lachgar was interfering in the union's internal elections used to nominate its organizational leadership. They alleged that Lachgar sought to make their union his fiefdom in order to advance his bid to become the Party's president. The factions within the union wrangled, and the internal elections were frozen. A coalition of 77 members of the union's governing assembly submitted a protest letter criticizing Lachgar's interference in the syndicate's affairs. Releasing a statement, the group asserted that Lachgar and the other socialist leaders needed to "take their hands off the union and liberate the unionists from all secret pressures exerted upon them."[34] On three separate occasions, the union's general assembly convened to elect a new leadership but failed because of divided votes; police and medical personnel attended the third meeting in the event of clashes breaking out between the different factions within the union.[35]

Whereas the government of Abbas al-Fassi was emboldened with an electoral mandate from the 2007 elections and prepared to reject labor demands, the unions were weak, disorganized, and divided prior to the unrest of 2010–2011. Given the internal discord within Morocco's labor unions, there were few reasons for al-Fassi to take their threats seriously. How could these public employees who could not keep their own house unified force Morocco's regime to give in to their material demands? Beginning in December 2010, however, the situation changed. The unrest that originated in Tunisia and spread across the Arab world would compel the regime to reconsider (and fear) the unions' threats.

Egypt and Tunisia: The Role of Labor Unions

Moroccan unionists watched as their counterparts in Tunisia and Egypt took to the streets in increasingly violent labor protests beginning in the mid-

2000s. In Tunisia, even before the protests of Sidi Bouzid, phosphate miners in Gafsa had organized a strike with protests that lasted eight days in January 2008.[36] These actions were reminiscent of earlier contentious episodes in the region, such as the 1984 bread riots that originated in Tunisia's marginalized interior provinces. Responding to the regime's request to reprimand its wayward members, the UGTT secretary-general expelled these miners from the union. The miners, who rejected orders from central headquarters in Tunis to disband, continued to strike until police overwhelmed the local union headquarters.[37] Although the mining protests of 2008 in Gafsa preceded the unrest of 2010–2011 in Tunisia, public opinion seemed to reinterpret the popular memory of these laborers—turning those once seen as surly strikers into prescient heroes who aided the downfall of Ben Ali's authoritarian regime.

When protests began in December 2010 in Sidi Bouzid after Mohamed Bouazizi's self-immolation, laborers from the UGTT joined protests as they spread throughout central Tunisia, to Gafsa, Gabes, and other smaller communities. After the overthrow of Ben Ali, information emerged that detailed the role of the UGTT in the popular protests that forced his exile. Although the UGTT's central office stayed loyal to Ben Ali's regime until its end, the union's regional offices took a forceful oppositional line.

In Egypt, likewise, labor unions were identified as vehicles of contestation even before the protests of January 2011. Beginning in the 1990s, Egypt introduced major structural adjustment changes that came to a climax in the mid-2000s: eighty different state-owned factories and industries were privatized, 27 per cent of the total number since the beginning of privatization in 1991. Mubarak had tasked his prime minister in July 2004 to carry out this process. From workers, the government received a response by way of increased strikes. Between 1998 and 2003, there had been approximately 100 strikes per year; this number grew to nearly 200 per year between 2004 and 2006.[38] By 2007, such labor actions nearly tripled across Egypt.[39] In December 2006, one prominent example of such unrest arose. That month, 20,000 workers in the region of al-Mahallah al-Kubra, one of Egypt's textile manufacturing centres, went on strike for three days in response to government plans to restructure contract agreements. While workers' contracts had traditionally been permanent, Mubarak's government planned to introduce temporary contracts that were renewable based on worker performance. There were other demands from the strikers for basic improvements: higher daily wages, improved factory conditions, and better injury compensation. Eventually the police broke the strike, although regime-labor tensions sizzled throughout 2010 and 2011.

Outside al-Mahallah al-Kubra, labor strikes increased dramatically across Egypt in the months leading up to the 25 January revolution. Labor protests in Tunisia and Egypt had set the stage. The time was ripe for Moroccan unionists to strike, pressing for their material demands, just as their counterparts had in neighboring Arab states.

Morocco's Mobilization: Rising Labor Unrest in 2010 and 2011

Although many of Morocco's unions faced infighting and other internal problems, they prepared to vocalize their demands to the regime and, if need be, mobilize mass protests with urban violence to elicit concessions. Taking inspiration from events in Egypt and Tunisia, where labor contestation rose sharply in the late 2000s, unionists took similar actions. Indeed, within the first eight months of 2010, labor strikes increased by eight per cent in Morocco.[40] These strikes included over 18,453 workers in 139 different institutions of the public sector, including municipalities, schools, hospitals, courts, and other state agencies.[41] One particularly important strike occurred on 4 November 2010, when 85 per cent of public sector workers stopped working. They occupied their desks and workstations, shutting down all activity in the public institutions. In some provinces, such as Oriental, 93 per cent of public employees ceased working.[42] This was preceded by a smaller strike on 26 October 2010, when journalists of the Syndicat National de la Presse Marocaine at Morocco's public television station, 2M, organized a strike over rumors of privatization.[43] Despite these labor actions, Morocco's Minister of Finance, Salaheddine Mezouar, remained intransigent. On 17 December 2010, he declared that the option to raise wages rested "in the hands of the government, not in the hands of anybody else." Referencing earlier offers to increase wages in May 2009, which the unions had rejected, he stressed that other priorities such as improving public infrastructure (roads, water, and electricity) would likely take priority over public employee wages in the finance law of 2011.[44]

The unions lambasted the state for its unwillingness to negotiate. Mohammed Yatim, leader of the Islamist union, declared on 26 January 2011 on Morocco's 2M television station that he held the Fassi government "fully responsible" for the increasing strikes in the public sector and that the government had demonstrated a complete "absence of a true desire to steer the social dialogue toward tangible benefits" for Morocco's working class.[45] Initial mobilizations from the unions backed up Yatim's confrontational words. As revolutionary unrest in Tunisia and Egypt erupted in December 2010 and January

2011, Moroccan unions also escalated their actions and took to the streets, inspired by the spontaneous mass protests in neighboring Arab countries. In the last week of December 2010, the unions announced that they would organize a major national strike that would encompass all public sector employees. The 72-hour strike occurred over the days of 8–10 January 2011, and featured an 80 per cent participation rate for public employees. In specific locales, like Sidi Ifni and Safi, participation in the strike included 95 and 90 per cent of public employees, respectively. On its last day, the strike culminated with a large protest that snaked through the streets of Rabat outside the Ministry of Public Works with over 1,000 participants. The unions released a statement calling for the "Fassi administration and the ministry to abide by previous agreements from past social dialogues with the unions" that had been reached in 2007, 2003, and earlier years.[46] They also voiced familiar demands: Extra compensation for public employees posted to small communities, reform for the system of promotion, and a new minimum wage of 3,500 dirhams per month (then equivalent to about $430).[47]

Rallying in solidarity, other unions offered their support for the public employees who had gone on strike and protested in Rabat. On 28 January 2011, a division of the socialist union known for its defiance, the FDT's phosphate miners, called for a protest to support the full implementation of law 6500 that guaranteed health insurance and retirement pensions for those in their industrial sector.[48] Likewise, on 30 January 2011, employees at the Casablanca branch of the Ministry of Finance launched a 48-hour strike because, according to the workers, of a desire to support "the right of employees to express their complaints and discontent" regarding their "collective grievances."[49] With mounting labor unrest at home, and increasing protests regionally, Prime Minister al-Fassi began to take closer notice of the unions' discontent, worrying that it might spin out of control and lead to urban violence, as it had in the 1980s and 1990s. He pledged to personally lead the government's talks with the unions, rather than delegating the task to the Minister of Public Works or another deputy, though he did not set a date for the negotiations.[50] There was no doubt that the specter of labor-driven urban violence had resurfaced in Morocco, motivating the regime to take union threats more seriously.

Although the unions' protests preceded those of Morocco's youth movement, the 20 February Movement for Change, the two groups found common cause. On 20 February, the youth movement launched a major, nationwide protest that included 53 different cities in all geographic corners of Morocco.

The movement claimed that over 238,000 Moroccans demonstrated, while the state estimated the number at only 37,000. The unions publicly endorsed the protests, ordering their members to go into the streets and join the mass marches. Participation in the demonstrations was greatest in the cities of Rabat and Casablanca, where 16,000 and 8,000 protestors, respectively, took to the streets.[51] Although the protests were generally nonviolent, one exception was in Hoceima, where five protestors died. Protestors in other cities of Northern Morocco, such as Tangier and Larache, burnt and destroyed considerable amounts of public and private property. A second and third round of protests, scheduled for March and April, would follow these initial 20 February 2011 protests. Whereas the protests in Morocco were more modest in size and generated less violence than those in Tunisia, Egypt, and Syria, they still represented a resurgence in popular mobilizations unseen in the country since the urban unrest of the 1980s and 1990s.

In response to the demonstrations of 20 February, as well as the previous surge of labor protests in 2010 and early 2011, the al-Fassi administration declared on 21 February that it wanted to return to the negotiating table with the unions. Sending messages to all the major labor unions, Prime Minister al-Fassi emphasized that a new social dialogue should be convened as quickly as possible. The Moroccan regime wanted "social peace at any price," one local journalist noted; wages would be increased to calm union anger.[52] Seeking to improve its position, however, the al-Fassi government stalled on the timeframe for the talks and announced that the state-labor negotiations would re-commence on 5 April 2011, following a two-day religious holiday, which would provide a cooling-off period.

The anger of unions, however, did not abate during the holiday break, and union organizers kept up the pressure against the state throughout the month of March. Between 23 and 31 March, three types of protesters took to the streets: unemployed graduates, health workers, and teachers. The unemployed graduates staged a sit-in in front of parliament, whereas the doctors and nurses demonstrated in front of the Ministry of Health.[53] On 26 March, the teachers' unions staged a large protest with tragic consequences. The protest, billed as the "largest demonstration in the history of Moroccan teachers' unions," occurred outside the Ministry of Education in Rabat and featured over a thousand participants. Although security forces had demonstrated restraint against using force on the youth demonstrators of the 20 February protests, they did not follow a similar course of action with the teachers. In confrontations with security agents, 65 teachers received serious injuries from police batons, and several were rushed to the hospital. On the following day, one teacher died of severe trauma to the head after slipping into a coma.[54]

In a newspaper editorial, Rachid Jarmouni—a teacher and participant in the protest—condemned the attacks on the teachers: We need to "defend the dignity of the men and women of education" and recognize these "flagrant abuses of human rights," he wrote. Jarmouni's editorial also epitomized the socio-economic angst felt by teachers, and, more generally, by all public employees. He decried large discrepancies in salaries between different types of government workers. How can a "public educator after 20 years of teaching experience continue to be paid 4,000 dirhams monthly ($492.00)," while, he continued, the "director of the public phosphate company [can] be given 250,000 dirhams ($30,766.00) per month?"[55] Several private sector unions, including the merchants of Casablanca's fruit and vegetable market, organized solidarity strikes in support of the public sector labor action, a rarity since private sector unions had been weakened by structural readjustment.[56]

Although the al-Fassi government signaled its willingness to negotiate, to stop the unions from re-mobilizing, the leaders of organized labor did not immediately embrace the prime minister's offer to re-start negotiations. Some of the unions publicly warned their members against too much optimism. Other unions boycotted the talks altogether, deciding instead to ratchet up the public pressure. In an editorial on 3 April 2011, Mohamed Yatim of the Islamist union cautioned that the state would need to "respect the agenda and method of negotiations agreed upon in past social dialogues" from 2007 and 2008, and also to provide "tangible answers to core labor demands, and principally, wage increases."[57] The leader of the socialists' union, the FDT, echoed these sentiments, saying, "The government must give signals relating to wage increases and also promotions."[58] One union—the CDT—boycotted the social dialogue and released a statement to the media, emphasizing that the state "continues to gain by drawing out and debating the talks' agenda, and by delaying the negotiations through forming committees. All of this means that the social dialogue is devoid of significance."[59] The CDT, by staying outside the negotiations, helped to maintain the pressure on the state, while the remaining unions entered into talks with the al-Fassi government. At the opening meeting of the social dialogue, four of Morocco's five major unions attended—the UMT, FDT, UGTM, and UNTM. However, few concrete proposals emerged from the first meeting of the social dialogue between the unions and the state, confirming the CDT's initial impressions.

The al-Fassi government also dragged its feet in the second round of talks, which were held on 7 April 2011. The prime minister's advisors did not offer a package of reforms addressing the unions' demands; rather, they continued to debate the topics of the agenda and to equivocate over the scheduled time-table of the negotiations. Seeking to escalate the pressure on the government, the unions made the next move. Frustrated, the Islamist unionists took the lead, with UNTM's negotiators storming out of the meeting during the talks. The UNTM's negotiators announced their rationale for leaving the talks early to a group of journalists, emphasizing that the al-Fassi government had "not come to the meeting with projects or proposals" to meet the unions' demands and that the negotiations had proceeded just like "previous iterations of the social dialogue" that had failed.[60] If the al-Fassi government would not offer concessions to the unions and present a clear plan of how to so implement these concessions, then the Islamist union threatened to join the CDT in a boycott of the entire social dialogue. "The government," said UNTM Secretary-General Mohamed Yatim, still has not provided "answers to other union demands, especially regarding additional promotions in the public sector, which it considers impossible at the current moment."[61] The unions showed that if their demands were not met, they would return to the streets to continue strikes and support mass demonstrations. With Prime Minister al-Fassi desperate to prevent the urban violence that has historically accompanied labor protests, his advisors scrambled to devise a way to meet the unions' material requests.

Responding to the demands of the unions, on 9 April 2011, the al-Fassi government presented an initial reform package that sketched out a proposal to raise workers' salaries, increase retirement pensions, and reform the promotion system. Specifically, the state's proposal agreed to raise the minimum wage, previously set at 2,110 dirhams per month (about $260.00), by 500 dirhams ($62.00) for public sector employees, beginning in July 2011. The proposed increase for private sector workers was much smaller—a monthly increase of 211 dirhams ($25.00). Although the income tax would remain at 38 per cent, the Fassi government vowed to increase support for pensioners who suffered from such policies.[62]

By flexing their muscles, the unions' public employees in the education, health, and justice sectors forced the al-Fassi government to offer concessions. Yet the unions did not accept al-Fassi's proposals immediately; rather, they undertook bargaining maneuvers to procure even greater benefits from the state. Each syndicate outlined a different proposal—each more generous than the one offered by the state. The UMT proposed the most ambitious package. Under their proposal, wages of workers would increase by 1,390 dirhams while the income tax would be reduced to 35 per cent. The UNTM advocated a monthly salary increase of 890 dirhams and reducing income tax to 33 per cent. The CDT—still boycotting the talks—favoured a 700-dirham boost to the monthly minimum wage, a 34 per cent income tax, and a 50 per cent larger retirement pension stipend.[63] The al-Fassi government reacted coolly to the unions' proposals. Even though Morocco had witnessed considerable internal unrest over the last few months, the al-Fassi government thought that the unions' articulated demands were unreasonable. The two sides, the elected government and labor syndicates, had reached a barrier in negotiations that seemed insurmountable.

To overcome the impasse, the unions met on 15 April 2011 to devise a common strategy and harmonize their demands; they collectively agreed that the government's offer was not sufficient. Working in tandem, the unions drafted a common list of demands that included a raise in wages and substantial promotion reform. Public employees would receive either 700 or 800 dirhams more per month, depending on their rank within the civil service hierarchy.[64] Lower-level public employees would receive the largest boost in salary, whereas the higher-level bureaucrats would get the smallest increase. Further, the unions' proposal mandated that these wage increases be retroactive to January 2011. The unions also demanded that 33 per cent of public employees be promoted in the civil service system immediately, also retroactive to January 2011. Because of the Moroccan state's budget shortfalls after 2008, such promotions had been frozen to balance the budget. With regard to pensions, the unions demanded that the minimum amount be increased to 1,000, rather than 600, dirhams. To make up for these additional budget expenditures on public sector salaries and retirement pensions, the unions' proposal called on the government to eliminate tax loopholes for the rich. A new financial regulation would make it illegal to claim more than 36,000 dirhams ($4,420.00) in tax exemptions, a tax evasion strategy used by Morocco's aristocratic and business elites. As these two social constituencies are often at odds with organized labor, the unions felt few qualms recommending policies that hurt their interests. Through their coordination, the unions developed a cohesive list of demands and overcame divisions in their policy preferences. Often separated by their respective party affiliations, ideological differences, and organizational histories, the Moroccan labor unions united to articulate a cohesive, combined set of material demands. Even the

CDT, which had boycotted earlier negotiation rounds of the social dialogue, took the decision to join the other unions in presenting this final portfolio of demands to the al-Fassi government.

On 26 April 2011, the unions and the government met for a final time with a compromise plan of wage, promotion, and pension reforms—a far more generous deal than the initial package offered by al-Fassi's negotiation team. Acceding to the unions' demands, the government agreed to a 600-dirham boost in wages (effective May 2011) for all public sector employees across all levels and ministries within the civil service administration. The government also confirmed that it would budget to increase the minimum wage of private sector workers in July 2011 by 10 per cent, and then boost it again in July 2012 by 5 per cent. By the end, the minimum wage would be set at approximately 2,437 dirhams monthly (about $300). The gradual increase in wages from May 2011 to July 2012 would, in total, represent almost a 330-dirham raise in the national minimum wage, far larger than the 211-dirham increase outlined in the first al-Fassi plan. No doubt, the promised wage increases were much larger for public sector employees than for the private sector ones. In securing a 600-dirham increase for their public sector workers—school teachers, court clerks, hospital nurses, and municipal bureaucrats—the unions had secured a major victory over the government. Union supporters were rewarded for launching strikes and organizing protests to vocalize their discontent with the socio-economic status quo.

Concerning the issues of pensions and promotions, the unions also secured major concessions from the regime in the final package of reforms. The al-Fassi government, in fact, adopted the unions' proposed changes in their entirety. The minimum retirement stipend for public employees, set at 600 dirhams per month, would be increased to 1,000 dirhams—an unprecedented raise of over 70 per cent for retirees.[65] The unions' proposal for rapid, immediate promotion of workers was also approved; the government promised that 33 per cent of employees would be promoted in January 2012 to compensate for previous delays and backlogs. In a press conference with journalists that was serenaded by the whizzing, snapping, and clicking of cameras, Prime Minister al-Fassi announced these changes. He was accompanied by the leaders of the five major unions—the UMT, FDT, UGTM, UNTM, and CDT—who posed beside him for photographs. Leveraging their role as "labor aristocrats," skilled workers in charge of state agencies, Morocco's public employees had compelled the regime to their will through union action. Fearful of the urban violence often accompanying past episodes of labor unrest, the regime had caved in and granted many of the unions' key material demands.

Conclusion and Implications

This chapter has recounted how Morocco's labor unions, building on a series of syndical strikes, sit-ins, and marches that began in the first eight months of 2010, took strategic advantage of the chaotic atmosphere and social discontent of the Arab uprisings to press for and secure major material demands. From this narrative of the political history of state-labor negotiations during this period, three important issues emerge.

The first issue relates to the unions' relationship with the regime. A skeptic might interpret the interactions between unionists and regime officials as an example of authoritarian allocation of rights in which a nondemocratic leader benevolently bestows privileges to a political actor or group in exchange for their pledges of loyalty.[66] According to Steven Heydemann this is one method of authoritarian resilience, a way that regimes "upgrade" to ensure their persistence in the face of opposition.[67] Morocco's monarch, indeed, is known for this strategy: The most prominent example comes from feminists during the family code (*mudawana*) debates of 2003–2004.[68] When political parties reached an impasse over the legal reforms, unable to reach a compromise, the feminists directly appealed to Mohammed VI, who subsequently promulgated a liberal family code law. Following the royal intervention on their behalf, feminists now count themselves as a core social constituency within the regime's coalition of support.

The success of the public employees' unions was not analogous to that of the situation of the feminists—victory by top-down, regime-allocated right. Rather, the unions forced the hand of Prime Minister Abbas al-Fassi to grant material concessions. Given the weakness of Morocco's economy after 2008, the regime never wanted to saddle the state budget with higher wages, better pensions, and more promotions for public employees. These were hard-won gains for the unionists, who undertook traditional tactics of state-labor negotiations—threatening to protest, bluffing to cancel talks, and exaggerating material demands—to exert pressure on the regime, which opposed any concession. Yet, in the context of the Arab uprisings, the unions' strategies became more efficacious; Morocco's regime took them more seriously and bent over backwards to appease labor demands. In the end, the regime's fear of urban violence that has become historically associated with labor union protests and strikes motivated it to forge social peace through palliative concessions.

The second issue concerns the activists of the 20 February Movement. A critic may want to know how these youth activists reacted to the unions' wheeling and dealing with the regime. Were they disappointed that the unionists did not embrace a broad democratization agenda beyond their narrow material demands? The answer seems to be no. Unlike the protestors in Tunisia and Egypt, who squatted in town squares for days and demanded regime change, members of the 20 February Movement neither occupied public spaces nor called for the king's removal. The protest camps were episodic, appeared once-per-month, and disassembled at the day's end. Because the majority of 20 February protestors did not ask *a priori* for the regime's dissolution but rather called for its reform, the unions' vertical negotiations with the state did not derail a broader project for revolutionary change. A future area of research, however, might explore if lateral negotiations occurred between the youth activists and the unionists, and whether the former sought to entice the latter to reject the regime's material concessions.

The third issue concerns the future of Morocco's labor movement. Even though the al-Fassi administration acquiesced to many of the Moroccan unions' core demands, this does not mean that the popular, socio-economic grievances epitomized by the labor unrest have been resolved. Nor, moreover, does it imply that the Moroccan state has evolved into one that prioritizes the interests of workers in urban areas over those of other key social constituencies, especially the rural aristocracy. Indeed, events in the phosphate-mining centre of Khouribga in July 2011 indicate that the socio-economic frustration of workers was not fully resolved by the union-government deal of April 2011. In this incident, miners stormed the local branch of the national phosphate company, Office Chérifien des Phosphates, and burnt, looted, and destroyed the building's interior, resulting in approximately $13 million in damages.[69] In clashes between miners and police, two lives were also lost during the riots. The miners, most of whom were unionized by the FDT and UMT, called for higher daily pay, safer work conditions, and better injury compensation, though the state did not meet their demands. This conflict demonstrated that, despite the union agreement of April 2011, the struggle for the full realization of labor rights continues in Morocco, and that achieving this goal will be long and arduous, and will likely include many more strikes, protests, and negotiations. This analysis has shown, however, that unions can best advance their cause by working in tandem to coordinate their opposition, articulate their demands, and seize propitious opportunities.

5

THE AMAZIGH MOVEMENT
IN A CHANGING NORTH AFRICA

Paul A. Silverstein

Commentators often characterize the political upheavals that took place across North Africa beginning in January 2011 as an "Arab uprising" or, more colloquially, as part of a larger "Arab Spring." Although the uprisings in the Arab world lasted longer than a single season, the allusion to the Prague Spring of 1968 does point to a set of parallels between Eastern Europe's transition from communist rule in the closing years of the twentieth century and the contemporary challenges to authoritarian regimes on the other side of the Mediterranean. These regimes were established at the height of the Cold War, even if they sometimes explicitly adopted policies of non-alignment. Indeed, one might well argue alongside North African scholar Maxime Ait Kaki,[1] that the end of the Cold War and the subsequent rise of neoliberal governance as a global model of sovereignty has provided the opportunity for North African citizens to re-think models of state-controlled political and cultural economies, and state-society relations more broadly. The recent uprisings arguably result, in delayed fashion, from such collective efforts.[2]

Likewise, by referring to these uprisings as "Arab," commentators emphasize the transnational dimensions of the revolts, linking the demonstrations in Egypt, Libya, Tunisia, Algeria, and Morocco to the upheavals in Bahrain, Syria, and Yemen—countries that all share histories of Ottoman/European imperialism, anti-colonial nationalism, and Islamist political contestation. Although the internal workings of the revolts in each country followed their own individual courses, the overlapping timing, demands, and methods point to a broader, networked challenge to these self-defined "Arab" states, a dynamic that calls into question the ultimately arbitrary geopolitical and academic distinctions between the "Middle East" and "North Africa," and between the "Mashreq" and the "Maghreb."

However, referring to the uprisings as "Arab" fails to take into account the ethno-linguistic heterogeneity of North Africa and the ways in which such internal diversity has shaped the challenges to state rule. In this chapter, I draw on the decades-long struggle for Berber/Amazigh rights to argue that the recent revolts follow a long fight for cultural and political inclusion that has been animated by a variety of challengers to authoritarian rule, themselves coming from a range of political persuasions, religious pieties, and ethnic identifications.[3] Indeed, over thirty years before the "Arab Spring," activists and scholars had already recognized a "Berber Spring" that had left behind an important legacy of political activism for North African citizens, particularly for those living in the Berber-speaking peripheries. If the recent uprisings called world attention to the plight and agency of small communities of Berber speakers in Tunisia and Libya, much larger swathes of self-identified Berbers (or "Imazighen") in Algeria and Morocco, aided by diasporic Berbers in Europe and North America, have been for decades outspoken in their demands for cultural and linguistic recognition and in their decrying of institutionalized socio-economic marginalization.[4] Indeed, since the late 1960s, Berber language and culture have become the object of sustained reflection, objectification, resistance, and cooptation in a high-stakes political game over the future of post-colonial North African nation-states heretofore unified under the mantle of Islam and Arabic language.[5] Until the mid-1990s, Amazigh activists, often young men aligned with Marxist oppositional movements,[6] were subject to arrest, detention, imprisonment, and violence for public displays of Berber language (Tamazight) and calls for its national recognition. More recently, the Algerian and Moroccan governments have co-opted Amazigh activists in their struggles against the Islamist opposition and have moved to incorporate Tamazight into the education and media systems as a public gesture of political openness and cultural tolerance, but they continue to suppress ongoing efforts by activists to forge economic and political autonomy in Berber-speaking communities.

In this chapter, I trace transformations in Amazigh militancy over the past fifty years. Its engagements have gradually shifted from particular demands for cultural and linguistic recognition toward a broader advocacy for social justice, political transparency, and economic equity that parallel those of student, labor, feminist, and human rights movements. These are demands that congealed in the 2011 mass demonstrations across North Africa and that explicitly sought to transcend extant ethnic and religious divisions within the region. Alongside these other groups, Amazigh activists lent organizational experience and know-how, a facility with social media, and a cult of martyrdom, which marked not only the Moroccan 20 February Movement but also the revolts in Libya and Tunisia in which Berber citizens were notably involved. Their long-term insistence on decentralization and diversity within the nation-state mapped out an alternative to top-down state-society relations and a model for post-authoritarian governance structures, while such horizontalism ultimately demonstrated similar tendencies to internal fragmentation and state co-optation in the uprisings, as it had throughout the history of the Amazigh movement. Today, the Amazigh movement's imagination of a broader cultural-geographic space of Tamazgha (Barbary) stretching from the Canary Islands to the Egyptian Siwa oasis continues to provide an alternate model for thinking beyond the narrow national interests that had sunk previous, official efforts to enact North African unity. Even as Amazigh activists remain fractured along generational, class, and indeed regional/national lines, their efforts at organizing through "world" federations, supranational bodies (for example, the United Nations), diasporic resources, and delocalized social media point to alternative vectors for rethinking North Africa beyond a set of discrete nation-states. The Amazigh movement thus provides a salient lens for examining contemporary social currents in North Africa.[7]

The Stakes of Amazigh Activism

Over the last fifty years, Amazigh activists have vacillated between articulating cultural/linguistic and sociopolitical demands; between quiescence and conflict; and between engagements at local, national, and transnational scales of belonging. Amazigh activists have had to repeatedly allay accusations of fostering separatism or of being vectors of external manipulation. In the first place, such suspicions derive from the lingering debris of French imperialism and the lasting influence of a set of colonial policies that reified observed cultural differences into hardened ethnic distinctions between "Arab" and "Berber," with the latter projected as carriers of some original Mediterranean culture: incipiently democratic, only superficially Islamized, and thus as potentially assimilable into French civilization. Colonial administrators inconsistently applied such distinctions into legal and educational reforms that specifically targeted Kabylia in Algeria and the largely Berber-speaking periphery (the so-called *bled es-siba*) in Morocco.[8]

Indeed, Moroccan nationalism takes as its origin point the collective response to the so-called "Berber Dahir" of 16 March 1930, a royal decree that reiterated an earlier 1914 *dahir* (royal decree) which instituted the jurisdiction of customary law (*'urf* in Arabic or *izref* in Berber) rather than Islamic law (*shari'ah*) in tribal areas identified as "Berber." Interpreting the pronouncement as a denial of Berbers' Muslim belonging, a group of young activists largely based in Salé and deeply influenced by the *salafi* (Islamic reformist) movement of the Lebanese scholar Rachid Rida and the Algerian *'alim* (Islamic scholar) Abdelhamid Ben Badis organized a broad call for nonviolent protests through the *latif* (Friday) prayers normally used for national calamities, eventually successfully petitioning Sultan Muhammad ben Youssef for its abrogation in 1934.[9] Subsequent anniversaries of the decree served as rallying moments for Moroccan nationalists who, similar to the Algerian activists associated with the 1920s *'ulema'* (Islamic scholar) movement, articulated a vision of a nation fused through Islam, with Berbers understood as earlier migrants from Yemen who were subsequently reintegrated into Arabo-Islamic civilization (*hadara*).[10] Amazigh activists' articulations of Berber ethno-cultural distinction thus risk not only being received as critiques of a particular political ideology, but also as calling into question the precise unifying principle of North African nations. Amazigh activists' recent calls for a democratic and secular state have similarly resulted in accusations of them being agents of foreign conspiracies to weaken or destroy the nation, whether by constituting a *hizb fransa* (a French party), or by being neo-imperialists or even Zionist sympathizers.

Beyond such anxieties of national cultural unity, ongoing suspicions of Berber sectarianism hinge on broader concerns over the territorial integrity of post-independence North African states. Certainly, Berber-speaking peripheries were among the last patches of resistance to the French colonial conquest, with Algerian Kabylia and the Moroccan High Atlas, anti-Atlas, and pre-

Sahara only submitting to military "pacification" efforts more than twenty years after the initial establishment of the colony. These same peripheries witnessed subsequent revolts against imperial rule, notably in Kabylia in 1871 and in the Moroccan northern Rif mountains under Abd el-Krim al-Khattabi from 1921 to 1926. During the 1950s, they would similarly become key sites for anti-colonial organization and military actions for nationalist forces. Indeed, self-described Berber leaders like Ramdane Abane, Krim Belkacem, and Mokhtar al-Soussi were central to the national revolutions, and Berberophone regions were made to pay a heavy price by the French colonial army for their support of the fighters.

But these were also the very same regions that, in the wake of independence, revolted against the centralizing rule of the National Liberation Front (FLN) in Algeria and the Istiqlal (Independence) party in Morocco. In Algeria, the Kabyle revolutionary leader Hocine Aït Ahmed led a ten-month insurrection beginning in September 1963 against what he called the "ethnic fascism" of the FLN regime. He and his organization, the Socialist Forces Front (FFS), were forced into exile in Europe. In Morocco, within a year of independence, the governor of the Tafilalt province, Addi ou Bihi, refused to accept the Rabat-based Ministry of Interior's nomination of local mayors (*quwwad*), jailed members of the Istiqlal party, and took direct control over the towns of Midelt and Rich.[11] In December of the following year, a number of Berber tribes in the northern Rif mountains fought a three-month rebellion against central state rule. The revolt followed the government's arrest of leaders of the rural-based, nascent political party, Popular Movement (MP), and the insurgents demanded neutral (non-Istiqlal) local administrators as well as more state investment in the region.[12] In 1972–1973, in conjunction with the attempted assassination of King Hassan II by army forces loyal to General Mohammed Oufkir, Berber groups in the Middle Atlas, High Atlas, and pre-Saharan southeast amassed arms and attempted a revolutionary secession.[13] The brutal, militarized suppressions of these challenges set a tone of police surveillance of civil society and arbitrary detentions of state challengers that would mark the regimes in both Algeria and Morocco until the end of the twentieth century.[14] While the militants involved in these various rebellions broadly understood their actions to be a continuation of the anti-colonial struggle at the vanguard of a popular revolution against ongoing state injustices, this subaltern narrative has historically run up against the enduring legitimacy of the military and monarchy as guarantors of national strength, thus tending to limit the traction of the localized uprisings.[15]

Given this historical experience and enduring sociopolitical and economic conditions of marginalization, the Amazigh movement had little room for maneuver, and faced an uphill struggle to convince Berber speakers to take on the risks of activism. For centuries, social mobility for rural Berber speakers across North Africa had been premised on alliances with *shurafa'* (lineages claiming descent from the Prophet), urban Arabic-speaking elites, or other groups avowing Arab, Andalusian, or Ottoman genealogies, whether through marriage, migration, education, or various forms of religious or temporal submission. While the French Protectorate had set up a structure of Francophone education and civil service for the children of Berber rural notables, after independence the state administrations, school systems, and militaries became progressively Arabized. Contemporary activists' bemoaning of the marginalization of Berber populations from the structures of power is belied by a significant number of soldiers and administrators of Berber background who achieved high positions in the state apparatus and, in some cases, became outspoken proponents of Arabization language and cultural policies. Even many of those Berbers outside of the high administrative ranks answered King Hassan II's call in 1975 to occupy the Western Sahara, finding themselves included in the patriotism surrounding the Green March and allaying suspicion of any latent sectarianism.

Many of those educated or nationally incorporated in this manner ended up turning their backs on their home villages (*tudarin* or *timizar* in Berber), maintaining minimal participation in local affairs, collecting revenue from inherited property from a distance, and only occasionally visiting relatives during holiday periods—though often still pre-arranging for their own burial in the village cemeteries. For these migrants, their maternal cultural and linguistic idioms came to represent a baseline heritage from which to measure their individual success. They thus integrated their personal narratives into a broader modernization discourse adopted by postcolonial states in which Berber arts, crafts, and ritual forms primarily served as national folklore, living remnants of a previous time.[16] If "the Berber" remained a "national signifier" in post-independence Algeria and Morocco, it was the heroic past that was signified, not the modern present—a patrimony of resistance rather than a contemporary model for a nation in the making.[17]

Militant Generations, State Recuperations

It was within this context of Arabization and migration that those whom Stéphanie Pouessel calls the "first generation" of Amazigh activists—primarily students and intellectuals based in Paris and Rabat during the mid-1960s—began to form cultural associations dedicated to recording and preserving Berber material and aesthetic forms, particularly oral poetry, folktales, music, handicrafts, epigraphy, archaeological artifacts, and architectural techniques.[18] In 1967, both the Berber Academy of Cultural Exchange and Research (ABERC), founded by Kabyle artists and scholars in Paris, and its sister organization, the Moroccan Association of Cultural Research and Exchange (AMREC), founded by students originating from the southern Sous valley, were established with a focus on Berber culture (*idles* in Berber) as an object of reflection and refinement. On the one hand, this move involved the delocalization of culture from its material conditions of production and the articulation of a common, standardized linguistic, semiotic, and aesthetic repertoire shared by all Berbers, regardless of regional specificities. On the other hand, this cultural logic projected a shared Berber tradition as commensurate with other popular arts, practices, and folklores extant within North Africa and beyond, as equally valued contributions to a broader national and world heritage. Indeed, the founding articles of the AMREC defines its task as contributing to "Moroccan cultural patrimony in general and the popular arts and literature in particular."[19] Much of the association's efforts has involved transcribing and translating Berber folktales into Arabic. In parallel, ABERC founders included the singer Taos Amrouche and the writer Mouloud Mammeri, whose life's work similarly involved translating the repertoire of Berber sung poetry (in Amrouche's case, from her mother,[20] in Mammeri's, from the oeuvre of traveling Kabyle bard Si Mhand ou Mhand) for European listeners and French readers. While their motivation derived in large part from the concern that post-independence state policies endangered a Berber way of life, by transforming lived and materially-grounded cultural practices into an inventory of nameable (semiotic/material) objects to be catalogued within national (and world) patrimony, the first generation of Amazigh activists succeeded in side-stepping state vigilance over Berber ethnic or regional sectarianism.[21]

By the late-1970s, the work of entextualizing Berber oral traditions, standardizing a uniform Berber language (Tamazight), and recuperating a script (Tifinagh) from fragmented Tuareg epigraphy—particularly accomplished by the ABERC and its successor association, the Berber Academy (*Agraw Amazigh*) under the aegis of ex-FFS militant Mohand-Arrav Bessaoud—came to have deeply symbolic value within an increasingly politicized North African environment. This period witnessed the rise of a Marxist opposition in Morocco, particularly on university campuses, as well as a growing sense of cultural and regional pride among a younger generation of Algerian Kabyles who rallied around the Tizi-Ouzou soccer team named the Sporting Youth of Kabylia (JSK), using the matches as opportunities to intone Berber songs and display banners written in Tifinagh.[22] When a lecture scheduled to be given by Mammeri on ancient Berber poetry at the University of Tizi-Ouzou was cancelled on 10 March 1980, students occupied the campus and solicited sympathy strikes and demonstrations among Kabyles across Algeria and France, voicing demands for the freedom of cultural and linguistic expression. On 20 April, police stormed the campus, detaining hundreds and injuring many, precipitating international public outrage.[23] The date is commemorated annually by Amazigh activists around the globe as *Tafsut Imazighen* (Berber Spring) and serves as an occasion for the celebration of Berber culture and the staging of demonstrations for Berber cultural, linguistic, and political rights.[24] As Maxime Ait Kaki claims, the events would motivate an entire generation of young militants to spontaneously take the lead in Berberist demands (*revendication*).[25] In Kabylia, detained student activists formed the Berber Cultural Movement (MCB), which would direct the next several decades of struggle for state recognition of Tamazight as a national and official language to be incorporated into the school system and media.[26]

The Tafsut similarly politicized the Berber question in Morocco. In the late 1970s and early 1980s, a "second generation" of activists, largely affiliated with the Marxist opposition, founded a number of Amazigh cultural associations in Rabat and Agadir, with a more deliberate program of promoting Berber language and culture as a central component of Moroccan identity. A number of these, including the lawyer Hassan Id Belkassem, founder of the Rabat-based Tamaynut that still dominates the Amazigh association scene across Morocco, and the professor Ali Sadiqi Azayku, served prison terms for questioning the Arab bases of Moroccan national identity. Like their Kabyle and diasporic colleagues, they proffered an alternate historical narrative of Berber presence in North Africa, rejecting the Khaldunian (and Salafi) Arabian genealogy to emphasize Berbers' Mediterranean and African roots, and highlighting heroic ancestors from the pre-Islamic period including the Numidian kings Jugurtha and Massinissa, the Christian theologian Saint Augustine, and the Jewish Shawiya queen Dihya Kahina who resisted the Arab invasion. These activists drew on the colonial ethnological archive to emphasize a distinct Berber character or spirit that had carried values of democracy, gender equality, and secularism forward from a primeval past, finding a number of those practices apparently still present in remote High Atlas villages and among desert Tuareg encampments to which younger activists traveled as cultural tourists on a quest for self-discovery. While their peregrinations outlined a greater Tamazgha, their model of Berber political culture provided a relevant contrast to the authoritarian regimes under which they lived. In this sense, their efforts melded their cultural engagements with a Marxist sociopolitical framework.

Ultimately, the spread of the Amazigh movement across the region—with hundreds of village-based cultural associations opening up across Algeria and Morocco by the early 1990s—forced the hands of both states. In Algeria, this corresponded with a broader popular challenge to single party FLN rule, particularly in the countrywide riots of October 1988, which resulted in the liberalization of the political system, the legalization of the FFS, and the founding of a new Kabylia-based political party, the Rally for Culture and Democracy (RCD), headed by MCB activist Saïd Sadi. The FFS and the RCD, through their respective branches of the MCB, would give the Amazigh movement an increasing political, if decidedly divided, voice, particularly in the context of the "civil war" that, after 1991, pitted the military government against an Islamist insurgency. While the FFS called for a negotiated political settlement, the RCD, with its strong platform of secularism (*laïcité*) would support the military's "eradicator" position, occasionally entering into coalition with various military-supported governments. Nonetheless, in 1994, the two groups were able to coordinate their actions in a yearlong school boycott (*la grève du cartable*) for the introduction of Tamazight into the educational system as, at minimum, a language of study, if not a language of instruction. The government ultimately responded with the creation of a High Commission on Amazighité (HCA) charged with overseeing the introduction of Tamazight into the school system and piloting the first classes in 1995. Similarly, the revised 1996 constitution recognized for the first time Amazighité as a "fundamental component of its identity," but maintained Arabic as the national and official language.[27] It further outlawed the creation of political parties with an explicitly linguistic, religious, racial, or regional charter.

Morocco has witnessed a similar, gradual process of state attempts at appropriating the Amazigh movement for its own low-intensity "war on terror." In 1994, seven teachers, most of whom were from the southeastern oasis town of Goulmima and were members of an Amazigh association called Tilelli (Freedom), were arrested after their participation in a May Day parade in nearby Errachidia, and for carrying banners written in Tifinagh. Police held them for several weeks, after which the courts sentenced three of them with prison terms and large fines. The three were later released on appeal and the charges subsequently dropped after the case received widespread international publicity and protests from Amazigh associations across the globe. Responding to the outcry, the Moroccan government promised reforms, with Prime Minister Abdellatif Filali opening channels for Berber-language programming in the national broadcast media and the late King Hassan II declaring in his August 1994 Throne Day speech that Amazigh "dialects" were "one of the components of the authenticity of our history" and should—in theory—be taught in state schools. After taking the throne in 1999, the new King Muhammad VI carried out the promises of his father.[28]

In response to this new opening, a group of 229 prominent activists signed a "Berber Manifesto" authored by Royal Academy educator and author Mohammed Chafik, calling for the rehabilitation of Berber culture and the introduction of Tamazight into the school system and public administration. In response, the King issued a *dahir* (royal decree) on 17 October 2001, establishing a Royal Institute of Amazigh Culture (IRCAM) to be headed by Chafik. The institute's 33-member administrative council was recruited through the Amazigh associational structure, with an open attempt to garner an equal representation of activists from the three major Berberophone regions in the Rif, the Middle Atlas, and the High Atlas/Sous. Amazigh militants with technical training and advanced degrees have likewise been incorporated into the institute's seven research centres charged with linguistic standardization, pedagogical development, artistic expression, anthropological analysis, historical preservation, translation and media promotion, and communication. Housed in a purpose-built, state-of-the-art facility whose monumental design incorporates a number of recognizable Amazigh motifs, the IRCAM has since produced textbooks and school curricula for the three major dialects of Moroccan Tamazight, all written in a modified Tifinagh, and classes are being offered in primary schools across rural Morocco. The IRCAM has also taken over the previous role of Amazigh cultural associations like AMREC in editing collections of Berber poetry, publishing studies of Berber history, translating world classics into Tamazight, producing two hours of daily programming on the 2M television channel, and organizing festivals to promote Berber arts, music, and ritual forms.[29] This royal appropriation of the Amazigh cause anticipated the 2011 constitutional reforms discussed below, and constituted a public claim to the monarchy's democratic openness to cultural diversity.

Such state promotion of Berber language and culture as a weapon in North African wars on terror created a significant dilemma for Amazigh militants whose legitimacy derived simultaneously from their multicultural discourse and their oppositional stance. While many activists willingly accepted positions in the new state administration and happily joined the battle against the Islamist insurgency, many younger militants of the "third generation" severely distrusted the HCA and IRCAM as but state lip service to multicultural democracy, designed to maintain the reduction of Berber culture to mere folklore without making any tangible changes to the socio-economic marginalization and contempt (*hogra*) Berber speakers still faced from the Algerian *Pouvoir* and Moroccan *Makhzen*. The Algerian civil war had particularly hardened younger Kabyles living in a state of insecurity that required, in many cases, the organizing of village-level self-defence militias (*groupes de légitime défense* or, in the military's lexicon, "patriots") to make up for the state's failures.[30] The assassination of political singer Lounès Matoub in June 1998 at the hands of unknown assailants, and the killing of teenager Mohammed (Massinissa) Guermah in April 2001 by military gendarmes, further underlined for many Kabyles the extant conditions of inequality, a lack of transparent justice, and their treatment as "second-class citizens" (*citoyens de seconde zone*). Accusing the Algerian government of ultimate responsibility for the two deaths, young Kabyle men took to the streets of the provincial capitals of Tizi Ouzou and Bejaïa, as well as other towns throughout the region, chanting "Government, Assassin" (*Pouvoir, Assassin*), attacking local government offices, and confronting government security forces. While the 1998 demonstrations died down after a week with minimal casualties, the 2001 "Black Spring" proved much more deadly, with at least 60 young men killed and over 300 injured by state troops, and aftershocks continuing throughout the year.[31]

For many of the younger Kabyles who confronted the gendarmes, the excessively cultural focus of the MCB and the political machinations of the FFS and RCD during the seemingly unending civil war delegitimized these institutions as agents of real change; indeed, local offices of the two parties were directly attacked in both the 1998 and 2001 demonstrations.[32] This dovetails with a broader tendency of the younger generation of activists across North Africa to disdain the formal political sphere in favour of a set of decentralized, grassroots efforts that are coordinated on a temporary basis in response to particular challenges. Indeed, in the wake of the 2001 violence, a new political actor in the form of the Coordination of 'Aarouch, Daïras and Communes (CADC or 'Aarouch) arose, uniting a series of nongovernmental, village-based decision-making bodies into a single negotiating partner with the state. The 'Aarouch managed to mobilize 500,000 people in a "black march" in Tizi Ouzou on 21 May 2001, that marked the end of the major violence, whereas the FFS and RCD political parties proved ineffective at coordinating the rioters. Alongside the CADC, former MCB leader and political folksinger Ferhat Mehenni founded a France-based Movement for the Autonomy of Kabylia (MAK) to advocate for the creation of autonomous local government bodies and security forces that would replace the Algiers-directed communal assemblies and gendarmerie. While the MAK recognizes the rights of the national (and, to its mind, future federal) state to maintain an army, regulate interregional commerce, and provide a single currency, it nonetheless proposes a separate Kabyle flag that would be hung alongside the Algerian one. In fact, throughout its proposition for a Project of Autonomy for Kabylia, it consistently presents Kabylia and Algeria as parallel entities: "Kabylia will be more open to Algerians, and Algeria to Kabyles."[33] In June 2010, Mehenni established a Provisional Government of Kabylia (Anavad Aqvayli Usdil) based in Paris and has continued to coordinate efforts from afar.[34]

The MAK's walking of a fine line between decentralization and sectarian separatism has been paralleled in similar efforts made by the "third generation" of Amazigh militants in Morocco who look to Kabylia as their collective "older sister."[35] Matoub has become a hero for younger activists across the country, particularly those members of the Amazigh Cultural Movement (MCA) grouped within the national university student union. Matoub's image and words are reproduced as graffiti across the landscape, and young men and women grow up singing and playing his militant anthems as part of a larger repertory of adopted Kabyle political folksong by Mehenni, Idir, Oulahlou, and others. These young activists and fellow travelers look to Kabyle broadcast and online media for their political news, particularly in the Rif and the southeastern pre-Sahara most proximate to the Algerian border. They support the JSK at a distance and have even founded local soccer teams using JSK colours and insignia, with players even naming themselves with emblematic Kabyle names (Idir, Ygurten, etc.). They have further adapted Kabyle tactics of sit-ins, marches, boycotts, and roadblocks for their own political actions.[36] As early as 1996, Tamaynut had advocated for Berber regional autonomy, as defined by the self-determination of economic, social, and cultural affairs.[37] Its members, mostly from the southern and southeastern regions of Morocco, keep in close contact with Kabyle militants over the Internet, host the latter when they visit Morocco, and plot their own visions of Berber autonomy through the discourse of the MAK and other such groups.

More than simply an agenda item, Berber regional autonomy in Morocco has been an object of recent conflicts that have pitted local activists against state officials and their legal resources. This has been in a manner reminiscent of the earlier struggles for regional self-determination of the late 1950s and early 1970s, if at a lower scale of intensity. Since the establishment of IRCAM, many Berber cultural associations from the High Atlas Mountains, the southern Sous valley, and the pre-Saharan southeast have recentered their activities around socio-economic development, environmental protection, and community education—treating these arenas as equivalently subject to a universal discourse of human rights. In recent years, these groups have been involved in protests against state efforts to expropriate collective (tribal) lands for municipal, national, or even private use. As I have detailed elsewhere, in February–March 2004, the Averroès Foundation for Education and Development based in the pre-Saharan town of Goulmima launched a sustained protest against the provincial governor's attempt to procure the cession of five hectares of collective land to a non-local private investor.[38] A smaller conflict erupted during the same period in neighboring Tinjdad over the state electric company's attempts to secure local land for the building of an electrical relay station. Members of the Association for Integration and Durable Development of the High Atlas region of the Tasemmit massif similarly attempted to block the state's establishment of a nature preserve for wild mouflon sheep that would have cut off village inhabitants from their grazing lands and easy access to local markets and educational centres. Three women from the area were sentenced to two months in prison for cutting a hole in the reserve's boundary fence to gain access to a water source, and the president of the association was correspondingly put on trial for his role in "inciting racial hatred, tribalism, inciting destruction of public property, threatening the public order."[39]

In the years that followed, activists founded federations demanding fiscal and territorial self-determination in the Rif, the southeast, and the Sous. They considered themselves part of a global movement of indigenous peoples, drawing inspiration from the struggles of Native American and Amazonian groups, and finding active solidarity with Berber speakers in Qaddafi's Libya and with the armed struggle to a create a Saharan republic of Azawad for Berber-speaking Tuaregs in Mali and Niger.[40] For Moroccan Amazigh activists, territorial control was inseparable from language rights as the conditions of possibility for a vibrant Berber future. As one of the banners raised by the protesters in Goulmima averred, "Our identity is in our land [Tamazirt] and our language [Tamazight]."[41]

North African Uprisings and Global Imaginaries

In the face of what Didier Le Saout has called the "Kabylization" of the Amazigh movement in Morocco, the Moroccan state has explicitly sought, in the words of Hassan Aourid, Berber scholar and then spokesman for the Palace, to "de-Kabylize" the Berber question.[42] They have done this largely by supporting activist aims surrounding language and culture, and prosecuting those whose actions call into question state functions or national territorial integrity. Indeed, one might read some of the amendments to the 2011 revised constitution as a preemptive effort to quell the rising discontent of the younger, radical militants, particularly given their strong participation in the 20 February Movement (M20F), both in the capital Rabat but also in provincial cities like Agadir, al-Hoceima, Errachidia, and Ouarzazate. In these demonstrations, Amazigh activists lent their tactical skills of mobilization and protest, learned in large part from their Kabyle counterparts, with Amazigh flags prominently displayed and in which images of the Rif War leader Abdelkrim al-Khattabi doubled as a sign of national sacrifice and Amazigh specificity. Whereas all previous constitutions since Morocco's independence in 1956 had specified the Moroccan nation as an "Islamic and fully sovereign state whose official language is Arabic," Article 5 of the new constitution specifies that "Arabic remains the official language of the State" but further stipulates that "Amazigh [sic] constitutes an official language of the State, as the common heritage of all Moroccans without exception."[43] Some Amazigh activists initially worried that the distinction between "the" versus "a" will maintain Tamazight's secondary status. And they remain skeptical over the timetable and effectiveness of the future law that will regulate when and how it becomes "official" within the education and media systems. But the state's embrace of Tamazight as an explicit element of national "heritage" (*patrimoine*) does represent a significant shift in the official national imagination away from a monolithic Arab nationalism.

The new constitution also addresses the Amazigh movement's claims to material, as well as linguistic, rights. If previous constitutional revisions centralized more and more power in the hands of the Rabat political elite, limiting rural administrators to simply enforcing "the law," the new constitution provides significantly more territorial pluralism. The first article defines

Morocco as a "constitutional, democratic, parliamentary and social monarchy" and describes its territorial organization as "decentralized, based on an advanced regionalization."[44] Seven additional articles elaborate, proposing new state efforts to foster local citizenship and human development across the regions (Articles 136 and 139). They outline a limited degree of local financial independence while assuring an "equitable allocation of resources, in order to reduce disparities between regions" (Articles 141 and 142). Like with the language policy, the practical details of such a decentralization program depends on a set of new laws that are yet to be written, while the autonomy movements have broadly taken a wait-and-see approach.

At the end of the day, many Moroccan Amazigh activists, like others associated with the M20F, criticized the revision process as non-transparent, rushed, and undemocratic, and the new constitution as heavy on political rhetoric but light on actual changes. The constitution invokes a greater separation of executive, legislative, and judicial powers but does not substantially alter the king's absolute authority or fundamentally change the structure of governance, as the second generation of Amazigh activists had long called for. It rhetorically guarantees wide civil rights, freedom of religious conscience, and social protections from economic insecurity and state corruption, but stops short of establishing a secular state envisioned by many within the Amazigh movement, or guaranteeing the implementation of these reforms. The M20F continued to press for change with monthly protests, but, in spite of its slogan of *Mamfakinch* ("We will not be disunited"), it quickly fragmented into the separate Marxian, feminist, Islamist, Sahraoui, and Amazigh oppositional tendencies from which it was formed.[45]

What is most surprising is that the Amazigh movement had agreed to coordinate their actions with these other challenger groups in the first place. For years, the younger generation of activists had refused to participate in the annual May Day celebrations organized by Marxist groups, whom the former accused of propagating a "Ba'athist" or "Arabo-Islamic" ideology. During the past fifteen years, on repeated occasions and across university campuses in the Moroccan south, MCA student militants have violently clashed with the Marxist Qa'idiyyin faction, even though many of the second generation of Amazigh activists cut their political teeth with members of the Qa'idiyyin faction. These clashes resulted in numerous hospitalizations and arrests. One of the central sources of tension was the MCA's refusal to participate in expressions of solidarity with the Palestinian cause, which more radical Amazigh militants view as an Arab nationalist canard deployed by North

African states to distract from local socio-economic and political problems. Like a number of Kabyle militants, some outspoken Amazigh activists have adopted philo-Semitic positions, have sought to reconcile Jewish and Berber populations, and have publicly advocated a normalization of relations with Israel.[46] Such philo-Semitism has generated accusations of a Zionist conspiracy, and prominent militants have even been accused of apostasy (*ridda*) for their avowed secularism, thus precluding many coordination efforts between Amazigh and Islamist associations.[47] Similar lines of ideological and material fracture divide Amazigh activists from the Sahrawi rights movement. Many Amazigh militants from southern Morocco view Sahrawis as competitors for resources and political attention, and many campus fights have broken out between the two groups.

The Sahrawi question is also one that has historically divided Algerian and Moroccan Amazigh activists who, for all of their supranational imagination of Tamazgha, continue to recursively identify through national lenses. While the Tuareg fight for an independent nation-state of Azawad has served as a cohesive symbol of resistance, around which transnational Amazigh militancy has come together, the Sahrawi struggle has been notably avoided. Since the mid-1990s, diaspora-based activists have spearheaded the creation of a World Amazigh Congress (CMA) that met for the first time in 1997 in the Canary Islands.[48] Delegates participated from across North Africa and the diaspora, including several from Tunisia and Libya, and many noted the profound emotions they felt in such unprecedented encounters.[49] Subsequent congresses were held in Lyon, Brussels, Roubaix, Nador, Tizi-Ouzou, Meknes, and, then, in Tunis (2014), at which point a subsequent meeting was planned for Tripoli (Libya). However, the various ideological and organizational disagreements between and among national representatives quickly fragmented these coordination efforts, resulting in two parallel CMAs holding rival congresses, with one of them ultimately distinguishing itself as the World Amazigh Assembly (AMA) in 2011. To a certain extent, this split parallels the preexisting one between the FFS and the RCD that had already fragmented the Algerian MCB and the French diaspora, but similar disputes had long divided the Moroccan movement between royalist, culturalist, and politically radical factions. Indeed, Moroccan delegates located themselves on either side of the split, sometimes with nominal members of the same association taking opposite positions. Such tendencies towards recursive scission arguably reflect a deeper dual organization structure within Kabyle village and Berber tribal life that, unlike in other segmentary lineage systems—as described by Ernest Gellner—can play itself out according to a logic of "me and my cousin against my brother."[50]

Although such institutional forms of Amazigh globalism have proven difficult to maintain, the Amazigh movement has succeeded in outlining a transnational vision of political action that stands in stark contrast to the failed efforts of North African states to establish an Arab Maghreb Union. Through long-standing use of new media and social media, diasporic resources, the ongoing online and offline exchanges between activists, Amazigh proponents, however disunited, have transcended North African geographic and geopolitical divides. As already discussed, the circulation of Berber folk music, videos, and texts, mostly produced in the diaspora by Kabyle artists, had a significant effect in expanding listeners' cognitive maps of *Amazighité*. More recently, the Paris-based BRTV satellite station, while essentially Kabyle in orientation, is far preferred across North Africa for Berber news and entertainment than national efforts at providing Berber-language programming. Similarly, websites like www.tamazgha.com, www.mondeberbere.com, and even www.kabyle.com, all maintained by Paris-based Amazigh associations, have become clearing houses for North African political information and discussions in Tamazight, French, and English by activist and non-activists around the globe.[51] Such websites have largely taken the place of the Amazigh-net LISTSERV, previously administered by activists based in North America. As cybercafés and mobile internet service have increasingly spread across North African peripheries, even remotely rural activists have become major contributors, with some even establishing their own village-based websites that reach out to a more targeted diaspora. These forms of media activism preceded, and arguably modelled, the Facebook pages and Twitter feeds that would prove so crucial in coordinating the 2011 demonstrations and uprisings.

One of the unexpected outcomes of these globalizing efforts has been the rapid incorporation of nascent Tunisian and Libyan Amazigh militancy into the broader movement. For years, individuals from these two countries had participated in online discussions and international fora, but authoritarian repression in both countries had all but squashed any institutional organizations. By 2008, several village-level cultural associations had been founded in Tunisia under the rubric of preserving "Berber patrimony."[52] In the wake of the overthrow of Ben Ali, several new associations were established with a national purview. The Tunisian Association of Amazigh Culture and the Amazigh Association for Culture and Patrimony both focused on the preservation and production of Berber arts and culture, much as the Moroccan AMREC had during the late 1960s. While the latter did seek the introduction of Tamazight into schools located in Berber-speaking areas, neither engaged in explicitly political demands, with the Amazigh Association for Culture and

Patrimony taking steps to distance itself from the CMA and other international Amazigh movements.[53]

By contrast, Libyan Amazigh activists have been much more outspoken in their demands for the official recognition of Tamazight, as well as for the creation of a democratic and secular state. Fighters from the Djebel Nefusa were central in the overthrow of Qaddafi, and the downfall of the Jamahiriyya brought them a measure of autonomy. Some communities took advantage of this de facto decentralization to post signs in Tamazight, often written in the Tifinagh script, hang Amazigh flags, and even engage in independent experiments with teaching Tamazight in primary schools. Tripoli-based activists began to publish a newspaper, *Tilelli*, and host a number of Berber arts and music festivals across the country. However, these grassroots efforts did not receive financial or otherwise documented support from the state. While the draft constitution promises to recognize Tamazight as one of several national languages, Arabic appeared to retain sole official status. More disturbingly, only two of the sixty seats of the Constitutional Assembly were reserved for Berber representatives, foreshadowing what many activists presumed would result in future political marginalization.[54] As a result, the Amazigh Supreme Council called for a boycott of the constitutional process. In an effort to force the issue, in November 2013, armed Amazigh militants occupied the Millitah port and threatened to shut down gas shipments across the Mediterranean.[55] While activists look to the history of Amazigh politics and its gains in Kabylia and Morocco, they also recognize their unique situation given the recent history of armed fighting and the current absence of an effective state structure. As one Tripoli-based activist reflected, "What's different from Algeria and Morocco is that the consciousness of the Amazigh people is stronger in Libya, because we've paid the price. We have had martyrs who gave their lives to preserve their language, and ensure they are part of the political environment of the new Libya for generations to come."[56]

Conclusion

Given these different conditions of state repression and rule, Amazigh activism should not be approached as a singular movement. Yet the activists' varied objectification and promotion of a marginalized language and culture do collectively call into question the Arab nationalist ideologies on which post-independence North African states were founded. The activists' long-standing discourse of democracy, decentralization, and diversity (whether described in those exact terms or not) largely dovetailed with the calls for transparency, social justice, and the rule of law made by demonstrators in the so-called "Arab Spring" uprisings, which likewise deployed electronic coordination, diasporic support, and street protest tactics similar to those utilized by Amazigh activists since the 1980 "Berber Spring."[57] While the 2011 coalitions did not last, they broadly succeeded in changing the playing field on which future struggles for greater cultural and political self-determination will take place—decentralized coordination of localized and ideologically diverse groups outside the formal political sphere.

But perhaps the greatest impact of the past fifty years of Amazigh activism in North Africa and the diaspora has been, in the words of Ait Kaki, the "re-Berberization of Berbers."[58] The vast majority of Berber speakers are decidedly not activists, who tend to be students or well-educated workers in the civil service or in the liberal professions. Indeed, most Berbers distrust activists, viewing them as playing politics for their own personal gain or bringing suspicion or the wrath of the state onto their local communities. Activists are potentially useful to the extent that their connections and organizational capacity makes them good intermediaries when family problems or neighborhood issues arise, but otherwise, activists—with some notable exceptions—are generally considered by the communities in which they live to be a necessary evil.[59]

Nonetheless, the Amazigh movement has fundamentally altered the communities in question. Where once "Berberness" was a quality to be hidden and disdained, now North Africans can publicly display being "Amazigh." Indeed, Berber fashion has arguably arisen across North Africa, not simply as a performance for foreign tourists, but as a set of aesthetics to be cultivated and displayed for oneself and one's everyday interlocutors, as an identity diacritic that can coexist alongside one's family reputation and national patriotism. Such personal performances have fostered an emerging industry of commoditized clothing, material culture, media, recordings, and a variety of knickknacks that one finds on sale in any upper- or lower-class *suq* (market) across the region.[60] Twenty years ago one could be jailed for displaying signs in Tifinagh, but now the script has shifted from being a symbol of rebellion to an aestheticized iconography within the urban visual field. As one activist precociously recounted to me in Goulmima in 2004, there are many ways to profit from Tamazight. From its Marxist origins to its neoliberal present, the Amazigh question thus fittingly charts contemporary social and political currents in North Africa.

6

THOU SHALT NOT SPEAK ONE LANGUAGE

SELF, SKILL, AND POLITICS
IN POST-ARAB SPRING MOROCCO

Charis Boutieri

The widespread movement of contestation that swept through urban Morocco during the Arab Spring (2011–2012), known as *Harakat 'ishrīn fibrāir* (20 February Movement), made *dārija* (Moroccan Arabic) central to its articulation of disaffection with economic hierarchies, existing institutional structures, and modes of socio-cultural engineering.[1] The majority of its street slogans and online campaigns, which featured on sympathetic websites such as Mamfakinch [We will not give in] and Lakome [To you], posited *dārija* as the voice of the "people" addressing "authority".[2] Authority was associated, on the one hand, with royal and governmental edicts in *fuṣḥā* (Classical Arabic) and, on the other, with elite symbolic and material capital most often contingent on *francophonie*. The widespread demands for *shughl* (work), *karāma* (dignity), and *'adāla ijtimā'iyya* (social justice) need to be seen in relation to the linguistic registers in which they were enunciated, not least because the

93

Moroccan state did exactly that. The new constitution, drafted by a consultative commission of eighteen members that King Mohammed VI appointed himself and ratified via referendum on 1 July 2011, took a considerably revised position towards Morocco's languages. Specifically, article five reinstated *fuṣḥā* as the official language of the country but added the *amazighiyya* (Amazigh/ Berber) as the second official language and proclaimed that it was to be promoted in public education and the wider public sphere. The article then proceeded to guarantee the state's preservation of *ḥassaniyya* (Hassani)—the Arabic Bedouin register spoken in the south of Morocco and Algeria, the contested Western Sahara territories, and the Sahel—as an integral component of *"al-hawiyya al-thaqāfiyya al-maghribiyya al-muwāḥḥada"* (the unified Moroccan cultural identity).[3] Without mentioning specific foreign languages, article five strongly encouraged their mastery with a view to intensify interaction with and integration into the global *"mujtamaʿ al-maʿrifa"* (knowledge society).[4] The constitutional article presented Morocco's "Arab and Berber" languages in the plural as constituents of a singular, authentic patrimony and as resources for the future.[5]

To an extent, this performance of recognition sanctioned what is already happening in private and public social interaction and in print, visual, and social media: an ever expanding and all the more visible multilingualism among Morocco's spoken Arab and Berber registers, between versions of Arabic, and between Arabic and foreign languages, mainly French and English. The weight of this constitutional performance lay in its marked shift from earlier official rhetoric around the languages and cultures of Morocco and, through this move, its signaling of the emergence of a new nation-state attuned to the role of diversity as an index of liberal democratization. Yet a celebration of this particular institutionalization of multilingualism should be cognizant of a number of caveats. First, the singularity of culture and patrimony pronounced in article five elides conspicuous fissures across class, regional, and gender lines that greatly impact the way differently positioned citizens apprehend "Moroccan-ness." Second, this linguistic configuration does not at all reflect the political economy of the country, which reserves little space for *fuṣḥā* speakers and even less for monolingual Amazighophone or *ḥassaniyya* speakers. In fact, this political economy traditionally depended on *francophonie* and is gradually leaning on the *anglophonie*. Third, this narrative of national reinvention is situated amidst international appeals from Morocco's economic patrons for legislatively safeguarded pluralism. In turn, such appeals for pluralism dovetail with the neoliberal enterprise on a global scale by foregrounding language and culture as objects of commodification within a presumably open arena of competition. Given the above, this chapter aims to probe the relationship between multilingualism and diversity with two aims: first, to examine the social impact of Moroccan multilingualism within the frame of global market capitalism, and, second, to use social experience to unsettle the assumed tautology between institutionalized diversity and liberal democratization.

Written long before the Arab Spring, Abdelfattah Kilito's polemical work *Lan Tatakalama Lughati* ("Thou Shalt Not Speak My Language"), introduces a scriptural-sounding prohibition in the realm of multilingualism in sharp contradistinction with its conventional interpretation as a marker of social and political pluralism.[6] His work places the phenomenon of bilingualism and the act of translation within the continually hegemonic military and scholarly relationship between Euro-America and the Middle East and North Africa. The equivocal title, both declarative and imperative, challenges utopic and elite postcolonial visions of multilingualism as joyous and nonviolent fusion—visions that repeatedly obscure the voraciousness of foreign languages (and their speakers) towards Arabophone language and culture. In this chapter, I modify Kilito's title to "Thou Shalt Not Speak One Language" in order to place this prohibition at the heart of an evolving Moroccan state and thus interrogate the state's agenda of multilingualism during this period of advanced neoliberalism. By advanced neoliberalism, I refer to the current period of global consolidation of a fifty-year long US-led market strategy of penetrating national economies, and to a matching ideology of self-reliance and self-management in an arena of unfettered competition.[7] In doing so, I adopt Kilito's explicitly political stance towards multilingualism and map it onto contemporary experiences of society, governance, and the market in Morocco. Going against the grain of national and international depictions of multilingualism, I question its status as preamble to social justice, economic redistribution, and institutional democratization.

More concretely, it is the contention of this chapter that official promotions of multilingualism partake in a broader neoliberal state strategy—in place since Morocco's adoption of structural adjustment measures through IMF loan packages starting in 1987 and free trade agreements with the European Union in 1996 and the United States in 2004—to shield highly stratified and unequal economic interests by placing the heavy burden of global adaptability on individual speakers as students, laborers, and citizens.[8] In its rhetoric, this strategy endorses individual multilingualism as instrument for balancing out opportunity and access among the population. This rhetorical endorsement at once disguises the difficulty of managing multiple languages, and absolves the state of its responsibility to rectify structural inequalities. Since multilingualism cum pluralism intersects a wide spectrum of public conversations in Morocco around the socialization of young Moroccans, the experience of cultural identification, and the running of institutions, it becomes a critical space in which to notice the antagonistic exchanges between the "people" and "authority". What makes these exchanges hard to unpack is that neither "authority" nor the "people" are easily delineated and cohesive entities that face each other in a transparent arena of institutional politics.

Students of Morocco, and the Maghreb more generally, may ask what is distinctive in the friction I unpack here from earlier mappings of language onto (unequal) demarcations of modernity and tradition, class, gender, and regional hierarchies, mappings that already have intense material and symbolic consequences. It would seem at first glance that the most recent promotion of multilingualism prizes open these earlier frames and offers new opportunities and ways of envisaging oneself in society. The hitch is that there is as much novelty here as legacy. In other words, policies on multilingualism reify previous hierarchies by recasting certain languages as those of modernity, opportunity, and progress within the actualities of global market capitalism. Simultaneously, though, the same policies push crucial questions on the role of diversity in socio-political transformation outside the sphere of representative politics. In sum, the chapter exposes current modes of discrimination that determine who is left out of national and global discourses on development. It also raises urgent questions about the possibility of public deliberation in an ostensibly developing and democratizing Morocco, questions that resonate with the wider Maghreb region and especially within the Algerian and Tunisian contexts.

Time and Space within the Global Linguistic Embrace

Language has been a central concern for historical, sociolinguistic, and postcolonial research, as well as in literary explorations of the Maghreb. Each of the above fields has addressed the geopolitical and symbolic motivations that defined, classified, and disseminated the various registers of the region in the pre-colonial, colonial, and postcolonial phases—bearing in mind that transition between these phases is considerably more indeterminate than the terms would imply. It is not coincidental that the attention devoted to language policy and practice in the Maghreb was significantly more sustained than that given to the Mashreq and Gulf areas. This attention no doubt springs from the modalities of the French colonial mission: its desire to map language onto racial differentiation; its deployment of language difference in dividing and better managing the population militarily, judicially, and economically; the distinctly pedagogical attitude of its imperialism; and its intense cultural and material involvement in Maghrebi societies post-independence.[9]

Earlier scholarship tended to reproduce the naturalization of dominant nationalist language ideologies as well as counter-claims for vernacularization and regionalization. Researchers working in the fields of sociolinguistics and critical theory unhinged language from claims to nature and authenticity and delved systematically into the social and political underpinnings of linguistic practice.[10] Literary production in *fuṣḥā*, *dārija*, or French during the second half of the twentieth century pushed in the same direction in experiential terms by foregrounding both the desire and impossibility of charting any language onto identity, itself a highly elusive concept.[11] In a way, this literature coincided with, or even prefigured, the analyses of recent sociological and anthropological research on Moroccan and Maghrebi speakers.[12] By virtue of its focus on language politics and their social impact, this chapter cannot do justice to the impact of unsanctioned communication and transcription codes offline and online. Along with the immense linguistic ingenuity of several art forms, these individual or collective linguistic experiments infinitely complicate the ideological projects in question.

The interdisciplinary conversation above delves into the inescapably social and, by consequence, political nature of speaking and thinking about language. Language is inherently ideological, whether we understand ideology more neutrally as the fact of formulating speech as purposive activity "in the sphere of interested human social action," or, more critically, as a process of mystification, that is, attempts at social control.[13] The latter view maintains that both ideas about language and the policing of language use overlap with fundamental social and political institutions. It is worth noting that in both definitions of ideology the very attempt to figure out the boundaries of a language—*fuṣḥā*, *dārija*, *amazīghiyya*, French, English, and so on—is metalinguistic and, therefore, rooted in and mediated through culturally intelligible scripts.

Along these lines, the nationalist project of Arabization—which is the scaffolding upon which Morocco's post-independence state-building project is based, as it has been in Algeria and Tunisia—hinged on the modernization

and generalization of "Classical Arabic".[14] Yet, neither modernization, generalization, nor "Classical Arabic" for that matter, are straightforward concepts
and processes. What is worse, terminology here becomes as much impediment
as clarification. In English, we refer to the Arabic promoted through
Arabization in North Africa and the Middle East more generally as "Modern
Standard Arabic". As Haeri points out, this translation is misleading because
it implies that linguistic transformation has been complete and that speakers
distinguish between Classical and Modern Standard Arabic conceptually and
practically.[15] In practice though, both formal and informal linguistic interactions shift constantly between these registers. We need to extend this flexibility to Morocco's so-called "vernaculars", a term often used as coterminous with
"mother tongues." Besides the fact that the concept "mother tongue" is multi-
referential and indeterminate, the product of debate as much as socialization,
everyday speaking offers the opportunity for infinite code-switching. For
instance, the Arabic of the Qur'ān imbues *dārija*-speaking across generations.
Furthermore, youth and middle-class professionals in urban centers tend to
code-switch between *dārija* and French. This negotiation between labelling
and usage is equally central to the Amazigh languages and has become integral
to the activism of the multifaceted Moroccan Amazigh movement.[16] English
will take on a more prominent role in the chapter's narration of events as they
have transpired, but overall I contend that despite significant strides, especially
after the Arab Spring, the language is not yet as institutionally or economically
entrenched as French. Therefore, Moroccan youth who do not emigrate to
Anglophone countries can participate in the global market locally (through
off-shore businesses, development initiatives, and so on) through *francophonie*.
Finally, in this chapter I have sidelined Spanish, a language with a strong presence in northern Morocco but of minor importance in the geographical location under study here.[17]

As suggested by the fluidity of linguistic boundaries, language ideologies
and the strategies for their promotion are sites for the study of society and
politics *tout court*, namely of the multidimensional power struggles between
those who attempt to dominate and those who respond, comply with, or
resist such attempts. Yet insofar as ideology is itself a multifaceted, evolving,
and contradictory process, it is imperative to maintain our curiosity around
how a diverse crowd such as decision makers, pundits, and speakers endlessly
reconfigure languages. It is surprising, but not, as I will go on to show, coincidental, how little these insights have informed the analysis of two focal
areas of social experience in Morocco: public education and global market

integration. The silencing of language ideologies from these two spaces of engagement allows this chapter to provide an original scholarly commentary on the flourishing social and political impetus for embracing multilingualism in Morocco. This chapter shows that this public celebration over multilingualism serves as a powerful political tool in the hands of the state through the twin gestures of institutionalization and de-politicization: namely, the state bureaucratizes diversity in ways that do not alleviate but in fact perpetuate the structural inequality of minorities (classed, linguistic, regional, gendered, and so on) and through measures that leave the elusive shape of Moroccan authoritarianism unscathed.

A Brave New Market World and its Second-Class Citizens

Detailed observations on the official direction and everyday experience of the languages of formal schooling and their role in the work environment allow us to ask pressing questions around continuity and change in Maghrebi societies along social, political, and economic lines: How do Moroccan and international neoliberal language policies use and reposition earlier linguistic hierarchies? What is the vision of socio-cultural and political engineering they promote? To what extent is the realignment of the Moroccan speaking-self with emerging work skills the local instantiation of a global phenomenon? Finally, how can we articulate the relationship between global market integration and the tenets of (neo)liberal democracy in the region?

When 18-year-old Simo, the younger brother of my friend Omama, passed his baccalaureate (nationally standardized exit exam) with flying colors, his family threw a large feast in their home in the old medina of Sla (Salé). Simo had been a stellar student throughout secondary school to the extent that he switched midway through his baccalaureate cycle from his neighborhood high school to the more distinguished Moulay Youssef in Rabat, located near the royal palace at the top of the central Avenue Mohamed V. Simo opted for a prestigious track of the scientific baccalaureate orientation, *sciences physiques* (physical sciences) that exclusively recruited well-performing students. Considering his relatively modest background—his family had a grocery store inside the old medina—Simo's achievement was huge: even though he had the wholehearted support of his family, Simo could not afford private tutoring and did not benefit from help with homework and exam preparation by any of his siblings, who had quit school in early stages, or his parents, who were primary school graduates. Shortly after the award of his baccalaureate, Simo, a graduate of the public (that is, state-funded) school system—Arabized since 1983—entered two *concours* (university entry exams) to gain access to the Faculty of Mathematics and Physics. Sadly, he failed them. The *concours* had a written and oral component, both in French. As Omama admitted to me, Simo coped with scientific terminology in French but could not demonstrate adequate oral skills in the language. While waiting for the *concours* of the following year, Simo took French lessons in one of the many private language centers of Sla, through which he managed to gain entrance to the Faculty of Mathematics. His dream was a postgraduate degree at INSEA (Institut National de Statistique et d'Economie Appliquée), a higher professional institution that produced *ingénieurs d'état* (highly qualified and scientifically trained analysts). This highly selective degree has customarily led to profitable employment, a rare occurrence in a country with an unemployment rate of 25 percent, and 40 percent among university graduates.[18]

His dream was short-lived. A year into his university degree, Simo was unable to follow his classes and failed a number of his exams. Translating his mathematical background into French from his Arabophone basic education to an entirely Francophone university degree was demanding enough, but understanding in-class communication was overly challenging. His sister Omama commented: "Do you see what happens? They break students early, showing them that they will not go anywhere with a public school education. You fail once, you fail twice, eventually you will quit; you are only human...". Indeed, Simo did not finish university and neither did he pursue an INSEA degree. He joined a second-rate private college for information technology and took English lessons in the same private language school in Sla in the hope of either joining a multinational company based in Morocco or seeking a future in Europe or the US. Omama and I agreed that students who sailed through university and the prestigious professional schools in Morocco usually attended bilingual private schools or private tuition centers. While officially obliged to teach the Arabophone curriculum during basic education, many private high schools add Francophone science classes and multiply the hours of French language instruction to help their students make the transition into higher education and the job market. It is no exaggeration to claim that it is largely by virtue of their linguistic skills that many private school students gain access to scientific and technical training, domains that the Moroccan state has postulated as symbols of its own development in economic and human capital terms.[19] Therefore, even though the triangular model of class stratification (working class, middle class, upper class) does not exactly fit the Moroccan landscape,[20] the category of class constitutes an important axis on which to gauge the social impact of language hierarchy on Moroccan students.

Simo's underprivileged family, who had placed their hopes for social ascension and financial security on his academic promise, was deeply disheartened by the derailing of his plans. One night during dinner, they raised the issue once more. Simo argued that the problem came from primary school, where his teachers, who were underpaid and as a result combined their public school employment with parallel private engagement, were indifferent and often absent: "We did not learn much in general and our language skills suffered the most because our teachers gave us very weak foundations." His mother Bouteina did not agree. She blamed herself and her husband for refusing to pay for supplementary evening and weekend lessons provided by private language centers. Her husband, Ahmed, to whom her critique was mainly addressed, chided his children for not rendering enough effort on their own: "I say, whoever works succeeds. You need to do more than what the school asks you, you need to read your own books, you need to try to have conversations in that language." Bouteina responded in a resigned tone: "I don't get it, in my time you could just go to school and university and become a professional or even an academic! Now you put all this effort, all your money, and you end up doing nothing." Simo lowered his gaze in embarrassment, shook his head, and said: "Who knows? Perhaps it's [due to] globalization…"

Simo's trajectory and his family's conversations condense the various links between official language policy and paths to social mobility and economic integration in the contemporary moment. Simo's difficulty with academic French speaks to the structural disadvantage of public school students, who generally belong to less privileged social strata, with regards to academic and professional promotion. His family's evaluation of their own responsibility for his inadequate multilingualism showcases the particular assembly of selves and skills within the frame of neoliberalism. This assembly may have found fertile ground in Morocco—such as a cultural resonance of success as the result of self-reliance—but what is important to bear in mind is that it places the weight of overcoming language and class barriers solely on the individual. From their top-down vantage point, the country's international lenders, such as the World Bank, have continuously deplored the inadequacies of the region's public educational systems and the lack of coherence of the latter with the job market. This technocratic assessment has traditionally reduced education to the product of effective streamlining in planning, financing, and demographics.[21] In this review, a curricular emphasis on science, technology, and foreign languages pairs with extra-curricular factors such as classroom size, teacher training, and gender equality in access. In response to this diagnosis, the Palace appointed the *Majlis al-Aʿla liʾl-Taʿlīm* (High Council for Education), an extra-governmental body of non-elected educational specialists. This essentially technocratic body assumed responsibility for the drastic transformation of educational structures to match the demands of a globally integrated Moroccan market. While not openly publicized, privatization became fundamental to the reconfiguration of the system of formal education. Besides encouraging the creation of privately run institutions, the commission suggested that municipalities, civil society organizations, and parents should partly finance state-subsidized schools.[22]

This managerial hijacking of education construes the language of instruction, the main impediment to Simo's academic promotion, as a commodity first and foremost, that is, a skill converted into economic revenue. Mr. Benslimane, a secondary school teacher of French, echoed this direction in his assessment: "Language has no value in itself, it is about the opportunities it offers. It is a means of social promotion, finding a place in the world. People are motivated by French because they extract (*tirent*) more from French. Arabic does not participate in this self-actualization (*épanouissement*)." Evidently, however, Arabic underpins other types of fulfilment not immediately liable to commodification, because in the same breath Mr. Benslimane declared his deep admiration for Classical Arabic poetry and his attachment to the language of the Qurʾān: "I love Arabic, I was cradled by the Qurʾān!"

Simo's story, the direction of policymaking regarding education, and Mr. Benslimane's statements about the role of language beg a set of queries: What is the salience of the post-independence policy of Arabization, the decolonizing and nation-building measure par excellence, in the current academic and professional landscape? After more than 60 years of independence, what is the position of the French language in Moroccan education and the job market? How can we interpret this position in view of the global displacement of French in favor of English? Despite the dominance of an instrumentalist view of language in market terms, language is not just instrumental for students, educators, educational technocrats, or states. Hence, the trouble with the systemic rearrangements that the World Bank proposed in 2007, and that the Moroccan government swiftly pursued in 2008 through its "Educational Emergency Plan," is that they sideline the multiple sides of linguistic experience and obscure the persistence of linguistic hierarchy inside Moroccan schooling since independence.

Public education in post-independence Morocco adopted the segregated colonial educational infrastructure that ensured elites attended special schools (Francophone French mission schools, bilingual private schools, and, increasingly, Anglophone schools) while the rest of the population received Arabophone instruction. This was also the case in Algeria and Tunisia despite some noticeable differences in the historical roots and implementation of *francophonie* in education, society, and state.[23] Even within Arabized public education, a double logic was in place: on the one hand, schools were geared towards the preservation of the officially sanctioned Arabo-Muslim culture that ensured the continuous legitimation of a religious dynasty and of pan-Arabism as regional paradigm. On the other hand, the same schools created the expectation that the majority of the population would be part of a developing and expanding labor force that would meet the demands of global market integration. What is particularly thorny about this double logic in Morocco is that these two goals did not hinge upon the same language. The result is that students like Simo are educated in Arabic up until their high school exit exam but shift to French as language of instruction at the university level—officially for scientific and technological subjects and unofficially for the arts and humanities.

A frequent technocratic response to this structural discrepancy is that some students are capable of managing basic and higher education in two languages, while also speaking *dārija* or *amazighiyya* at home and working on their English skills or on another foreign language. In their discussion, Simo and his family reproduced this idea of personal responsibility and entrepreneurship, which, as mentioned, is indicative of a particular articulation of the successful neoliberal self. Yet the manifest failings of such a narrative are demonstrated by recurring statistics of alarmingly low rates of retention inside public schools. According to UNICEF, while net enrolment in primary school education for the period 2008–2012 was 95.6% for girls and 90.7% for boys, secondary school attendance dropped to 36.1% for girls and 38.7% for boys. University exam access is currently calculated at a shocking 7% of the entire schooled population.[24] As Simo's trajectory indicates, the burdensome linguistic demands of the public school and the inadequate support within the system to meet such demands play a large role in student failure or abandonment of basic education. This foreclosure of academic opportunity has grave ramifications for young Moroccans, especially if we consider the hegemonic rhetoric of the "knowledge society", a euphemism for the "knowledge economy"; the latter pushing for the substitution of specialized production skills with the generic and adaptable skills of communication, leadership, and technological aptitude.[25] Based on this rhetoric, language skills, notably in the languages most influential within the global market, are critical to professional success. Even though the question of the language of instruction in public education has lately become the object of an open public debate—as I discuss in the next section—the Ministry of Education continues to fragment educational tracks based on language ability, thus exacerbating the already debilitating effects of educational multilingualism. Case in point: the coalition government elected in the aftermath of constitutional reform established a Francophone baccalaureate track option within the ostensibly Arabophone public educational system in September 2013.[26]

In an interview, intellectual and long-time advocate for Amazigh cultural rights, Mohamed Chafik refers to Moroccan public education as the equivalent of the system in Aldous Huxley's dystopia *Brave New World*, a novel set within an imaginary future regime where reproductive technologies are manipulated to create a genetically stratified population.[27] Drawing on this idea of social engineering, Chafik calls public school graduates "group B," essentially second-class citizens. Even though he shies away from blaming Palace initiatives for language policy, he accuses the "government" of intentional betrayal of the population through a poorly designed, "rushed," and "fanatical" Arabization of education and society.[28] More specifically, students who were products of educational Arabization invested in a state-centered vision of development that would guarantee transition from pedagogy to socio-economic incorporation. Yet, given that neither higher education nor the job market outside the public sector converted their operations into Arabic, this transition never ensured the social mobility of Arabophone graduates. More gravely, the state that was supposed to fulfil these expectations began to operate with new objectives. These objectives required restrictions in the financing of the very institutions that would shape and direct social mobility, such as schools and universities. As suggested by Melani McAlister, shifts of this sort are products of "convergence of historical events, overlapping representations and diverse vested interests [that] come together in a powerful, if historically contingent, accord that is productive of a new common sense."[29] What I understand by "convergence" and "overlap" is the broader transformation of the function of the state and its ramifications on a new entrepreneurial model of citizenship introduced within the United States in the late 1960s and disseminated across the global south through US and multilateral funding agencies. As Shana Cohen shows for Morocco, Mohamed

Benrabah for Algeria, and Elizabeth Buckner for Syria, the effects of global fiscal crises in the 1970s and 1980s on North Africa and the Middle East and their consequent adoption of structural adjustment packages—foreign investment that made long-term funding dependent on domestic policy reform—imposed restrictions on state spending and encouraged the privatization of wide sections of social activity, including education.[30]

Multilingualism fitted well with the relatively unfettered foreign investment in the Moroccan economy that affected infrastructure, industry, tourism, and the outsourcing of international businesses and the banking sector. Through these focal points, multilingualism came to inform the concept of "work skills". Scholars of education have frequently expressed skepticism over the definition and inculcation of valuable work skills that pair education with the neoliberal value of flexible accumulation, essentially turning all possible forms of sociality and "being" into specific types of exchanges.[31] In the Moroccan context, what may at first glance appear as opportunity for public school and university graduates—entry into an international market arena of labor and ostensibly fair competition—actually functions as foreclosure. Given Arabization, multilingualism depends on the individual efforts of students and families. Competition that hinges on multilingualism has had another effect on the languages of Morocco: it has breathed new life into surviving colonial and postcolonial ideas about the value of certain languages over others. For example, French is not only the language of imperial domination or Western-imported modernity, but also the register of work opportunity in a theoretically globalized Moroccan—as well as Algerian and Tunisian—workforce. I use the term theoretical here to emphasize the discrepancy between the participation of Global South youth in transnational business endeavors, and persistent inequalities in their physical and professional transnational mobility. In this flattening of the meaning of languages, both the Classical Arabic of public schooling and Arabic vernaculars lag behind French and English. Given the continuous relegation of Arabic registers with respect to foreign languages, it comes as no surprise that many Moroccans are deeply skeptical about the standardization of Tamazight and its integration into the public school system.[32]

Even when linguistic mastery allows access to new workspaces, one still faces the inequalities built into the operations of global market integration. On 20 August 2013, the 59th anniversary of the consolidation of the Moroccan anti-colonial struggle, King Mohammed VI's address to the nation explicitly encouraged the mastery of foreign languages by students who wished to compete in emerging areas of the Moroccan economy such as the "car industry, call centers, and the aeronautic industry."[33] These emerging areas necessitate a brief comparison. Arguably, call center employees of Orange France Telecom in Casablanca and engineers in the Renault car industry in Tangiers—assuming that some Moroccan engineers are indeed hired—have vastly differential access to the world of international corporations and substantially diverse compensation. Out of the public school graduates who resort to call center jobs to fund their university studies or as a first stage in their professionalization, very few consider call centers a step to social mobility within or outside Morocco. Essentially, call center employees use none of their basic or university educational skills. The only thing that this precariously employed youth and the Francophone engineers at the Renault industry or at the new TGV have in common is that their ability to work is contingent on their mastery of French.

In a very real sense, then, the thousands of graduate employees in call centers constitute both second-class citizens in their own state and second-class employees in the global scene. This begs the question: what is the role and function of the Arabized public school? In fact, this role was seriously contested long before the events of the Arab Spring. For one, the burgeoning associations of unemployed graduates, who staffed the *Harakat 'ishrīn fibrāir*, and subsequently the National Committee for the Support of the Movement (CNSAM), have long doubted the purpose of public schools in contemporary Moroccan society.[34] A prevalent student turn towards privatization through private schooling or parallel lessons, noteworthy dropout rates from formal education, and palpable enthusiasm towards alternative spaces of learning such as cyberspace, suggest that citizens are negotiating significant gaps in formal education. In short, the state has gutted the very institution that was meant to guarantee social justice and the redistribution of resources in the post-independence developing period.

The function of multilingualism in view of these gaps is very important. In his historical analysis of the alliance between a corporatized state mechanism and the promotion of multiculturalism in the United States (at school, on campuses, and in administrations) titled "Second-Hand Dreams," Vijay Prashad presents a compelling narrative around the political usage of multiplicity.[35] Starting from the aftermath of the Civil Rights Act (1964) and its erasure of racial discrimination in legislative terms, Prashad shows that the welfare US state where these heretofore second-class citizens sought equality was already obsolete by the end of the 1960s. As this state pulled away from the redistribution of tax revenue into provisions for all citizens, it made achievement and integration of the diverse populations of the United States dependent on their own merit and determination. However, for the already underprivileged, material and structural inequalities seriously impeded their participation in the competition for resources, and entrepreneurship remained an uneven upward struggle. The neoliberal state did not alleviate, but actually made use of, this imbalance in three ways: it instituted multiculturalism as a formal acknowledgement of diversity, which glossed over important differences between and within the various "cultures"; claimed colour-blindness as a strategy of promoting the idea of individual merit in ascension and success; and held certain minorities as examples for imitation over others and as justification of the latter's inability to respond to seemingly equal state and market opportunities. Given the close encounter between the two states through diplomacy, direct investment, and the receipt of IMF and other types of aid since the 1980s, it is fair to assume that the Moroccan state under Hassan II and later under Mohamed VI adopted an equivalent ideological rhetoric that could render legitimacy to neoliberal change. This ideological rhetoric was necessary for the attainment of consent within liberal democracies, but it was perhaps equally crucial for the legitimization of developing democracies (or, more cynically, the façade of democracy in these countries) in the eyes of the international community.[36] Besides Morocco, Tunisia under Ben Ali constitutes a prime example of the adoption of the language of liberalization, which in action decoded liberalism as an economic principle of laissez faire and not as political pluralism. In short, the Moroccan exceptionalism promoted by post-Arab Spring constitution via institutionalized multilingualism serves similar functions to US policy around diversity that has sustained the myth of American exceptionalism.

The specific paradox in both cases is that whereas the state presents multilingualism as coterminous with political pluralism, it shifts the handling of multilingualism in technocratic arenas and therefore outside the realm of institutional politics (elections, parliamentary debate, and ministry-led policies). As we will see below for Morocco, social currents such as campaigns for the promotion of *dārija* in education operate in a deceptive sphere of public deliberation. Even though a civil society language of rights becomes more confident and more visible, technocratic expertise shrinks the power of representation and strengthens the executive branch causing a democratic deficit at the very moment it purports to encourage democratization.

Language(s) and the Anti-Politics of Diversity

In October 2013, Noureddine Ayouche, businessman and founder of Zakoura Education, a non-governmental organization for the reintegration of previously unschooled children into public education, held a workshop titled "Sabīl al-najāḥ, le Chemin de la réussite" (Pathway to Success). This international workshop, in collaboration with the Fondation du Roi Abdul-Aziz al-Saoud, presented several findings that corroborate the widely discussed crisis of public education in the country. Even though this recognition is hardly new, the workshop was groundbreaking in putting forward the question of the language of instruction as fundamental to the tackling of educational dilemmas. Specifically, the workshop proceedings stated that the dropout rate of 350,000 students per year was intimately linked with the abrupt transition of Darijophone and Amazighophone students into the textual culture of *fuṣḥā* in the first grade and, soon afterwards, of French in the fourth grade. They also indicated that, by the end of the primary education cycle (six years), only 6 percent of students mastered Arabic and a mere 1 per cent mastered French. Preschool education did not assist with a transition from *dārija* or *amazīghiyya* to *fuṣḥā* since 67 percent of pre-school children attended *msids* (traditional religious schools), which focus on the memorization of *fuṣḥā* sounds and forms with little emphasis on comprehension.[37]

Ayouche's workshop triggered a parliamentary and media outcry as well as widespread public discussion because of its recommendation to establish the "mother tongues" of Morocco, *dārija* and *amazighiyya*, as languages of instruction in pre-school and early primary school classes. Ayouche was accused of undermining the Arabo-Muslim foundations of Moroccan cultural unity and, by extension, alliances between Morocco and other Arabophone and Muslim countries in the region. Given the ideological potency of the allegations, one would have expected the televised debate between Noureddine Ayouche and the eminent historian and novelist Abdallah Laroui on the talk show *"Mubāsharatan ma'kum"* (Directly with you) to become a heated politicized argument between conflicting camps: the *fuṣḥā* camp represented by Laroui versus the vernacular camp (*dārija* and the Amazigh languages) defended by Ayouche.[38] Instead, the debate quickly shifted to technical comments on the nature of language pedagogy in the classroom, the linguistic and experiential overlap between official language and the vernaculars, and the role of international expertise in implementing language policy across the developing world. For instance, both contributors agreed that a well-thought out, progressive imbrication of the vernaculars with *fuṣḥā* in the

Moroccan curriculum would prevent students from experiencing the school as rupture. They disagreed on the shape of this linguistic amalgam: Ayouche spoke of *dārija mtwasta*, a coded, elevated, intermediate *dārija* that would gradually morph into *fuṣḥā* in the fourth grade, while Laroui proposed a *fuṣḥā mbasta*, a simplified *fuṣḥā* closer to oral communication. Remarkably, the labelling of this amalgam was of lesser importance to the contributors. When the talk show host interjected to ask: "So how would we call this language, *dārija* or *fuṣḥā*?" Ayouche replied nonchalantly: "This is not of my concern." This is a significant disclaimer precisely because it glosses over two extremely vexed political issues: the potential role of so-labelled "minority" languages such as *amazighiyya* in the pedagogical transition of primary school students from orality to textuality, and the neutralization of the use of *dārija* in a state-run institution like a school. This neutralization is rather uncharacteristic of the Moroccan state, which has historically dictated the omission of *dārija* and Darijophone cultural production from public school curricula.

To a degree, the very fact that the above debate took place on national television signals a shift from the hegemonic cultural politics of the state under Hassan II. Drawing on an Arabo-Muslim national narrative as the panacea to the divide and rule highly racialized policies of the French protectorate, both the post-independence monarchy and the ruling nationalist party (*al-Istiqlāl*) had carefully policed articulations of Moroccan identity. This policing led to the banning of publications and artistic products that rendered visible alternative cultural repertoires. There is little doubt that the state agenda in question resonated with some components of the Moroccan public that feel attached and committed to *fuṣḥā*, but it did not however resonate with all. The debate on national culture and languages survived beyond the Arab Spring. After the constitutional reform of 2011, the newly elected PJD party intervened in state television by increasing broadcasting on religious topics and in *fuṣḥā*. Its campaign for *al-Fān al-Nadhīf* (morally appropriate art) received some public support or, at least, benefited from public tolerance. As a response to the PJD campaign, in the name of linguistic, cultural, and ethical pluralism, Khalil Boukhari, editor of the weekly Francophone magazine *Tel Quel*, and others opposed what they saw as a PJD attempt to moralize the Moroccan public sphere through *fuṣḥā*. They launched an advocacy campaign to protect Moroccan pluralism through the founding of the Action Group for Free Culture.[39]

Besides these public confrontations, advocates of *dārija* continue their projects of translation, journalism, and play and novel writing. Their choice of language and topics seem to converge on the belief that cultural production in *dārija* allows the masses to have access to knowledge and public deliberation, which in turn enables processes of socio-cultural pluralism and institutional democratization.[40] The activity of *dārija* production and the visions that undergird it evinces of a social current that is gaining ground beyond the domain of primary education. Certainly, these visions are neither straightforward nor unproblematic: for one, the standardization of *dārija* entails a series of difficult negotiations around language miscegenation and linguistic boundaries, alphabet choice, and hierarchies of location that are far from merely technical. Second, an attempt to pluralize culture and politics through *dārija* still needs to grapple with the highly vulnerable position of monolingual Arabophone speakers within the Moroccan economy as discussed in the previous section.

There are other reasons for caution against the correlation of public debates and cultural activity with political pluralism. Despite increased public discussion, there are still instances where the state represses the use of vernaculars either through legal persecution or through the subtler method of financial bleeding of endeavors deemed threatening to the state's official cultural politics.[41] Moreover, the co-option of artists and cultural producers that have previously been antagonistic to official cultural rhetoric is systematic though constantly evolving in character.[42] Specifically, these former antagonists become model dissenters and function as symbols of the state's multiculturalism insofar as they stop demanding drastic institutional reform. This co-option functions through recognition, financing, and inclusion in exclusive circles of power. One instance of this strategy is the shift from the suppression of the Amazigh activist movements from the 1970s onwards into the official shaping of a model minority through the creation of the IRCAM (Institut Royal pour La Culture Amazighe) by royal *dhahīr* (edict).[43] The founding of IRCAM, essentially a research center and lobbying group, aptly demonstrates that the openness of the conversation around multilingualism, and multiculturalism more generally, is often encouraged as technocratic intervention. Notably, this arrangement presents itself outside the realm of institutional politics.

This technocratic sleight of hand appears apolitical, but it serves a number of political purposes. In her analysis of the trajectory of institutional reform in Morocco in 2011, Beatrice Hibou introduced the concept of "anti-politics" as the overarching interpretive and agentive frame of public and institutional action.[44] She argued that the foregrounding of technocratic expertise to address democratization advances a public understanding of reform as neutral and apolitical. On the contrary, politics is qualified as a quintessentially divisive and self-interested activity. A parallel in the domain of language policy would be the forgetting of the colonial and antagonistic past of the French language within the Maghrebi context and its mutation into the language of global work competition. What happens next is that technocrats, members of both the business elite and civil society, take over domains of governance such as educational restructuring. Their actions precede, and in fact make insignificant, public deliberation that would otherwise need to happen through debate and the rules of political representation. It should be highlighted that such gestures resonate strongly with the neoliberal transformation of state and society far more broadly than just in Morocco or the region. In this transformation, technical expertise acts as civil society pretending to be a nonaligned buffer from the potential excesses of the state. A significant consequence of this transformation is that it releases elected state officials—members of councils or parliaments—from the duty and risk of matching public demand with policy. What is specific about the Moroccan case is that both technocratic decision-making and civil society lie in the vicinity of the Palace, which is an ambiguous political mechanism. This makes the domain of resistance appear particularly unclear because oppositional actors are well aware that a change in the mode of representation, typically imagined to be central to a democratic state, cannot result in the meaningful transformation of governance.[45]

The elucidation of technocracy sheds some light onto Ayouche's workshop and the ensuing debate around the pedagogical language of instruction. A central figure in both the Moroccan business world and civil society, and close to the King himself as he repeatedly admitted, Ayouche promoted certain theses on language and education that invite further discussion. According to his workshop's proceedings, produced by educational experts from Zakoura Education, the World Bank, the American Institute of Research, and Microsoft, one of the major assets of the Moroccan educational system is that it is supervised by a monarchical regime "that is durable and that, according to the constitution, has the right to overlook the strategic issues of the country."[46] Indeed, three royal advisers, Omar Azziman, Fouad Ali el-Himma, and Rashid Benmokhtar, who became Minister of National Education soon afterwards, attended Ayouche's workshop. Such figures, like el-Himma, were active in institutional politics, but withdrew from elections before 2011 and joined the royal cabinet as consultants. Moroccan press and political commentators have considered these consultants so central to the running of the country that they referred to them as a "shadow cabinet."[47] The implication of this statement is that the executive structures of the country remain bicephalous, namely the elected executive body is subordinated by the one appointed by the King, even after reforms to the role of monarchical authority in the summer of 2011.

It is worth connecting the attendance of such royal advisors at the workshop with the King's 20 August 2013 speech referenced above.[48] In that speech, the King assumed patronage over educational reform and reintroduced the High Educational Commission, a body that he appointed in 2008 and charged with the mission to overhaul the educational system in response to World Bank recommendations. Placing himself outside party politics, "I belong to no political party and take part in no election," Mohamed VI assumed patronage of the domain of education which "should not be included in the sphere of purely political matters, nor should its management be subjected to outbidding tactics or party politics."[49] In view of this statement, the King's subsequent call for "broad-based, constructive debates on all the major issue of concern to the nation" becomes particularly enigmatic.[50] Where and by whom will the debate take place considering that education is taken out of the hands of the elected representatives of the public? The correspondence between the August speech and the fall workshop that followed is unquestionable. Not only do both occasions reinstate the importance of patriotism and of respect for morality and hierarchy (all predictable metonyms for the monarchy), but they also push for entrepreneurship as the guiding spirit of educational aspiration. Entrepreneurship, for Ayouche's report, entails instilling the spirit of initiative in young people and in mobilizing "parents and local communities, teachers, economic actors and high executives of businesses in favor of improving the quality of education."[51] The overlap between monarchical supervision over decision-making and the encouragement of social entrepreneurship based on principles of self-management is intriguing. The overlap demonstrates just how smoothly neoliberalism works with the rhetoric and platform of liberal democracy at the moment of doing away with conventional democratic features such as equal rights of representation and economic opportunity.

Another example of affinity between neoliberal reform and Palace objectives that circuitously produces a coherent state narrative about language is the workshop's suggestion that English should become the institutional language of technology and science in research and industry alike.[52] This suggestion built on an existing official turn towards English, evident in

Minister of Higher Education Lahcen Daoudi's bill proposal to make English essential to completing a doctorate degree in the fields of engineering and medicine.[53] To an extent, student desire for this language mirrors the official turn from French towards English. In an interview in summer 2011, an inspector-coordinator for English at high school level underscored the trend across the country: even though English is an optional foreign language course in secondary school, about 85 percent of students opt for it yearly. Thanks to teacher and student initiatives, a few schools had instituted extracurricular English clubs that published their own newsletter. Moreover, students usually took it upon themselves to learn the language through cyberspace (surfing, chatting), music, and satellite TV. However, besides this public desire for learning the language, the appointment of royal adviser Rashid Benmokhtar, former dean of the first Anglophone private university al-Akhawayn, as Minister of National Education suggests that the Palace is starting to endorse, if not strategically promote, English in a still Arabophone public schooling system.

In comparison with the historical inflexibility of *francophonie* as it maps onto class stratification and its connotations as the register of imperialism, it would seem that English can offer opportunities for social ascension and a more impartial overture to the global scene. This may be the case in the future, but, for the moment, English dovetails comfortably with the privatization of education and thus becomes the symbol of new imbrications between Moroccan elites and the global, mainly UK and US, economy. Tellingly, in Morocco, considered a hub of *francophonie* with at least thirteen cultural centers and about thirty mission schools, extracurricular English classes take places at the British Council, the American Language Center, AMIDEAST, and numerous smaller language centers that keep mushrooming across the country. Notably, all these institutions are private, as is the University of al-Akhawayn with fees that reach $8,000 per year. The equally private International Institute for Higher Education in Morocco (IIHEM) in Rabat offers Anglophone undergraduate and graduate degrees in popular market areas such as business, management, finance, and internet technology that the American Association to Advance Collegiate Schools of Business (AACSB) ratifies.

The official encouragement of individuals and communities to take matters in their own hands, the centrality of technical expertise in education and governance, as well as a push for English in scientific and technological advancement are familiar traits of neoliberalism across the global south and beyond. For example, it is not a coincidence that Tawfiq Jelassi, Tunisian Minister of Higher Education, Scientific Research, Information and Communication Technologies within the caretaker government of technocrats in power from January to October 2014, openly promoted English-language training and a pedagogical turn towards "education for self-employment."[54] Instead of settling with neo-liberalism's own assertions about the value of the principle of competition for economic progress and political pluralism, it is crucial to trace the historical, social, and political framework onto which neoliberalism engenders new expectations and anxieties. What is left unresolved in this matching of Moroccan, Tunisian, and other realities of learning and working to global recommendations is the harmonization of entrepreneurship and foreign language with social justice. Thus far, neither of the two appears to create novel opportunities for the previously marginalized, but, on the contrary, exacerbate the substantial gap in fluency, skills, and access between the elites and the masses, and, by extension, between urban centers and rural peripheries. What is more, the official production of the Moroccan multilingual entrepreneurial self ensures that neoliberal ideologies and policies can support and sustain a monarchy that combines elements of liberal pluralism (its endorsement of free trade and moderate social and political reform) with despotism (centralization of executive power in the figure of the monarch). From this angle, it is no wonder that the international community, already happy with Morocco's role in anti-terrorism and the control of migration flows, did not react to the abnormalities of the Moroccan state's rushed constitutional reform in June 2011. The same community did not criticize the ambiguities of the new constitution that offered few changes in the structuring of decision-making at the same time as it solidified monarchical control.[55]

Multilingualism Revisited

The official recognition of linguistic plurality from the 1990s onwards that found its most audacious expression in Morocco's 2011 constitution is undeniably a shift from the mono-cultural post-independence narrative and its transfiguration into exclusive and autocratic modes of governance. It is nevertheless premature if not naïve to view this shift as the actualization of cultural and political pluralism, which according to a modernist liberal imaginary is the pillar of democratization and instrumental to social justice and the redistribution of resources. In fact, the encouragement to view multilingualism this way by both Maghrebi states and their international patrons is indicative of the neoliberal appropriation of diversity at the service of global market integration and the demise of the welfare system, however rudimentary it may have been. Times have indeed changed since the French Protectorate, the aftermath of independence, and nation building efforts in the Maghreb. Yet, as I have argued, it is by throwing languages in new patterns of circulation that the current state demarcates novel relations of inequality.

Beyond the social impact of multilingualism in the period of global market capitalism, there are urgent political questions that intersect language reform. The Moroccan state appears to work towards ridding itself of the obligation to make diversity a catalyst for deep institutional and economic transformations. As a result, social currents that support certain languages in the public, educational, or work sphere cannot target the state—as institutional mechanism approachable through processes of representation—as the addressee of their claims to opportunity and equality. Even more gravely, deference to technocratic management and official recognition of multilingualism dovetail so well with established liberal market democracies that they actually serve as evidence of democratization *avant la lettre*, and despite many indicators that point to the closing down of pluralizing processes in Morocco. When the promises of multilingualism and neoliberal democratization prove false, the underprivileged recipients of both agendas may venture another effort to imagine the future of Morocco and the Maghreb more widely. In that instance, it will become urgent for the deliberating public to envisage how languages will feature in and support deep economic and political transformation.

7

THE POLITICS OF THE HARATIN SOCIAL MOVEMENT IN MAURITANIA, 1978–2014

Zekeria Ould Ahmed Salem

The Islamic Republic of Mauritania is often referred to as "slavery's last stronghold."[1] Mauritania has earned this unenviable title due to the existence of descent-based domestic slavery in the country despite successive abolition decrees put in place since the 1960s. Advocating for the eradication of slavery and its vestiges, El-Hor (meaning "free man" or "freed man" in Arabic) is a social organization that has been present on Mauritania's political scene for almost four decades. Launched as an underground movement in March 1978 by a handful of young activists, El-Hor presented itself as an organization for the liberation and emancipation of the Haratin, a group in Mauritanian society whose made up for slaves, former slaves, and their descendants. Having ties to Black African ethnic groups, with whom they share their ethno-racial origin, and the Arab-Berber group, with whom they share their language and culture (Moorish and Arabic), the Haratin are important players in the demographic and cultural equation at the heart of Mauritanian national identity. This social movement, led exclusively by victims of slavery and their descendants within a social and political environment where the social condition of the Haratin community was emerging as a critical issue, projected a pioneering character. Even though the forms of resistance enacted by the Haratin have begun to attract the attention of some scholars,[2] the many changes brought about through the movement have not been thoroughly examined.[3] The purpose of this chapter is to help fill this gap in the body of research. This is especially important for influencing scholarship in Mauritania's wider region, where racial and ethnic issues are often overlooked by analysts of social currents.

I draw on qualitative data collected in the field over approximately ten years in order to understand how the Haratin have sought equality and justice primarily through fighting the stigmas attached to slavery (and the relics of slavery), and by challenging the political marginalization that has secured their subordination. My analysis will explore the context in which the Haratin movement began, the evolution of the rhetoric it has used to articulate dissent, its politics, and the growing diversity of the organizations that have devoted themselves to the Haratin cause. I outline the ways in which the generational divide among activists has shaped the movement's actions without changing its core demands. I devote attention in the second part of the chapter to analyzing the patterns of conflict and cooperation over time, not only within the movement, but also in its rather ambiguous relationships with other social and political actors. I seek to explain how the complex intersectionality of ethnic and cultural identities has made it difficult at times for non-Haratin communities to accept the legitimacy of the Haratin cause. This has led social movements defending the Haratin cause to take unexpected forms, especially in the context of the "political liberalization parenthesis" that has opened from time to time in the country since the early 1990s in the wake of the so-called "third wave of democratization" in North-West Africa. I then argue that not only has the Haratin movement been an important player in Mauritania's various attempts at democratization, but also that, despite its shortcomings and setbacks, the so-called "political liberalization" process in the country has allowed the Haratin movement the opportunity to advance its social and political agendas. This advancement is illustrated through the political careers of the two major figures of the Haratin movement: Messaoud Ould Boulkheir, the father-figure of the El-Hor movement, and Biram Ould Dah Abeid, the aspiring and outspoken radical leader of the Haratin social movement who has recently attracted international media coverage.[4] The trajectory of these two leaders exemplifies the historic changes that affected the movement, as well as the general trend I trace in this chapter.

A Complex Social Context

Mauritania is an impoverished country with a population of three and a half million. Despite its abundant mining and fishing resources, the country is so crippled by corruption and bad governance that it still relies heavily on foreign aid. Mauritania is governed by a military-dominated autocracy, with elections serving to legitimize the power of the latest strongman and providing a façade of democracy. The country has experienced six coups d'etat since 1978, the latest of which occurred in August 2008, bringing the former general Mohamed Ould Abdel Aziz to power. Located on the west coast of Africa, this is a Sahel-Saharan state that straddles Sub-Saharan and northern Africa, a geography that has led to Mauritania's multi-ethnic population. Noel Foster describes the Mauritanian socio-political equation as follows:

> Two out of five Mauritanians are the descendants of slaves, facing discrimination in a society where the vestiges of slavery impede reconciliation and where many contend slavery still persists. Mauritania's black African population suffered grievously from government-sponsored ethnic violence twenty years ago, and an unfinished reconciliation since. And an exclusionary, predatory elite continues to preside over an overwhelmingly destitute population, the vast majority of whom survive on less than two dollars a day.[5]

Exact statistics on the ethnic makeup of Mauritania are not available since political sensitivities prevent such questions from being asked on national censuses. In the absence of official figures, most experts estimate that between 25 to 30 percent of this Arab-African country's population consists of non-Arabic speaking ethnic groups that self-identify as "Black Africans" (in French: Négro-Africains). These "Black Africans" belong to three ethnic groups: Haalpulaar (Fulbe/Fulani), Soninke, and Wolof. The majority of the population, however, speaks Arabic and were traditionally called "Moors" in colonial literature, but its members call themselves *Bizan* ("the whites" in *ḥassaniyya*, the local colloquial Arabic). However, it is estimated that the majority of the *Bizan* population is racially black since it is composed of Haratin.[6] The origin of this term is unknown; it is also used in Algeria and Morocco, and refers only to freed Arabic-speaking black slaves. Increasingly, however, it has come to refer not only to former slaves and their descendants, but also to present-day slaves (*'abid*; sing. *'abd*). Both so-called "domestic" slavery and "traditional" (or hereditary) slavery continue to exist in Mauritania, but to a degree that is difficult to estimate due to the lack of statistical data. However, if Mauritania remains a post-slavery nation—where slavery is no longer legal but where slaves still suffer from the vestiges of their former condition through social stigmatization although the system was abolished institutionally—it is mainly because traditional social structures of inequality are still meaningful in this country where society remains strongly hierarchical and racialized.

Slavery and Social Hierarchies

Within traditional *Bizan* society, to which the Haratin belong, slavery is part of a tribal and hierarchical social structure that is built upon the principle of inequality by birth. Though all individuals are members of tribes (*qabaîl*, sing. *qabila*), these are themselves divided into religious tribes (*zawaya*) and warrior tribes (*hassan*). But more importantly, within each tribe, the "free" members are considered superior to their servants, namely the griots (*iggawin*), artisans (*mâalmine*), herders (*aznaga*), and finally slaves (*ʿabid*) or freed slaves (*haratin*). Slaves and freed slaves are the lowest groups in the social hierarchy.

Because of the nomadic traditions that were prevalent throughout the country until the late 1970s, exploitation (including sexual exploitation), forced labor in the areas of agriculture and livestock breeding, and the sale and granting of slaves were integrated parts of the local social system. Traditionally, slaves were private property to be loaned, given away, sold, or exploited. They had no right to marry without the consent of their masters, to own or inherit property, or to testify in court. As a result, slaves lived in a condition of "social death" and economic exploitation, especially the women. In the Mauritanian slavery system, slavery is hereditary and passed through the mother's line; therefore, female slaves (*likhdam*, sing. *khadem*) were expected to be the producers of new slaves for their masters.[7]

Though slavery in Mauritania is not always linked to race alone, it has survived in Arab-Berber society, where Haratin are black (*sudan*) and the masters are white (*bizan*). Among the Black Mauritanian societies living on the right bank of the Senegal River, slavery has mostly disappeared,[8] yet its stigma remains powerful in present-day social relations. The anthropologist Ousmane Kamara has noted that in this region "the ideology of caste means that being a slave is part of your very personal substance."[9] Therefore, despite sharing a common racial identity with the predominantly black larger society, black Mauritanians of slave origin who live on the right bank of the Senegal River are prohibited from marrying outside of their caste, are forbidden from owning land in villages or holding other property rights, and are generally treated with contempt. Black Mauritanians of slave decent (*maccudo* in Fulbe, *komo* in Soninke, *jaam* in Wolof) are even deprived of some religious rights, such as the right to serve as an imam of a mosque within the Wolof, Haalpulaar, or Soninke groups. Incidentally, over the past decade or so, the Haratin themselves have seized on this right, at least in the big cities.[10]

Since the French colonial era (1904–1960), Mauritanian political authorities have responded to the realities of slavery in the country by vacillating between denial, embarrassment, and laissez-faire tolerance. The colonial administration largely tolerated the existence and practice of slavery in order to avoid offending the elite families and tribal leaders. The colonizers even went so far as to tacitly sanction the practice by invoking the "Islamic" nature of "traditional slavery."[11] In postcolonial times, the official discourse remained largely the same for similar reasons. Successive governments seem to have assumed that the practice would eventually vanish on its own as part of the natural march towards "modernity," an enduring assumption that proved to be inaccurate. Today, the Haratin slavery problem is both a hotly disputed issue and a disturbing reality on the ground.

Slavery: Between Past and Present

Each year, human rights organizations bring to light dozens of cases of "hereditary traditional slavery," even if the anti-slavery activists usually refrain from invoking figures of the actual number of victims for fear of what a census may reveal. Today's slavery takes the form of unpaid domestic or agro-pastoral work, forced concubinage, the loaning and inheriting of slaves, the seizure of slaves' inheritances by their masters, and dividing slave families and distributing the children of slaves among the family members of their masters. Slaves are often abused and treated as chattel. In rural areas, slaves (including Haratin) are also excluded from owning tribal lands even though they are the ones who cultivate them. In the traditionally segregated slave hamlets (*adabay*, pl. *adwaba*) that still exist in most parts of the eastern and southwestern parts of the country, public services such as education and healthcare are often absent.[12]

The Islamic sanctification of the institution of slavery plays a significant role in the Mauritanian Sunni-Maliki *maddhab* (school of jurisprudence) to the extent that Haratin activists often say, with irony, that slavery is a, "sacred institution." As a sacred institution, it must be desacralized among religious people and not simply abolished within the law. In Mauritania, the chains of servitude are also psychological. Master-slave dynamics vary widely, but the most pressing element of coercion is often religious. Slaves have become so convinced of slavery's lawfulness, including within the realm of religion, that they often do not challenge their own status.

An old and popular proverb states that "the paradise of the slave is under the feet of the master." In the Islamic Republic of Mauritania, despite the equality supposedly guaranteed under the law, the courts have used Islamic law to defend slavery as "lawful" in Islam. In a country where nearly half of the population is illiterate or destitute, manumission (the act of freeing a slave) is considered illegitimate, (even by the enslaved victims, who are themselves Muslim) unless their freedom is granted by their owners. In a country where the population has long managed to keep the state bureaucracy and judicial system at bay, and where traditional hierarchies continue to be relevant for individuals, abolition remains theoretical.

Under pressure from activists and the international community, the law on the "criminalization of slavery" was passed in 2007 although the Abolition Act had existed since 1981. The United Nations Special Rapporteur on Contemporary Forms of Slavery, Gulnara Shahinian, noted after a visit to Mauritania in November 2009 that "serious cases of slavery, both in its traditional and modern forms, persist in Mauritania."[13] In 2013, Walk Free, an Australian non-governmental organization (NGO), created a global slavery index and named Mauritania the country with the highest prevalence of hereditary slavery in the world. According to Walk Free, slavery is "deeply rooted" in Mauritania where "it is estimated that there are 140,000 to 160,000 people reduced to slavery" out of a population of "only 3.8 million inhabitants."[14] Additionally, one of the winners of the United Nations Human Rights Award for 2013 is Biram Ould Dah Abeid, President of the Initiative for the Resurgence of the Abolitionist Movement (IRA-Mauritania), an organization created in 2007. In 2012, the government (dominated by *Bizan*, the white Moors) introduced a new constitutional provision labelling slavery "a crime against humanity." In March 2013, and at the request of the United Nations, the authorities agreed to set up a "National Agency for the Fight against the Legacy of Slavery" tasked with implementing the "roadmap for the eradication of slavery." In January 2014, the government also resolved to create a "Special Court" for judging "crimes of slavery." As a result, the number of trials for acts of slavery today have increased compared to the post-independence era after 1960 in part because acts of slavery were only described as such from 2011 onwards, and due to the work of Haratin activists. Previously, the justice system used euphemisms such as "family conflicts" and labor/land ownership disputes", to describe litigation involving masters and slaves.[15]

Be this as it may, even after the abolition act of 1981 many former slaves continue to live, for the most part, in a situation of complete economic, social, and political subjection.[16] They live in a situation of economic subordination taking on the most despised jobs. Because of the significance of the tribal framework in local society, many relationships are still based on tradition; for example, "fictive kinship" between former masters and former slaves of the same tribe is still meaningful to both.[17] This is especially important in such a poor country where state resources are scarce and never equally distributed, and the only social or economic security comes from their tribal network and relationships. This makes it even more difficult for Haratin, who are almost exclusively poor, to imagine being separated from their so-called former masters. Despite what is assumed by activists to be their important demographic significance, Haratin are still heavily marked by the legacy of slavery. Most of them still live under conditions of social dependency and poverty.

The situation of the Haratin remains a major social and political issue in Mauritania. The fact that it is now a part of the political and social discourse owes much to the activism of the anti-slavery movement and its successive iterations.

The Long March of the Haratin

The fight to end the persistence of hereditary slavery continues in Mauritania today. As of 2014, the organizations that contribute to the continuation of the Haratin movement are of three distinct types: first, the El-Hor organization, to which many activists continue to claim allegiance; second, the NGOs involved in the fight against slavery, such as SOS-Slaves or the Initiative for the Resurgence of the Abolitionist Movement (IRA); third, a myriad of smaller (and sometimes temporary) movements and initiatives that spring up informally and sporadically and that attempt to frame the issue of slavery in new terms. To understand and analyze the progressive diversification of the Haratin movement, we first need to retrace its genesis and progression since the 1970s.

The Birth and Transformation of El-Hor

In Mauritania, the anti-slavery movement appeared only when the social and economic infrastructure that had been propping up slavery began to collapse. Three important factors were at play in this process. The first factor was severe ecological droughts from 1972 to 1975 that undermined the agro-pastoral economy on which the lifestyle of Moorish society was based, driving former nomads and their slaves into urban centers.[18] The droughts and the following displacement left many slaves in poverty, but also in many cases led to *de facto* freedom. The second factor was Mauritania's war in Western Sahara between 1975 and 1978. This conflict relied heavily on Haratin who, in turn, benefited from the war, which provided access to paid work opportunities and basic literacy training offered by the army, both of which fostered emancipation on an individual level. The third and less prominent factor was the entry of a number of young graduates of Haratin origin into the workforce. It is no coincidence that El-Hor came into being in 1978, precisely the year in which all of these processes appeared to bear fruit.

El-Hor was created on 5 March 1978, by a few members of the small group of educated Haratin elite. The most famous of these were Messaoud Ould Boulkheir, Boubacar Ould Messaoud, Bilal Ould Werzeg, and Mohamed Lemine Ould Ahmed. The newly established El-Hor published a charter stating their ideas and the goals of their movement.[19] They immediately proclaimed the autonomy of their movement and its "national, non-racial, anti-segregationist and anti-chauvinist" principles. The creators of El-Hor also specified from the first sentences of their charter the main factors leading them to found the movement:

> The inequalities suffered by the Haratin are fundamentally inspired by religion, exacerbated by an abusive interpretation of the religion by the privileged elite, and maintained by the ambiguity or the almost total silence of the country's laws. These inequalities are not only economic, social, political and religious in nature, but are also inherent in a mentality deeply rooted in centuries of psychological conditioning. To fight all these abuses is the raison d'être of El-Hor (Article III).[20]

The El Hor charter goes on to list some of the key practices still prevalent in Mauritania that lend to the persistence of slavery, such as the land tenure system, bonded labor, and discrimination in access to education. El-Hor demanded that the government act quickly in order to "remove all the contradictions that exist between Muslim and modern law, especially those concerning the status of the slave, namely: the problem of the slave's legal incapacity (property rights, testimony, inheritance), and matrimonial problems (marriage, cohabitation)."[21]

This pamphlet caused widespread debate, and El-Hor quickly entered the public sphere. Once it was public, the movement began organizing social networks and creating local cells. El-Hor spread its message, which focused on concepts such as consciousness-raising among slaves in the rural areas and impoverished suburban neighborhoods where most Haratin lived. Two of the main markers of the movement were that it was nonviolent and operated underground, though the latter changed over time as various organizations within the Haratin defence movement began publishing tracts and manifestos, holding sit-ins in front of government buildings, staging hunger strikes, orchestrating international media coverage, raising public awareness, alerting foreign western powers, and organizing marches through cities, villages, and towns around the country. At a more institutional level, as soon as they were able, members of the movement tried to create political parties, run for elections, establish workers' unions, and set up non-governmental organizations.

El-Hor was born in the final days of the regime of Moktar Ould Daddah, the country's first president, who was ousted in a coup d'état in July 1978. The first public demonstrations of El-Hor coincided with a phase of remarkable instability in state power. In April 1979, Colonel Mohamed Khouna Ould Haidalla replaced Colonels Moustapha Ould Mohamed Saleck and Mohamed Mahmoud Ould Mohamed Louly, who had been successive heads of state since the 1978 coup. Despite the instability, the activists were able to make their voices heard well beyond the Mauritanian borders. For example, the London-based organization Anti-Slavery International swiftly lent their support to El-Hor, sending a mission to assess the phenomenon of slavery in the country and publishing a report on their findings.[22]

In February 1980, a rumor that a slave girl called Mbarka had been sold in Atar—the capital city of the Adrar region—immediately triggered a wave of protests and marches under the auspices of the El-Hor movement. In March of that year, several leaders of the movement were arrested and then put on trial in Rosso (in the southwest) the following July. The main leaders of the movement were sentenced to prison terms of up to three months.

The paradoxical result of this mobilization and the ensuing trial was that the "Military Committee of National Salvation," the country's ruling party at that time, passed a law abolishing slavery in November 1981. It would eventually become evident, however, that the Abolition Act was more of a political gesture to calm the national and international outcry than a genuine legal and political call for change.

Nonetheless, and despite the ambiguities of the legal text, the new law did still appear to be an important concession to the El-Hor Movement. Not only did the enactment of the law have the immediate effect of reducing social tensions in the country, but it also meant that the government was officially acknowledging the legitimacy of the Haratin struggle.

The leaders of El-Hor were not given the positions of power they demanded in their manifesto until after the December 1984 coup in which Colonel Ould Taya overthrew President Colonel Ould Haidalla. In 1985, one of the main leaders of the organization, Messaoud Ould Boulkheir, was appointed Minister for Rural Development. This was the first time that a person from a Haratin background had reached the ministerial level of government administration. The rise of Haratin to important positions continued, becoming more commonplace and culminating in the appointment of Sghair Ould M'bareck, a former member of El-Hor, to the position of Prime Minister from 2003 to 2005. From 2007 to 2014, Messaoud Ould Boulkheir himself was elected and served as President (Speaker) of the National Assembly.

Starting in the second half of the 1980s, the process of integrating the Haratin elite into the ruling class came at a cost. The mobilization of the El-Hor slowed to a stop for five consecutive years (1985–1990), and it was only on the eve of the so-called democratization process in 1991 that the Haratin leadership became involved in official politics. This would prove to become an important turn in the trajectory of the movement—as well as for the country itself—as I will show in the following section.

The Haratin Movement and "Authoritarian Democratization"

The Haratin leaders were not only active in the democratic debate that sprang up in the country in 1991, but they also played a part in the inception of the emerging civil society and in the new independent workers' unions that were created in the context of the country's turn toward "liberalization." It was from the Haratin's dual position at the nucleus of both politics and civil society that they would raise anew the question of slavery. At the same time, there were internal divisions between the ranks of El-Hor. This process of bringing the slavery issue permanently into the public discourse followed a tumultuous path that needs to be retraced carefully.

A Spearhead of the "Democratic Demand?"

El-Hor's engagement in the struggle for democratization was initiated at the first signs of openness on the part of the military regime. In October 1986, President Ould Taya decided to hold municipal elections, supposedly, as he put it, to democratize the country from below. If the first local elections of 1986 allowed the Haratin to come close to standing as members of other electoral lists, the second municipal election of 1990 enabled El-Hor to "unofficially" present (the movement had never been recognized by the authorities) a list of candidates in Nouakchott, the country's capital. This list, led by Messaoud Ould Boulkheir, then -President of El-Hor, did not win the municipality but did enjoy relative success that revealed the significance of a community that was making tangible political, social, and demographic progress.[23] Across the country, El-Hor activists gained experience at electoral mobilization through the list of candidates sponsored by the movement that would later be used when the "third wave of democratization" hit Mauritania in 1991.

Soon enough, the leaders of El-Hor were escalating political disputes with the government of Maaouya Ould Taya. Though some founding members left the movement to side with the regime, one influential group, led by Messaoud Ould Boulkheir and Boubacar Ould Messaoud, took the opposite path. These leaders were among those who addressed open letters to President Ould Taya denouncing the extrajudicial executions of Black African army members (from the Haalpuaar/Fulbe ethnic group) between 1989 and 1991, demanding the establishment of an independent commission to investigate the alleged massacres, and requesting a genuine multiparty system and effective rule of law.

On 15 April 1991, under internal and external pressure, President Ould Taya announced the establishment of a pluralist democracy. In the wake of the promulgation of a new constitution, all stripes of political opponents of the regime came together in July 1991 in a United Democratic Front for Change (Front démocratique uni pour le changement or FDUC). This organization was quickly transformed into a legal political party as the first "pluralist" elections were set to take place as early as January and March 1992. The new party was now called the Union of Democratic Forces (Union des Forces Démocratiques or UFD), and its members immediately elected the president of El-Hor, Messaoud Ould Boulkheir, as the party's coordinator. But, for lack of unanimity, Ould Boulkheir failed to win the nomination for the presidential election of 24 January 1992. The party then put forward an external candidate, Ahmed Ould Daddah, who in turn failed to beat the autocrat Colonel M. Ould Taya. In the aftermath of this bitter opposition defeat, a new party called UFD/New Era (UFD/*Ere Nouvelle*) was created around the leadership of Ould Daddah. El-Hor cadres felt increasingly marginalized within the new party. Unhappy with the way the larger Haratin issue was being treated within the UFD/EN, the movement published a lengthy document that traced its own struggle and also discussed its now uncomfortable position within the party.[24] But it was only in 1994 that the Haratin leaders left the UFD/EN to create Action for Change (*Action pour le Changement*, or AC), a political party led by Messaoud Ould Boulkheir and established in 1995.[25] This new phase brought the so-called "radical" wing of the Haratin social movement into an institutional political framework, a major shift that would have a significant future impact.

Party Autonomy, Activist Diversification, and the Instrumentalization of the Haratin Cause

AC was the first political party to be completely controlled by Haratin, and its very existence was taken as a sign that El-Hor was radicalizing. Among its main demands were the implementation of the law against slavery and the end of anti-black racism in the country. The party was accused by some government proxies of creating a "Black racial party," since the movement had agreed to join forces with some Black African nationalists. In the context of the time, the creation of this party was no trivial matter. The Haratin cause as a social movement was no longer the monopoly of El-Hor and various actors began to espouse the cause. Within the country, each party (including that of the government) wanted to have its own "Haratin component," while abroad, the question of slavery was hijacked by other non-Haratin political groups (the exiled political opposition, the Afro-Mauritanian diaspora, etc.) with the primary aim of destabilizing the M. Ould Taya regime.[26]

The creation of AC was not the only initiative aimed at fostering greater independence for the Haratin movement, which sought to serve as the representative of the entire Haratin community despite the fact that the Haratin themselves were not united. Even though the majority of Haratin were poor and illiterate, the community of former slaves was also diverse in terms of their living conditions, access to education, income, and personal aspirations. This diversity informed the strategy of AC, which tried to organize in such a way as to have political clout on the one hand, and to be able to reach the varied groups within its target population on the other.

As part of these goals, AC created a workers' union called the Free Confederation of Workers of Mauritania (Confédération Libre des Travailleurs de Mauritanie or CLTM) in 1995. That same year, another AC party member and a founder of El-Hor, Boubacar Ould Messaoud, set up an

NGO called SOS-Slaves. In 1995, this organization published a "Note on Slavery in Mauritania" that preceded the annual reports it produced between 1996 and 2005. In these reports, SOS-Slaves exposed and denounced an average of thirty to forty cases every year involving unpaid bonded labor, runaway slaves, dispossession of slave land, "property grabbing" of slaves, identity theft at the hands of slave-owners, and physical violence. Despite the few cases that were resolved thanks to the press campaigns launched by SOS-Slaves, the organization repeatedly accused the state of lacking any real desire to eradicate slavery, punish perpetrators, and protect victims in accordance with the law.[27]

By dramatizing the issue of slavery through the framework of human rights and their defence, the NGO shifted the approach of the Haratin cause from mere party politics to human rights and civil society advocacy. This shift was all the more important since Mauritania was undergoing a democratic setback after the first wave of democratization.

Between Politics and Human Rights: New Life for the Haratin Cause

The creation of SOS-Slaves played an important role in the slow evolution of the debate on Haratin and slavery in Mauritania. Since the debate was revived in the independent media, thanks in particular to the democratization of 1991, it had come to be discussed in two very different ways. According to El-Hor activists, traditional slavery could persist in the country because of the government's inaction towards the perpetrators. In contrast, supporters of the regime took the stance that since slavery was illegal, it simply no longer existed—though they did acknowledge the need to address slavery's economic and social vestiges. The government preferred to talk about eradicating the effects of a "cultural" phenomenon that had been legally abolished, while the human rights associations demanded the recognition of slavery as a persistent reality and the enforcement of existing anti-slavery laws. To the successive governments (dominated by *Bizan* groups of free origin), the judicial system was not the appropriate arena for resolving what they referred to as the "legacy of the past," whereas Haratin activists were demanding an end to impunity for "masters" who were caught still using their former slaves and abusing them. Because of this, the government repeatedly accused Haratin activists of "fabricating slavery" in order to "destabilize" a country supposedly "otherwise united."

Those members of El-Hor who had joined the regime were even commissioned by the government to confront their fellow Haratin on this issue. In 1997, they set up the government-sponsored Committee for the Eradication

of the Legacy of Slavery in Mauritania (CRESEM). This group even received
the public support of President Ould Taya, which in turn triggered a national
debate that revealed once again the hardening of positions around the issue.[28]
It was this tension that ultimately affected the future of AC in the Mauritanian
political scene. AC had enjoyed relative success in the parliamentary elections
of 2001 with the election of four (out of a total of 76) members of parliament,
including Messaoud Ould Boulkheir himself. Despite this minor success, the
government looked with disfavor on the participation of any AC leaders at the
UN's World Conference against Racism held in Durban in September 2001.
M. Ould Taya, who was re-elected in 1997 for a new term of six years, was
now taking ruthless action against opponents, including banning the UFD/
EN in January 2001. The AC party was banned in January 2002 when M.
Ould Boulkheir denounced the persistence of slavery and the marginalization
of the Haratin during a parliament hearing session.

Subsequently, M. Ould Boulkheir and his political allies were denied the
opportunity to create a new party called the "Convention for Change." It was
only in 2003 that the pro-Libyan nationalist Moorish Arabists of the Progressive
People's Alliance (Alliance Populaire Progressiste or PPA), an elitist party that
was losing ground, invited Messaoud Ould Boulkheir and his companions
(both Haratin and Black Africans) to join them. Messaoud Ould Boulkheir
became the President of the APP, with El-Hor the driving force behind it. This
unlikely alliance of habitually opposed micro-nationalisms had two consequences: it allowed El-Hor to stand as the synthesis of all ethnic groups in
Mauritania, and it allowed the Arabists, who automatically became a minority
current in the APP, to become more open towards the non-Arab Mauritanians.

Meanwhile, between 2003 and 2005, the political climate in Mauritania
seriously deteriorated. Ould Taya was re-elected for a third term in November
2003 under controversial circumstances. The political situation appeared to
be deadlocked with no options for peaceful change. Between June 2003 and
August 2004, at least two coups were foiled, but on 3 August 2005, Ould Taya
was overthrown by his own personal guards organized under the name of the
Military Committee for Justice and Democracy (CMJD). This era of "transition" opened up new opportunities for the Haratin movement.

The New Democratic Experiment and the Transformation of the
Haratin Movement

The August 2005 ouster of President Ould Taya by the CMJD eventually
sealed, in March 2007, a transition to democracy that was considered "exem-

plary" by the international community, as well as by local political actors. A coalition led by President Cheikh Abdallahi came to power. Although his party won only five seats in the 2006 parliamentary elections and a meagre 7 per cent in the presidential election, M. Ould Boulkheir decided in the second round to support Cheikh Abdallahi in exchange for some four ministerial posts for his party and the presidency of the National Assembly for himself. He also demanded that the first law to be passed by the new parliament would be to criminalize slavery. He argued that the abolition act of 1981 had not specified penalties for "masters" convicted of slavery. In keeping with its pre-election commitment, the new regime passed a law criminalizing slavery on 9 August 2007. This advance was duly hailed by the APP and its President, M. Ould Boulkheir.

However, at the national level, political events quickly accelerated and moved in an unexpected direction. The new democratic government elected in March 2007 was quickly challenged by part of its own parliamentary majority that was covertly supported by powerful army factions. On 6 August 2008, President Cheikh Abdallahi was overthrown by a military committee chaired by Colonel Mohamed Ould Abdel Aziz leading Mauritania into a period of unprecedented political and institutional crisis.

As President of the National Assembly, and still faithful to the legitimate regime of Ould Cheikh Abdallahi, Ould Boulkheir assumed leadership of a civic resistance movement called the "National Front for the Development of Democracy" (Front National de Développement de la Démocratie or FNDD). This group consisted of elected officials, political parties, NGOs, and independent personalities from a variety of backgrounds. The FNDD managed to maintain mobilization against the coup for over a year and urged the international community to refuse to recognize the new regime. Protests against the coup and pressure for a return to democracy were intense. International mediation led to a political settlement called the Dakar agreement, which was signed in Senegal in June 2009. As part of the settlement the deposed president agreed to resign. A presidential election was held in July 2009 in which Ould Boulkheir would run as the sole FNDD candidate.[29]

For the first time in history, a Haratin had the chance to become a public symbol of the struggle for democracy and social justice that largely transcended ethnic divisions. When the election took place on 18 July 2009, Ould Boulkheir came in second with nearly 17 percent of the vote, behind the coup leader General Ould Abdel Aziz who was elected in the first round with over 52 percent of the vote. Recognizing the results, the Haratin leader remained

President of the National Assembly, which surprisingly had not been dissolved after the coup. He continued to play a prominent role in the political life of the country until the parliamentary elections of November 2013, when he lost his seat as a result of his party's boycott of that election.

El-Hor continued to exist in theory during these developments. Indeed, since 2007, Ould Boulkheir had expressed his desire to see El-Hor absorbed by the APP party, but several activists who were also members of the APP categorically rejected this option. Some of his opponents (including Samory Ould Bèye and Mohamed Bourbos) were expelled from the party in 2010 and went on to create their own party named Al-Moustaghbal (The Future). This small group that has no elected members in the parliament or elsewhere, since 2010 has been the only party to openly speak in the name of the original El-Hor. El-Hor, which has been sidelined for so long, appears in the view of many to belong to the past. Indeed, on the ground, new generations of Haratin have begun to organize. They are successfully trying to reopen the Haratin and slavery debate on an entirely new basis.

IRA and the Second Life of the Haratin Movement

Paradoxically, the 2007 law criminalizing slavery merely served to revive the mobilization of new generations of Haratin who openly favored the radicalization of the movement. Some initiatives, however, stood out. For example, in 2008, a United Front for Haratin Action (Front Uni pour l'Action des Haratines, or FUAH) drew attention to itself by publishing a document entitled "50 Years of Systematic Exclusion and Marginalization of the Haratin."

However, as of 2015, the new organization that is effectively shifting the Haratin social movement toward a whole new level of radicalism is the Initiative for the Resurgence of the Abolitionist Movement (IRA-Mauritania).

Created in 2007 by Biram Dah Abeid, a former Secretary General of SOS-Slaves, IRA-Mauritania endeavored to frame the problem of slavery in new ways, with methods and discourse aiming at destabilizing the political and religious elites. In terms of reviving national interest in the Haratin community, the unauthorized IRA-Mauritania developed its activities in several directions including denouncing the use of Islam as a justification of the inferiority and the exclusion of the Haratin, the determination to bring all alleged cases of slavery before the courts of law, and taking a stance against bonded labor and domestic slavery.

To Biram Ould Dah Abeid, founding president of IRA, it was essential to fight what he called the "Bizan hegemony in Mauritania," of which the "official version of Islam" was the main instrument used to maintain that hegemony. For Ould Dah Abeid, "this is a top priority."[30] Therefore, he often criticized "the silence of the *ulama* in the face of the persistence of slavery," as well as their "willingness to manipulate the sacred texts to encourage the crime of slavery."[31] The IRA also reached a major milestone in this campaign when, on 27 April 2012, its activists organized the public burning of several books of Islamic law, including copies of the *Mukhtaṣar* (*Abridged*) the widely used and revered book of Maliki Sunni jurisprudence written in the fourteenth century by Khalil ibn Iṣhaq al-Jundi (d. 1365). Even if the burning of "blasphemous" books launched cries of "Allahu Akbar,"[32] the outrage was enormous across the country. The leader of the IRA was immediately imprisoned and charged with "blasphemy," though his case was dismissed four months later under national and international pressure.

The burning of religious books by IRA activists was triggered by one particular event. On 26 March 2012, the Supreme Court of Mauritania granted freedom to Cheikh Ould Hassine who had been sentenced on 21 November 2011 by the Criminal Court of Nouakchott to two years' imprisonment for the "practice of slavery."[33] The defendant was charged with exploiting two young boys who were "slaves by birth," and whom the defendant had been forcing into labor as goatherds: Said Ould Salka (aged 13) and his younger brother Yarg Ould Salka (aged 8 years).

The IRA's struggle against impunity of those using bonded labor had started long before this particular case, however. The actions of the IRA (sit-ins, demonstrations, clashes with the police) had, in January 2011, already led the courts to assign a six-month prison sentence to a woman accused of employing a thirteen-year-old girl without payment. But the woman, who was the first person in the history of the country to be sentenced for slavery, was later released. Ironically, after that case, Ould Abeid was put on trial, along with other activists, for organizing an "unauthorized demonstration" and for "membership [in] an illegal organization," namely the IRA. All convicted activists were ultimately released at the end of February 2011 following a presidential pardon.

Thanks to the efforts of the IRA, the Mauritanian government began responding to the issue, and President Ould Abdel Aziz said he would enforce the laws against domestic slavery. The wind of the Arab Spring was already beginning to blow across the region and in promising to enforce anti-slavery laws, the government hoped to avoid fueling social tensions.

The Arab Spring Effect

Like many parts of the word, the Arab Spring's ripple effect reached Mauritania. Wanting to take advantage of the opportunity presented by the events in Tunisia and Egypt, various protest groups (youth, women, public servants, the unemployed, and others) took to the streets or camped outside the presidential palace in downtown Nouakchott, the capital city. Yacoub Ould Dahoud, aged 43, would die later from injuries sustained when he set himself on fire outside the Senate in January 2011.[34]

The Arab Spring foregrounded demands for equality, economic justice, and respect for human rights. As these were all values championed by the Haratin social movement, Haratin activists were poised to play a leading role in the protest campaigns. Some of the Haratin movements were able to capitalize on their increasingly recognized image as activists against social exclusion, economic exploitation, marginalization, and poverty. Though the ideals were the same, the discourse of the activists had changed. They no longer focused on passing a new law or on integration from above of elites from the community. Instead, they raised the issue of resource-sharing, social justice, and economic equity. This change of emphasis was evident during the recent mobilizations.

In this multi-ethnic society plagued by incessant turmoil, the demand for inclusion and equality for the Haratin has outlasted the feverish protests that spread to Mauritania in unison with other Arab countries. In April 2013, well after the major waves of Arab protests had subsided, all Haratin organizations united in a show of solidarity to publish a Manifesto for Haratin Rights. This publication underlined, once again, the Haratin marginalization and the demand for equality between all Mauritanians. It also demanded a form of affirmative action for the Haratin for the first time.

This demand was not viewed favorably by wider Mauritanian society. In fact, when the sponsors of this manifesto decided to organize a national march in April 2014, they were unable to convince non-Haratin to join them until they changed the name of the rally to exclude any reference to the Haratin. The march ultimately was called "March for Rights" instead of the "March of the Haratin," as it was initially planned, and provides an example of how, in Mauritania, any mobilization that is exclusively Haratin tends to face indirect opposition from the mainstream elite (including the Haratin elite). Although non-Haratin social movements, political parties, and the media tend to agree in principle that the Haratin cause is "just," paradoxically the cause does not enjoy much support from these groups. This paradox is indicative of the ways in which the Haratin social movement is seen by other players in the national political scene. It also indicates that relations between the Haratin movement and other political and social actors remains as ambiguous as the status and condition of the Haratin community in Mauritania today.

The Haratin and the Others: Conflicts and/or Cooperation?

Despite their ambiguous status, the continued activism of the Haratin movement succeeded in placing the issue of slavery on the official agenda of most political actors. Unlike in the 1970s, Mauritanian politicians can no longer afford to ignore the issue. In today's Mauritania, everyone is fully aware that the community of former slaves is a major player in the ethnic and political makeup and structure of the country. At the same time, the Haratin have largely held a monopoly on the defense of their cause since it has been largely neglected by other social and political actors.

This position is hardly new, however. It is also hardly new that the dynamic of conflict and cooperation affecting the Haratin themselves within the various social movements they have created over time revolved around the very definition of their identity and belonging. Since very early on, El-Hor was affected by internal struggles over "Haratin identity." In the late 1980s, El-Hor split into two groups. One group considered the Haratin indisputably "Arab." A second group wanted to stick with the Charter of El-Hor, under which Haratin identity is considered distinct from all other ethnic groups, be they African or Arab. In order to grasp what is at stake through this debate on Haratin identity, one must consider three key historical moments: the inception of El-Hor in 1978; the major ethnic crisis that Mauritania experienced between 1987 and 1991; and finally, the creation of SOS-Slaves and the IRA. Most importantly, at these various historic moments, it appears that the debate over the ethnic problems in Mauritania as well as over the identity of the Haratin is closely related on one hand to the patterns of conflicts and cooperation that are taking shape in this context, and, on the other hand, to the role played by international pressures on the local government.

Internal Dissents, "National Interest" and the Haratin Identity

In 1978, the creation of El Hor came as a shock to Mauritanian society. Nobody welcomed an anti-slavery movement led by the Haratin, who, as a result, felt obliged to specify in their literature that their movement sought to promote "brotherhood" between Haratin and other communities.[35] However, general mistrust of El-Hor increased, especially when the organization asserted, soon after its formation, that the Haratin identity is separate from all others, while at the same time espousing a "racial" cause.

Ever since, successive regimes continue to maintain a striking paradox: denying the reality of the problem of slavery and the exclusion of Haratin, while at the same time adopting measures meant to combat these "non-existent" issues theoretically. From the government's perspective, taking pro-Haratin measures generally involved bowing to foreign pressures and, to a lesser extent, domestic pressures. The ambiguous positions of successive regimes on abolition enjoyed the support of an important part of the Arab and Black African (non-Arabic-speaking) Mauritanian elites. State-sponsored campaigns against the activists of El-Hor often benefited from the complicity of the other non-Haratin political actors and, to a lesser extent, from some of the Haratin elite. For example, in the late 1970s, El-Hor faced a high level of domestic hostility because of its contentious and repeated claims that it was unique to other underground movements in that it was not representing the interests of any external group. This claim was made in a political context wherein the majority of political groups were affiliated with foreign ideologies, such as Pan-Africanism (for Black African movements), Pan-Arabism (the model for many Nasserist or Ba'athist Arab nationalist groups), and proletarian internationalism (the reference point for leftist movements).

Although El-Hor faced hostility at home, its early orientation towards the promotion of human rights—and being one of the few organizations with such a focus—brought the group support internationally. In contrast, other underground groups were backed by foreign and/or neighboring countries (France, Morocco, Senegal, Algeria, Libya), furthering their own interests by influencing domestic Mauritanian politics through local actors. El Hor has never been shown to have allied with a foreign power, a source of pride for its leaders.

Despised and ignored by their Black African peers in the Senegal River Valley where slavery was regarded as an internal issue peculiar to the "Arab" community, Haratin activists were also accused by the very group to which they belonged (the Moors) of preaching division within the *Bizan*. This image would become even more pronounced later during the ethnic crisis that started in the mid-1980s and set the Black African and Arab-Berber groups against one another.

Haratin and the Ethnic Crisis

The lack of coexistence between ethnic groups is a chronic political problem in Mauritania, but, in the mid-1980s, the problem took a sharp turn for the worse. In 1986, the Forces de Libération Africaines de Mauritanie (the African Liberation Forces of Mauritania or FLAM) were created by Fulbe/Fulani elites. This radicalization of some Black Mauritanians took a new turn when army officers close to FLAM tried unsuccessfully to mount an ethnic coup d'état in 1987. The coup leaders were tried and executed by the government of Colonel Ould Taya. The founders of the FLAM were imprisoned, killed, or exiled. The situation worsened with the crisis in April 1989 that set Mauritania against Senegal. During riots that were likely staged by the respective governments, nationals of each country were killed and imprisoned spurring further protests in both countries. In Mauritania, the Haratin were accused of hunting down Senegalese people and, by extension, Black African Mauritanians, as both belong to the same ethnic groups. The government expelled nearly 80,000 black Mauritanians to Senegal and Mali creating an unprecedented humanitarian and regional political crisis.[36] In the process, nearly 300 Mauritanian soldiers from the Senegal River Valley were killed in a bloody purge in an army barracks in 1990 and 1991.

As a result of the ethnic tensions, pressure on El-Hor increased. Some of its leaders who openly supported Ould Taya's regime felt obliged to also endorse its Arab nationalism. Others wanted to distance themselves from both the Arab and Black African groups equally. For the Haratin activists who supported the authorities during the ethnic crisis, their actions carried three consequences: first, it presupposed that a purely Arab identity was to be ascribed to the Haratin; second, it implied solidarity with the human rights violations committed by the military regime against Black Mauritanians; and third, it meant effectively abandoning the struggle against slavery. In fact, supporting the official discourse implied agreement with the stance that since slavery had been made illegal, it no longer existed; slavery was to be discussed only in terms of the vestiges of an abolished institution, in accordance with official discourse.

To Arab-Berber nationalists as well as to members of Black African organizations, the uncomfortable position of some Haratin represented an opportunity to appropriate the movement for the sake of their own rivalry. It was also during this period when the network of the Iraqi Ba'ath party of Mauritania, well established within the regime and opposed to any non-Arab identity being ascribed to the country, developed a strategy of inclusion towards the Haratin. The party went so far as to publish a strategy paper that advocated this inclusion.[37] As for FLAM, they claimed to speak for all the "Blacks of Mauritania." The movement's underground newsletter was even called Bilal, after the emancipated slave and companion of the Prophet Muhammad. The name was also a nod to the Haratin, the only group in Mauritania to typically use this forename.

After they had gone into exile, some Black African activists began to appropriate the cause of the Haratin in their international campaigns against the regime in Nouakchott, which they accused of perpetuating enslavement of all Mauritanian black people. The objective was not to alleviate the plight of the Haratin, but rather to use it as an instrument for achieving their political goals. Some Haratin opposed this appropriation vigorously and publicly. For example, in 1989, Boubacar Ould Messaoud noted: "My skin is not a political program... An attempt is being made to establish a link between the activism of some elements that are the self-appointed spokesmen of a Black Mauritanian pseudo-community and the issue of slavery... In 1980, the fight against slavery was being carried out by El-Hor, not by them."[38] Messaoud Ould Boulkheir himself refuted this political recuperation. To him,

> slavery also exists in the Black African milieu.... The Black African slave, in his society, in his mind, is condemned to die as a slave, just like his children.... [The Black Africans] prefer to present slavery as a specifically Moorish institution and refuse to say what is really happening among them.[39]

This critical attitude towards the non-Arabic-speaking black community did not prevent El-Hor activists from dissociating themselves from the government and its human rights violations against Black Africans. The creation of the AC party and, especially, the APP had shown the Haratin's willingness to create a multi-ethnic coalition. Nevertheless, the introduction of the multiparty system itself in 1991 put an even greater emphasis on the isolation of the Haratin within the political landscape. The way in which the launching of the organization SOS-Slaves and that of the radical organization IRA would later be regarded by other partners/opponents in the political scene seems to suggest that the former slaves' fight against inequality was not always fully endorsed by non-Haratin, even though they may have thought it was indeed legitimate.

This rather complex relationship between the Haratin and other activists should not blur the complexity of the various layers of Haratin self-identification and the ways in which it impacts the patterns of conflicts and cooperation inside their own community. In fact, it is impossible to know for sure to what extent the majority of Haratin are supportive of the discourse developed by the most radical activists. Some members of the Haratin community are simply against any form of militancy. Many Haratin are socially affiliated with their tribe/village/traditional community rather than with their social class of former slaves and their descendants, with this sense of belonging varying at the individual level. In the absence of further studies, it is still unclear how anti-slavery movements and activists are viewed by various members of the Haratin community. The Haratin experience is hardly uniform, with the paths to emancipation varying historically from one region of the country to another as well as from one Haratin group or individual to another. The Haratin community has continued to evolve in different directions, even though Haratin are now almost absent among the political and economic elite and can claim few members even among the small local middle class. Despite the political and personal prestige the founding members of El-Hor gained at the national level, they have failed to unite their community. However, the Haratin movements have clearly succeeded in giving credibility to the Haratin as a social category that is able to contribute to the shaping of the political scene. The circle of those who are willing to formally join a Haratin movement without being of Haratin origin is exceptional, especially given that even among Haratin only a tiny minority of activists join social movements. Mauritania is a country where activism is perceived as an "illegitimate" activity, and belonging to an "ethnic" or "radical" political non-governmental organization is considered politically incorrect.

Conclusion

The experience of NGOs, such as SOS-Slaves or the IRA shows a new phase in the evolution of the patterns of conflicts and cooperation between Haratin activists and other players in the social and political arena in a context marked both by the radicalism of some activists and a radical change in the markers of action.

According to Boubacar Messaoud,[40] its president, one of the initial ambitions of SOS-Slaves had been to unite the descendants of both masters and slaves within one anti-slavery organization.[41] The objective was to mainstream the anti-slavery struggle and expand it outside of the Haratin community. He thought that a cause this just would be able to reunite people from all Mauritanian ethnic backgrounds. In fact, the organization had, at first, been successful in obtaining the support of only a handful (less than ten) of non-Haratin national figures known for their political independence, but, subsequently, only one person (Jemal Ould Yessa, a famous activist based in Paris) out of ten remained involved with SOS-Slaves as of February 2015. All other non-Haratin sympathizers had distanced themselves from the NGO. It is true, however, that, at least until 2005 (when SOS-Slaves was recognized by the state as an NGO, albeit under international pressure), participating in the activities of SOS-Slaves could lead directly to jail, as Boubacar Messaoud and his comrades had experienced repeatedly. As freedom of expression improved in Mauritania at the turn of the twenty-first century, the anti-slavery activists operated openly and almost without constraints.

Now, the issue of slavery is no longer taboo and non-Haratin politicians seem to view the fight against the legacy of slavery as legitimate, even though they remain external actors and seem to favor an instrumental approach to the issue. For example, because its overall political strategy seems to target marginalized groups, the Islamist party Tawasul (the national chapter of the Muslim Brotherhood network) published a "strategy paper" in 2011 as a contribution to the fight against slavery for the emancipation of the Haratin. The paper was essentially a pledge for "positive discrimination" in favor of the victims of slavery and the Haratin community as a whole. However, this interest was apparently only theoretical since Haratin are rare among the leadership of this party. For example, of the seventeen Tawassul members elected to the National Assembly in November 2013, only one is Haratin. It is true, however, that some Tawasul intellectuals and leaders support the claims made by the most radical Haratin. For example, when—in a controversial 2012 move—Birame Ould Dah Abeid burned several Islamic books, Mohamed al-Mukhtar al-Shinqiti (based in Qatar and close to Yusuf al-Qaradawi) downplayed the seriousness of the offense and took the opportunity to call for Muslim legal scholars to issue new legal opinions condemning slavery.[42]

Overall, friends of the Haratin activists remain rare in the *Bizan* community. The mainstream elite is inclined to make accusations of extremism toward anyone who mentions Haratin marginalization. Paradoxically, this attitude is shared within the political parties of the majority as well as within opposition parties led by non-Haratin. IRA sympathizers among the Black African community have increased in recent years because of their claim to fight against "Arab-Berber hegemony" and to defend victims of abuse in all communities. For this reason, IRA sympathizers have been able to attract support from Fulani nationalists. Ever since, the IRA has been considered by the government to be dangerously racialist. The IRA is denied official recognition, and its members are monitored, imprisoned, and persecuted. Birame Ould Abeid has won many international prizes and awards and has been invited to speak before the United States Senate Committee on Human Rights, as well as the Forum of the Civil Society, organized in conjunction with the USA-Africa Summit in August 2014 in Washington, DC. The increasing support that the IRA has secured on the international level has encouraged Ould Dah to enter the corridors of politics. He and his group tried to set up a political party, but the government immediately rejected their application. However, the leader Dah ran for president in the June 2014 election and was able to win 9 percent of the vote, which, although modest, ranked him in second place behind the incumbent president Ould Abdel Aziz who won with more than 82 percent of the vote.[43] Even if Biram Ould Dah secured his rank only because all the opposition leaders boycotted the election, coming in second still represented an important shift toward increasing interest in party politics and elections on the part of the new generation of Haratin human rights activists. This mirrors the path followed by their predecessors such as Messaoud Ould Boulkheir.

The launching of the Haratin movement in the late 1970s marked both the growth of a peaceful social current in Mauritania and the rapid public emergence of a social group embodying that social current. Apart from some sporadic and isolated revolts, the institution of slavery had never been challenged in an organized manner before. Today, there remains a close connection between the persistence of slavery on the one hand, and the current situation of the Haratin on the other—both of which are hotly debated issues. The quest for full citizenship for Haratin, which is now supported by a variety of groups that increasingly agree on the importance of putting an end to the marginalization of the Haratin community, has taken on the eradication of slavery as its battle cry. Despite the persistence of narrow political agendas among sharply divided national ethnic groups, pro-Haratin movements have collectively succeeded in embodying the quest for equality and justice in Mauritania. As the demographic and symbolic weight of their community continues to increase, the various Haratin social movements are even more likely to continue to play a crucial role in the social and political development of the country. It is too early to tell how the continuing "politicization" of this once peaceful social current by its most radical representatives will affect the debate over the interrelated issues of the eradication of slavery and the future of the Haratin community in Mauritania. It does, however, indicate that these discussions will be ever more central to Mauritanian politics for years to come.

8

KEEPING UP WITH THE TIMES

THE GROWTH OF SUPPORT FROM NON-STATE ACTORS
FOR THE POLISARIO LIBERATION MOVEMENT

Alice Wilson

The era of decolonization in the 1960s and 1970s saw the founding of a number of armed movements, often in post-colonial contexts, seeking to capture state power. In the context of the Cold War, the support of state actors for these movements was, in many cases, of crucial importance. Nevertheless, following the collapse of the Soviet Union, it has been argued that if the support of states continues to be important, the support of non-state actors has become increasingly significant for armed movements that seek to capture state power.[1] The conflict in Syria that developed out of the 2011 uprisings certainly seems to illustrate this trend. Alongside support from outside state actors such as Russia, there have also been private donations from wealthy individuals, especially in the Gulf, who have equipped brigades and contributed to the proliferation of armed rival groups.[2]

If a post-Cold War trend is for armed movements to draw on the support of both state and non-state actors, how might a movement that began in the

Cold War era, and has continued to benefit from the strong support of a state ally, nevertheless have adapted over time? In this chapter, I examine this question for the longstanding armed liberation movement for Western Sahara. From its early days, the Polisario Front (henceforth Polisario) appeared to be a typical anti-colonial liberation movement—one of several that, as Christopher Clapham suggests, could be categorized as among the four kinds of armed movements operating in Africa in the late twentieth century.[3] Since shortly after its foundation, Polisario has benefitted from significant support from neighboring Algeria. Crucially, this support includes the provision of safe haven in Algeria, along with diplomatic and material support.

Over its four decades of existence, however, Polisario itself, the international context in which it operates, and the situation of the people whom it claims to represent, have inevitably changed. Many dimensions of these transformations, both in Polisario's environment and in its own policies, have been studied, such as Polisario's shift to explicit acceptance of a market economy, its attempts to democratize, and its attempted embrace of a human rights agenda. Taking these shifts as a springboard in this chapter, I focus my analysis on the political impact of the changing importance of the support of state and non-state actors for Polisario, an area that has not yet been fully explored. I argue that for Polisario, as for other armed movements in the 1990s and 2000s, the support of non-state actors has become increasingly important. In Polisario's case, these non-state actors include the growing Sahrawi diaspora, especially the diaspora in Spain, but also new Non-Government Organizations (NGOs) and multi-lateral organizations' forms of support, such as sponsorship for infrastructure or government personnel in the Sahrawi refugee camps. To clarify, I do not wish to overlook the importance of support for Polisario from non-state actors in the Cold War period. Indeed, as I shall discuss, Polisario benefitted in its early years from the support of European activists and NGOs. Rather, I seek to show how in the post-Cold War period the support of non-state actors has both proliferated and increased in importance in the sense that it has allowed Polisario to undertake new kinds of activities above and beyond those it could undertake with only the support of state actors such as Algeria.

The growth of non-state forms of support for Polisario has had implications beyond the scope of traditional state support. First, the rise of these new forms of support suggests that Polisario is an "up-to-date" armed movement, in the sense that its transformations include having developed a growing range of non-state allies. Second, these new forms of support mean that the oft-foregrounded description that Polisario is an Algerian-backed movement needs to be supplemented in order to take into account the increasing significance of non-state actors' support for Polisario.[4] I see both of these factors as having contributed to Polisario's resilience as a liberation movement, even though it has not been able to achieve self-determination in some forty years of struggle. Third, the rise in the importance of support from non-state actors foregrounds an interesting tension, or flexibility, for Polisario. Whilst the states that have supported Polisario, including Algeria, have supported it as an armed movement, the support of non-state actors is more ambiguous. Some non-state actors in the Sahrawi diaspora are vocal in explicitly supporting Polisario as an armed movement, and demand a return to war. Nevertheless, the activities of NGOs and multilateral organizations focus on civilian initiatives. This suggests a potential future tension that Polisario might not, in the long term, be able to satisfy both kinds of supporters. In the meantime, however, although Polisario has not disarmed, the support it receives for civilian initiatives has allowed it to pursue activities comparable to those of unarmed social movements in the region (for example, cultural activities, art festivals, and an annual cinema festival). The support of non-state actors has become a significant resource that allows Polisario to blur the boundaries of being an armed vs. an unarmed movement. While this very ambiguity may raise questions about Polisario's future retention of different supporters, for now it seems to be a contributing factor to Polisario's resilience as a movement that seeks state power.

It might seem strange to make the focus of this chapter a discussion of the transformations of Polisario when the Western Sahara conflict more broadly has become synonymous with stalemate. Yet it is one of the premises of this study that the very overall appearance of continuity in the Western Sahara conflict has led to important analytical oversights. Seeking to explore one of these oversights, in this chapter I do not attempt a broad discussion of the Western Sahara conflict.[5] Instead, I focus specifically on how Polisario has transformed itself and the support networks from which it benefits. Interested in how continued attention to longstanding support from Algeria may have led analysts to overlook the growing importance of support from other, non-state actors, this chapter does not attempt to analyze how much Algeria may allegedly influence Polisario.[6] It looks at how Polisario undertakes new activities—thanks to the support of other actors—that were not facilitated by Algerian support. In order to address this, I draw on both existing studies of the movement and experiences from extensive fieldwork in the Sahrawi refugee camps from 2006–2014.[7] The chapter proceeds as follows: First, I briefly discuss the increasing importance of the support of non-state actors for armed movements since the end of the Cold War. I then turn to the case of Polisario, examining its beginnings as a typical anti-colonial liberation movement, and then subsequent economic, political, and demographic transformations in light of which Polisario has either shifted policy or stuck to longstanding principles. I go on to describe non-state forms of support that, in this changed context, have become increasingly important. Finally, I examine the broader implications of these new, intensifying forms of support for Polisario's position as this support has blurred the boundary between an armed and unarmed movement.

Support for Armed Movements

In the 1960s and 1970s, the confluence of demand for decolonization and radical leftist political mobilization saw the emergence of a number of armed movements seeking to capture state power in Africa, the Middle East, Asia, and in post-colonial states in Latin America. In the Cold War context of superpower rivalry, these movements attracted the intervention and support, or opposition, of states, which often proved crucial to these movements' trajectories.[8] Yet in the 1990s, the decade following the end of the Cold War, this situation was modified—a shift that has been highlighted in the policy-focused report, *Trends in Outside Support for Insurgent Movements*, published by Byman et al. in 2001.[9] Written to inform policy-makers and scholars of post-Cold War insurgency, the report undertakes a comparative analysis of 74 post-Cold War insurgencies in order to review shifts in the kinds of support that have been important to armed movements seeking to capture state power. The authors recognize that the support of states remained crucial for many insurgent movements, especially in the provision of safe havens for armed insurgents. Yet, Byman et al. argue that the support of non-state actors became increasingly significant in the wake of the end of the Cold War. Taking up the cases of diasporas, refugee populations, religious groups, wealthy individuals, aid agencies, and human rights groups, the authors examine how such non-state actors have, directly or indirectly, provided increasingly significant support for armed movements.

For instance, in the case of diasporas, the authors take up the example of the Tamil diaspora and the Liberation Tigers of Tamil Eelam (LTTE), and suggest that diasporas can provide political support, such as lobbying, organizing demonstrations, and raising awareness, as well as financial support. As regards the Tamil diaspora and the LTTE, it is reported that Tamils outside Sri Lanka donated money voluntarily, but were also subject to intimidation if funds were not forthcoming. In 1999, Tamil families in Canada were expected to pay $240 a year, and it is estimated that the Tamil diaspora of the UK, Canada, and Australia combined might have provided as much funding as $1.5 million a month.[10] Turning to the relationship between refugees and armed insurgencies, the authors of the report are interested in how refugee communities may provide a breeding ground for the creation and maintenance of an armed group. They take up the case of the Taliban as an example of a movement that was forged among Afghan refugees in religious schools in Pakistan. The authors discuss several further types of potential support, including material and intellectual resources from religious organizations; financial support from wealthy individuals; international humanitarian aid, though the authors suggest that this may be preyed upon by insurgents; and political support for armed movements from human rights organizations who may report on alleged abuses committed during counter-insurgencies.

A number of the underlying assumptions in this report merit scrutiny. Armed movements seeking to capture state power do not necessarily prey upon aid, but may seek it out as an opportunity to demonstrate their capacity for governance by distributing it appropriately to a civilian population.[11] The specific historical circumstances under which refugee communities coalesce around particular political discourses must be examined, rather than assumptions made that refugee communities are inherently disposed to particular forms of politicization.[12] It is beyond the scope of the present discussion to explore fully such avenues. My purpose for now is to take up the report's proposal that the support of non-state actors has, since the Cold War, become increasingly important for armed movements and to consider this suggestion in relation to Polisario. Polisario is indeed one of the cases included in this report, yet it is analyzed as one of the movements for which only the support of a state (Algeria) is noted, rather than the support of any of the other kinds of non-state actors. This chapter argues, however, that Polisario is most helpfully understood as a movement that has come to benefit significantly from the support of non-state actors. First, though, I consider the origins of Polisario, and the early emergence of crucial support from neighboring Algeria.

The Beginnings of Polisario

Founded in 1973, Polisario arose in a context of incipient nationalist anti-colonial sentiment in Spanish Sahara. Although Spain had acquired coastal territory near the Canary Islands in 1884–5, it only "pacified" the territory in 1934. Its exploitation of the resources in the territory accelerated from the 1950s, as Spain turned its attention to phosphate and fishing waters. In the context of something of a late start to intense colonial intervention in the Spanish Sahara, nationalist sentiment among the inhabitants of the territory has been traced to the 1950s.[13] Several factors contributed to its emergence.[14] The colonial experience itself fostered the emergence of nationalist sentiments, as colonial subjects became "saharianos" and "saharauis" to their colonizers.[15] Likewise, factors such as the rise in sedentary habits of a formerly mobile pastoralist population, the international context of UN declarations (from 1964) regarding the right of the people of Western Sahara to self-determination, and the increased local usage of radios that gave access to discussions within an international context, contributed to the rise of Sahrawi nationalism.

An early Sahrawi nationalist movement, active from the late 1960s, was crushed by Spain in 1970.[16] However, a new movement emerged in the early 1970s that consisted in large part of Sahrawi students studying in Moroccan universities. This group was led by a young Sahrawi man named Elwali Mustapha Sayed. Some of the students involved had grown up in southern Morocco; indeed, many Sahrawi families had left the territory of Spanish Sahara after Spain and France jointly put down an uprising against colonial rule in 1958. Intending to form a new liberation movement, in 1972, this group began approaching foreign governments in search of aid. They contacted Libya, Mauritania, Algeria, and Iraq.[17] While the group also sought help from Morocco, its activities and demonstrations became subject to harassment from Morocco. Making contacts with young Sahrawi men from across the areas where Sahrawis lived, from southern Morocco to Spanish Sahara, southwest Algeria, and northern Mauritania, Mustapha Sayed moved his center of activities away from Morocco to northern Mauritania. He assembled a group of supporters somewhere near the border between Mauritania and Spanish Sahara and, on 10 May 1973, founded the Popular Front for the Liberation of Saguia al Hamra and Rio de Oro, or Polisario Front (the name is based on the Spanish acronym). Polisario began a guerrilla campaign of attacks against Spanish targets, such as military bases and the phosphate mining installations.

Still in its formative period, Polisario sought the help of states that might be inclined to aid the formation of an anti-colonial liberation movement. Libya provided considerable help at the early stage, supplying arms (although this provision was hampered by the fact that Algeria did not allow Libyan arms to cross Algerian territory to reach Polisario).[18] Libya also allowed the movement to set up an office in Tripoli and permitted the first Polisario radio programs to be broadcast from Libya to Spanish Sahara.[19] For its part, Mauritania had allowed the movement's leaders to assemble in northern Mauritania, from where the group planned its first attacks on Spanish Sahara.[20]

Polisario did not, however, initially benefit from state support from Algeria. In the 1972 resolution of the border dispute between Morocco and Algeria, one "largely tacit condition" had been Morocco's plans to divide Spanish Sahara between itself and Mauritania.[21] The Algerian president at that time, Houari Boumedienne, made several statements privately and publicly as late as July 1974, indicating his support for such an agreement between Morocco and Mauritania.[22] Algeria has been described as initially "unconvinced that [Polisario] carried significant weight".[23]

Yet in early 1975, Algeria revised its position. A range of reasons for Algeria's change of position have been discussed.[24] As it became clearer that Morocco intended to claim much of Spanish Sahara for itself, it was suggested that Algeria feared the threat to regional domination posed by an expanded Morocco. In addition, Algeria could not retain its international reputation as a champion of liberation movements and self-determination without supporting Polisario, and so it soon began providing material and diplomatic support.

In February 1975, the Algerian armed forces commenced training for five hundred Polisario fighters.[25] Algeria also allowed the Polisario leadership to make their own base around the Algerian military base of Tindouf in southwest Algeria.[26] The oasis city of Tindouf was founded in 1852 by members of the Tajakant tribe, and in 1895 was attacked by members of the Rbaybāt tribe, one of the tribes that later came to identify as Sahrawi. Persons who would later identify, or be identified, as Sahrawis had remained living in the vicinity of Tindouf, so in 1975 the city and surrounding region already hosted Sahrawis. Further adding to Tindouf's attractiveness as a base location for the leadership of a Sahrawi nationalist movement was that it was only about 50km from the border with Spanish Sahara.

As the conflict for sovereignty over the former Spanish colony took shape, Algeria's help took on crucial dimensions. Under pressure from Polisario attacks and from the UN, Spain had begun preparations to withdraw from the territory and took steps to hold a referendum on self-determination. A UN visit to the territory in May 1975 noted overwhelming popular support for Polisario and for independence. Nevertheless, Morocco and Mauritania submitted claims to sovereignty over the territory, which were assessed by an advisory finding of the International Court of Justice. The Court's finding of October 1975 was in favor of the right to self-determination of the people of Western Sahara. Nevertheless, a few days later, Morocco arranged the Green March of thousands of Moroccan civilians as a symbolic reclaiming of the Sahara. Shortly after, Spain consented to the Madrid Accords, with Morocco and Mauritania, by which Spain agreed to hand the territory over to be divided between them. In November 1975, Morocco and Mauritania began to annex the territory. Although Mauritania withdrew in 1979, Morocco has continued to annex the larger, westerly portion of Western Sahara, with its cities, coastline, and phosphate resources. During the 1980s, Morocco built a series of military walls, later connected to form one continuous wall, to keep Polisario out of the areas under Moroccan control. This resulted in a de facto partition of the territory between the portion to the west of the wall, a Moroccan-controlled area, and the portion to the east of the wall, a Polisario-controlled area.

In the wake of the joint annexation of the territory, Polisario, which had begun fighting Spain, found itself fighting Morocco and Mauritania. In this context, Algerian support for the movement was crucial. In the period of active warfare—between Polisario and Morocco, from 1975 until the UN-brokered ceasefire of 1991, and between Polisario and Mauritania, from 1975 until Mauritania's withdrawal in 1979—Algeria provided military equipment for Polisario's army, the Sahrawi People's Liberation Army (SPLA).[27] Perhaps, though, Algeria's most significant support for Polisario was its provision of safe haven in the Tindouf region.

This haven near Tindouf served not only the Polisario leadership, but also Sahrawi civilians displaced from the territory. From early 1976, displaced Sahrawi civilians gathered in refugee camps near Tindouf. The number of refugees has always been contested, but some estimates suggest that there were between 100,000–160,000 by the early twenty-first century.[28] Authority over the refugee camps was delegated by Algeria to Polisario. As a result, Polisario found in the refugee camps not only a secure headquarters in which to base their political leadership, but also a protected space in which they could take on, in exile, the daily practical work of the state-like governing of a civilian population. Indeed, on 27 February 1975, the day after the last Spanish officers left Spanish Sahara, Polisario founded a state authority for Western Sahara, the Sahrawi Arab Democratic Republic (SADR). A some-times indistinguishable fusion of SADR and Polisario began to govern the refugee camps and the refugee population as a state authority. Over time, this governing authority developed a state-like apparatus. This included a penal code, courts of law, prisons, a parliament, customs houses, border controls, and a police force.

The fact that Algeria provided a safe haven for Polisario and Sahrawi refugees feeds into other forms of ongoing support offered by Algeria to Polisario, up to the present. These include diplomatic support in formal contexts, such as the UN and other international forums. An extension of this continuing diplomatic support is Algeria's facilitation of visas for foreign visitors to the refugee camps as well as passports for (some) Sahrawi refugees—although the criteria on which these passports are awarded (or not) to Sahrawi refugees who apply for reasons other than Polisario business are shrouded in controversy.[29] Another form of diplomatic support provided by Algeria is the willingness of Algeria to interface on Polisario's behalf, through its own Algerian Red Crescent (ARC), with international aid organizations such as the World Food Program. Organizations such as these only work with partners from a state whom they recognize, and therefore will not work with the Sahrawi Red Crescent (SRC). The ARC passes on all aid to the SRC, however, and the latter administers this aid on a daily basis to the refugees. By making these forums and resources available, this cooperation between the ARC and the SRC allows the governing authorities in the refugee camps to act, in practice, like a state authority. In addition to these forms of support, Algeria is one of several countries that educates Sahrawi refugee students for free, helping to provide refugee camps with a pool of educated potential workers.

The importance and range of Algerian support for Polisario from the early years to the present does not preclude the importance of other forms of support, from both state and non-state actors. Polisario has pursued the support of other states, with fluctuating success in gaining recognition from these states.[30] The movement has also benefitted, since the mid-1970s, from the support of civil society solidarity organizations, especially those based in Europe. These activists campaigned in support of self-determination and contributed to the welfare services within the refugee camps.[31] In the context of the transformation of the international stage and of Polisario itself from the 1990s, though, the importance of the support of non-state actors would increase, as the next sections explore.

A Time of Transitions

Global political and economic trends of the 1990s, from the end of the Cold War to the break-up of socialist economies and the following wave of democratization movements, brought about their own impacts upon the Western Sahara conflict. Transitions in both the international environment and in Polisario's own policies have received considerable scholarly attention. I briefly review transitions and overriding continuity, and then discuss the political impact of these changes regarding the support of state and non-state actors.

In 1991, Polisario transitioned from war to ceasefire, which unleashed an unsuccessful series of UN plans for a referendum on self-determination and face-to-face negotiations between Morocco and Polisario. But the ceasefire has proved a more auspicious setting for other developments in Polisario's policies and the lives of Sahrawis in the different geographical areas affected by the conflict. Once active warfare was put on hold, and yet it became clear that efforts at conflict resolution were failing, the Sahrawi population in the Moroccan-controlled areas became a new center of Sahrawi resistance. The frequency of demonstrations and protests intensified in 2005, leading Sahrawis to refer to what they saw as their Intifada.[32] Polisario wholly supported these demonstrations, broadcasting reports on its radio and television programs, and organizing "solidarity" demonstrations in the refugee camps. Nonviolent protest and its repression in the Moroccan-controlled areas have become new frontiers of the conflict since the end of active warfare, even though international interest in these demonstrations—including Western Sahara's largest uprising to date, which took place on the eve of the Arab Spring—has been low.[33]

As for the refugee camps, they have undergone multiple transformations since the ceasefire. Tracing Polisario's political and ideological shifts is not straightforward. Polisario seeks to keep its ideological cards close to its chest, and access to internal politics is extremely limited for non-Sahrawis, and sometimes even for Sahrawis. For example, the Polisario General Congress of over 1,000 directly elected delegates takes place behind doors closed to non-delegates. Nevertheless, an increased pursuit of democratic reforms since the ceasefire period represents a major shift. It was spurred not only by a desire to align with international trends but also by internal demands, such as the demands made by protesting refugees in 1988. The SADR Parliament's power to hold ministers accountable has increased, and quotas encouraging the election of women have been introduced.[34] In pursuing these reforms, Polisario vies with Morocco (which has pursued its own path of reforms) to be recognized as the "more democratic" government. Again echoing international trends, Polisario shifted from its early socialist focus on collectivized resources and labor to constitutional recognition for a market economy in a post-independence Western Sahara.[35] In practice, the refugee camps already have informal markets of commoditized goods and labor.[36] Trade in commodities and commoditized labor in the refugee camps is fueled by refugee incomes from a number of sources: local and intra-Saharan trade, pensions for former Spanish colonial employees, NGO and international organization salaries for local employees, development projects run by various NGOs, gifts from philanthropists such as European families who have hosted Sahrawi refugee children during summer programs, and remittances from Sahrawi migrants working abroad, especially in Spain. The refugee camps are now connected to the vicissitudes of the global economy through multiple routes beyond aid. Migration from, and sometimes back to, the refugee camps has also boomed.[37] While Polisario has undergone a number of transformations since the 1990s, there are also important points of continuity in its stance. It has eschewed some transformations undergone by other armed liberation movements. Since its foundation, Polisario has maintained its claim to be the sole representative of the people of Western Sahara. One consequence of this commitment is that, although Polisario has undergone a program of attempted internal democratization, it has not made the transition to a landscape of multi-party representation. Some armed movements have made this transition by becoming political parties, such as Frelimo and Renamo in Mozambique, and the Free Aceh Movement in Indonesia. In the case of Palestine, where, like in Western Sahara, the conflict over territory remains unresolved and the PLO remains an armed movement, different factions of the PLO have taken on the role of political parties and compete in elections in the West Bank and Gaza. Polisario, however, has evaded any such development.

The absence of multiple political parties for pro-independence Sahrawis does not preclude opportunities for the expression of dissent and criticism targeting Polisario. On the contrary, there are movements of dissent within Polisario. For example, in the mid-2000s there was a pro-war movement among Sahrawis in the refugee camps and in the diaspora, known as *khaṭṭ ashahīd* (the movement of martyrs, literally "the line of the martyr"). This group nevertheless claimed not to be against Polisario but rather to seek its reform. In the Sahrawi diaspora in Spain, there are also groups, especially of young Sahrawis, that similarly call for the reform of Polisario while stressing that they are not seeking its downfall—a phenomenon that has been dubbed "non-dissident dissidence."[38]

Ultimately, Polisario—like the PLO—has remained an armed movement. Polisario maintains an army, the Sahrawi Popular Liberation Army, which is stationed in the Polisario-controlled areas of Western Sahara. Several of the families that I came to know over the course of my fieldwork in the refugee camps had male family members serving in the army. In some cases, they were on duty in the pasturelands for stints of a few months per year. When off duty in the refugee camps, those who could find opportunities took paid civilian work, such as driving taxis. In other cases, men migrated to Spain for the greater part of the year but were still nominally part of the SPLA.

The nominal connection of migrants to the SPLA became more concrete at times. The electoral system in the refugee camps assigned voters to a constituency according to how they "served" the liberation struggle, resulting in the army having its own electoral constituencies. One of my interlocutors, Hamma, a middle-aged father, was a migrant in Spain, but was back in the refugee camps at the time of elections for the Polisario General Congress in late 2007.[39] Though a migrant for most of the year, since he was also officially a member of the SPLA, he attended a military voting station on election day in order to cast a vote (only to find that he was not allowed to cast his ballot because he did not wear a military uniform to the polls). Migrants have also proven willing to heed the call for arms. In 2001, when the Paris-Dakar rally organizers neglected to seek the permission of Polisario to allow vehicles to cross Western Sahara, Polisario issued a call to take up arms, and some migrants responded, returning from Spain to the refugee camps.[40]

Polisario's commitment to remaining an armed movement—albeit one maintaining a ceasefire—has closed off some diplomatic doors for the movement. For instance, Polisario and Sahrawis are unable to take part in forums such as the Unrepresented Nations and Peoples Organization (UNPO) attended by people in similar situations of living in territories of unresolved status, such as Tibet and Somaliland.[41] The fact that Polisario remains armed has opened the door to accusations from political opponents that it takes part in armed terrorist activities in north-west Sahara, although neither the United States nor the European Union have named Polisario as a terrorist organization. While Polisario's commitment to armed resistance comes at a diplomatic cost and carries risks to its reputation, it also provides it with considerable internal legitimacy. In the Moroccan-controlled areas, where SADR television can be watched (clandestinely) in Sahrawi homes, images of the SPLA may be met with spontaneous exclamations of appreciation, and, in the refugee camps, women typically ululate at the mere mention of the SPLA. By skilfully nuancing its stance with regard to political violence, Polisario also courts international legitimacy. While the Polisario leadership may make public mention of the possibility of a return to war should peaceful efforts at conflict resolution collapse, it directs great attention to Sahrawis' nonviolent protests in Moroccan-controlled areas (and Morocco's sometimes violent responses). Thus, Polisario foregrounds its commitment to nonviolent resistance, and accuses Morocco of using illegitimate violence against unarmed civilians. Through such a nuanced position with regard to political violence, Polisario courts legitimacy from both internal and international audiences.

Although Polisario has stuck unwaveringly to certain principles, such as its claimed monopoly on the representation of the people of Western Sahara and its status as an armed movement, in the last two and half decades it has also undergone political, economic, and demographic transformations. I turn now to the political impact of these changes in regard to the balance of support from state and non-state actors for Polisario.

New Horizons: The Support of Non-State Actors

Polisario is often discussed as an "Algerian-backed movement." While it certainly is true that Polisario benefits from the support of its strong ally, Algeria, I suggest that the political, economic, and demographic changes that Polisario has undergone since the 1990s have led to a growth in the importance of support from non-state actors. Byman et al. argue that this has been the case for other armed movements since the Cold War. In fact, some of the very sources of non-state support discussed by Byman et al. for other movements have also grown in importance for Polisario. In this section, I consider the increasing significance of the Sahrawi diaspora, the international solidarity movement, and multi-lateral aid agencies. Somewhat ironically, because the Polisario leadership is in exile in Algeria, the Sahrawi diaspora is not the only "distance" population with whom Polisario engages, as it also maintains connections with Sahrawis in Moroccan-controlled Western Sahara and southern Morocco. While Sahrawis in Moroccan-controlled areas engage in political activities aimed at Sahrawi and international audiences—ranging in political ilk from pro-self-determination demonstrations to membership in Morocco's council for Sahrawi tribal leaders (the Royal Consultative Council for Saharan Affairs or (CORCAS)—in this chapter, I focus on the diaspora. Support for Polisario from Sahrawis in Moroccan-controlled areas is important for Polisario's legitimacy as the representative of the Sahrawi people. It has also allowed Polisario to develop a discourse of demand for attention to human rights. Of particular interest here, though, is the extent to which the diaspora, along with the international solidarity movement and the aid industry, can be understood as a non-state actor which has offered Polisario forms of support that complement and, at times, go beyond the remit of support from a state actor such as Algeria.

Since the mid-1990s, a growing Sahrawi diaspora has developed. The most significant Sahrawi migrant community in this diaspora is located in Spain. In her study of Sahrawi migrants in Spain, Carmen Gómez Martín describes how the first generation of refugee migrants in the mid-1990s were highly educated graduates, typically educated in Cuba thanks to Cuba's policy allowing Sahrawi students to be educated there for free.[42] These migrants left the refugee camps disillusioned with the UN's failure to implement a referendum on self-determination and with the limited possibilities for skilled and paid work in the refugee camps. The number of Sahrawi refugee migrants heading to Spain (and other European destinations) grew in the 2000s, as more and more refugees became frustrated with both the lack of political change in the conflict and with the limited economic possibilities of earning a living to help their families. Refugee ration levels decreased sharply in 2005, as the World Food Program reduced the number of eligible refugees from 158,000 to 90,000.[43] Refugee families could no longer manage on the ration levels they were receiving, making supplementary forms of income essential to a family's survival. Not all Sahrawis in Spain hail from the refugee camps; some have migrated from Moroccan-controlled areas. Nevertheless, Gómez Martín estimates that, because of the precarious conditions in which Sahrawis from the Moroccan-controlled areas may find themselves during migration, such as in illegal crossings to the Canary Islands, the majority of the Sahrawis in Spain migrated from the refugee camps.

According to Gómez Martín, the relationship between Sahrawi migrants in Spain and Polisario has been tense. At first, those who left the refugee camps were seen as having abandoned the self-determination cause, and therefore received little help from Polisario. Some refugees who requested Algerian passports (a request made in most cases through the SADR Ministry of the Interior) experienced lengthy delays, leading to controversy surrounding the extent to which Polisario may have sought to impede migration—and a feared "emptying" of the refugee camps—by delaying refugees' requests for passports. Yet there is also speculation that obstacles to some refugees receiving Algerian passports may not originate with Polisario, but perhaps in Algeria, and ultimately as a result of pressure from Spain and the EU to reduce migration from North Africa to Europe.[44]

Another tension in the relationship between migrants and Polisario started in 2005, when migrants began forming associations in Spain. These associations drew attention to the situation of Western Sahara and sought to provide help to other migrants seeking to attain the legal right to remain in Spain.[45] According to Gómez Martín, Polisario was initially suspicious that these associations might threaten Polisario's claimed status as the sole representative of the people of Western Sahara.

Migrants have deployed a number of strategies to counter these various suspicions, Gómez Martín suggests. For example, just as the diasporic communities of other conflict zones have taken on active roles in their attempts to influence conflict in their homeland (to varying effects—sometimes encouraging peace, sometimes sustaining conflict), many Sahrawis in Europe have campaigned actively to draw attention to their case for self-determination.[46] As is the case for other diasporas, the Sahrawi diaspora is heterogeneous, with various groups voicing different demands. Some associations of Sahrawi migrants have over time begun to voice radical demands that Polisario return to war—although the membership of pro-war groups mentioned by Gómez Martín is small (ten and forty members, respectively).[47] In other cases, without vocally advocating a return to war, migrants have adopted a discourse of fighting for the cause from a distance—not only by campaigning, but also by returning regularly to the refugee camps for visits when work conditions (and travel papers) permit. Crucially, many of them send remittances to family members in the refugee camps. Gómez Martín estimates that in the early twenty-first century, a Sahrawi migrant working in Spain might send between 500 and 2,000 euros a year to family members in the refugee camps.[48]

After an initially tense relationship between Polisario and the emerging Sahrawi diaspora, Gómez Martín argues that, starting around 2003, Polisario adopted a more positive attitude toward migration.[49] The presence of a Sahrawi diaspora in Spain was a *fait accompli*, but Gómez Martín also draws particular attention to Polisario's realization of the economic importance of migrants who provide help for family members back in the refugee camps, usually in the form of remittances.[50] Gómez Martín does not describe any examples of official payments being requested directly by Polisario from Sahrawi migrants, in the manner of the LTTE's collection of contributions from the Tamil diaspora. The migrants' associations collect monthly or annual contributions from members, but these funds appear to be used to support their own activities (see below).[51] Nevertheless, Gómez Martín cites the president of the association of Sahrawi migrants in Cataluña, regarding his view that help from Sahrawi migrants has taken on national importance: "We contributed with our money to the development of infrastructure of the Sahrawi state in exile, and allowed it to carry out its work more easily."[52]

Polisario's initially wary attitude toward Sahrawi migrants, and the potential (and unclear) extent to which Polisario may be implicated in failing to facilitate some refugees' applications for Algerian passports that would allow them to attempt to migrate to Spain, have been attributed to Polisario's putative fears that the rise of migration may signal the weakening of the refugee camps. But perhaps the situation could be read differently. In a sense, it could be argued that rather than the diaspora being merely a potential drain and threat to the survival of the refugee camps, the diaspora, and its remittances, also allow the refugee camps to survive. One interesting illustration of the diaspora's commitment to the refugee camps as a center of the Sahrawi community is the fact that some of the migrant associations organize paperwork for fellow migrants who have died in Spain so that they may be repatriated and buried in the refugee camps.[53] In 2008, members of the Sahrawi refugee family with whom I lived in Smara camp (named after the city of Smara in Western Sahara) attended the funeral of a Sahrawi refugee migrant who had died in Spain and whose body had been repatriated to be buried at the graveyard in Smara camp. In the view of this host family, and indeed other Sahrawi refugees with whom I spoke, the migrants' association used their collective funds to help pay for the repatriation of the body. Thanks to such help, the relatives in the refugee camps—including those persons whom the man had supported through his work in Spain—could attend his burial.

The Sahrawi diaspora in Spain has taken on an increasingly significant role in relation to Polisario, providing much-needed economic infusions into the refugee camps and improving the material circumstances of those who continue to live there. Yet the diaspora is by no means alone in providing new forms of income for the refugee camps, and, as a result, new forms of support for Polisario. While aid organizations were active in providing help for the refugee camps in the 1970s and 1980s, as previously noted, the improved access to the refugee camps since the ceasefire has led to a proliferation of such aid. A visitor to the refugee camps in 2007/2008 would have encountered a wide range of active aid projects and evidence of past projects. Examples of these included an NGO from the Basque country that provided micro credit loans for refugees to set up small businesses; a Spanish organization working to introduce recycling facilities in the refugee camps to raise awareness among the refugees about waste disposal and recycling; and several other Spanish solidarity associations that funded the building or renovation of primary schools that now bear the associations' names.

In theory, the activities of these different organizations were coordinated through the SADR Ministry of Cooperation, as any aid project operating in the refugee camps was required to be administered through this entity. According to some NGO employees with whom I talked in 2007 and 2008, an important forum for the coordination of aid activities in the refugee camps was the annual European Conference of Support to the Sahrawi People (EUCOCO). These conferences have been taking place in European cities since the beginning of the Western Sahara conflict. The forty-second EUCOCO conference took place in Paris in 2017. NGO workers who had previously attended such conferences on behalf of their organizations explained to me that at one of the conference workshops, the humanitarian needs of the refugee camps were discussed, and plans were made regarding which projects to undertake and fund.

The funding made available through aid organizations, especially those based in Spain where there is a strong national network of support for Western Sahara, is of the level needed to make a significant impact on the refugee camps. In 2005, in the Basque country alone, the Basque Parliament, solidarity associations, local governments and regional funders (such as Euskal Fondoa) made a total contribution of 1,631,091 euros to humanitarian aid in the refugee camps.[54] In 2006, when the refugee camps were hit by strong floods that destroyed many homes and other buildings, the aid from the Basque country increased to 2,931,776 euros.[55] In the view of refugees, these solidarity associations, such as those who attended EUCOCO, funded not only services in the refugee camps, but also infrastructure, such as the intra-refugee camp tarmac roads that Algeria failed to provide.

Multilateral aid institutions also provided support for Polisario and its governance activities. The UNHCR expanded its activities in the refugee camps in 2008. A program officer from UNHCR whom I interviewed in July 2008 explained that the UNHCR's relationship with Polisario had not always been straightforward. The UNHCR exerts a high degree of administrative control over some of the refugee camps where it operates. This including conducting a census of the population and providing them with forms of identification. However Polisario has not agreed for the UNHCR to take on such roles in the refugee camps near Tindouf. Since Polisario, in fusion with SADR, claimed to take responsibility for protecting the legal rights of the refugees as citizens of SADR, in 2008 the UNHCR mission in the refugee camps explored possibilities of assisting the SADR Ministry of Justice in assuring refugees' legal rights. One project that had already been carried out was the creation of a legal library at the ministry of justice that was equipped with computers and internet access.[56] The UNHCR was also planning to conduct training for legal professionals, especially in the field of human rights.

In November of 2008, one of the SADR judges explained to me that he was negotiating with the UNHCR to secure funding to further strengthen the SADR legal structures. At the time, SADR paid its judges a wage of around 50 euros a month, but found that this was not enough to retain some judges, who preferred instead to migrate in the hope of finding better paid work in Europe.[57] The SADR Ministry of Justice had approached the UNHCR asking for funding for a number of new initiatives: a wage of 100 dollars per month for twenty-two judges (who would continue to receive their SADR wages as well); further training in human rights; a printer for printing official paper for legal documents; funding to distribute legal documents in order to make them more widely known among specialists as well as citizens; the renovation of the Criminal Court; and the building of a home for the High Court, which at the time had no permanent location and convened only when necessary. This judge later told me that the UNHCR had agreed to provide funding for most of these requests. In this way, the multi-lateral aid sector has ended up sponsoring one of the SADR ministries—even though it does not itself recognize SADR.

It is clear that in the late 2000s, Polisario—in its fusion with the state authority that it had founded, SADR—enjoyed a number of sources of support that were not directly forthcoming from states. The Sahrawi diaspora in Spain provided new economic inputs to the refugee camps. Although some members of the diaspora were vocal critics of Polisario, their dissent was "non-dissident" to the extent that they still supported Polisario as a liberation movement. Foreign NGOs had vastly expanded the range of activities that they supported in the refugee camps, including education, training, and welfare initiatives. Multi-lateral aid also supported the expansion of the governance capacities of Polisario's SADR. This rise in the importance of support for Polisario from non-state actors is interesting in its own right. I conclude by discussing the wider implications of this development.

A Transformed Movement

This chapter has reviewed the multiple political, economic, and demographic transformations that Polisario has undergone, and has explored some political consequences of these transformations, namely that Polisario has diversified the actors to whom it can turn for support. These now include a range of non-state actors, whose support is arguably of ever-increasing importance to Polisario, both politically and economically. This shift is important for understanding Polisario and for a broader understanding of movements of popular mobilization in the Maghreb and beyond.

First, the intensification of support for Polisario from non-state actors suggests that the movement has indeed transformed itself. After emerging as a Cold War armed movement that was heavily reliant on the support of state actors, Polisario has assumed a new guise. Today, Polisario enjoys increasingly significant support from non-state actors, as Byman et al. argue has been the case for other armed movements in the post-Cold War period. Although Polisario, alongside the PLO, is a longstanding armed movement seeking to capture state power, it is certainly not a relic. Rather, it has transformed itself and remained current by efforts such as the described development of non-state support.

Second, the new sources of support for Polisario from non-state actors— the Sahrawi diaspora, NGOs in Europe and beyond, and new forms of multilateral aid—mean that Polisario is most helpfully conceptualized in broader terms than as an Algerian-backed movement. The importance of other sources of support for Polisario is growing. Crucially, these other sources of support— the diaspora, which looks to the refugee camps as a metaphorical center; EUCOCO, which organizes the funding of multiple projects in the refugee camps; and the sponsorship of SADR governmental activities by a multi-lateral organization such as UNHCR—allow Polisario to pursue activities that Algerian state support did not allow it to undertake.

Both the fact that Polisario has been able to transform itself and remain "up-to-date" as an armed movement and the fact that it has fostered new forms of non-state support bespeak the resilience of Polisario as a liberation movement that appears to be primed to continue, even in the absence of progress toward achieving the goal of national liberation.

The third, and final dimension explored here regarding the transformation of Polisario into a movement increasingly backed by non-state actors is the extent to which the support of non-state actors outlines both a tension and flexibility within Polisario. The states that have supported Polisario have supported an armed movement, with some of those states having emerged from armed movements themselves. On the other hand, support from non-state actors for Polisario as an armed movement has not necessarily been clear cut.

The Sahrawi diaspora has some vocal members who demand a return to war, while aid from NGOs and multi-lateral organizations has markedly focused on civilian activities in the refugee camps: legal services, welfare services, education and training for young people, etc. The non-state sources of support for Polisario harbor a potential division, then, between those who are more explicit in their support for Polisario as an armed movement, and those who are more explicit in supporting Polisario as the governing authority of a civilian population allowing or enabling the implementation of social and economic development projects.

The addition of new and significant forms of support for Polisario may thus expose Polisario to fresh tensions in the future. If Polisario continues with the current ceasefire, it may eventually lose the support of those who demand a return to war. Similarly, a return to war might expose Polisario to the risk of losing other forms of support on which it increasingly relies. In the early twenty-first century, Polisario not only managed this tension but also seemed to draw some benefit from the fact that, despite being an armed movement, it was able to garner support that focuses on civilian initiatives in the refugee camps. The international attention from civilian and solidarity groups to the cause of Western Sahara has allowed Polisario to pursue activities comparable to the forms of visibility deployed by unarmed social movements in the region, such as the Berber movement in Algeria.[58] Polisario's musical groups, such as "Estrella Polisaria," perform on international tours arranged and supported by Western Sahara activists. Polisario runs cultural festivals, an annual cinema festival (FiSahara), and an art festival (ARTifariti) in the Polisario-controlled areas of Western Sahara.[59] The festivals bring returning and first-time visitors to the camps, who are billeted with refugee families for homestays. Refugees look forward to these events as high points in the year. Families beyond the camp where the cinema festival is hosted, including refugees from other camps, travel to the festival site to stay with friends or relatives and enjoy the films, meet visitors, and form their own views as to which director should receive the prize of an albino camel for the best film. By appealing to an international civilian audience through such innovative means, Polisario strengthens its political base and presents itself as much more than an armed liberation movement.

In conclusion, paying attention to the increasing support of non-state actors for Polisario is important for several reasons. It is important for understanding Polisario as a movement that, although hailing from a classic Cold War scenario of receiving support from state actors, has followed the trend set by other armed movements to develop the support of a range of actors. It is also significant for recognizing how Polisario, despite remaining an armed movement, has been able to adopt activities comparable to those of other unarmed social movements in the Maghreb by attracting this support from non-state actors. Finally, it is important to note that it may be crucial to the success of armed movements to blur the boundary between being an armed and an unarmed movement. Although it is unclear how such a blending of armed and unarmed mobilization might affect future support for Polisario from its state and non-state advocates. For now, this blurring of boundaries seems to have contributed to Polisario's resilience as a liberation movement.

9

FILM AND CULTURAL DISSENT IN TUNISIA

Nouri Gana

"By indirections find directions out."
Shakespeare, *Hamlet* (2.2.66)

In post-revolutionary Tunisia, there is hardly a public debate over any pressing political, economic, or social issue—ranging from national security, tourism and labor strikes, to accountable governance and institutional reform—that does not ultimately devolve into a "blamestorming" exercise. In each area, the participants apportion blame for the deterioration of the state of affairs (*taraddī al-ʾawḍāʿ*) to figures of the *ancien régime* of Ben Ali or discredit or champion others, establishing their own revolutionary credentials in the process. This obsessive return to the pre-revolutionary situation in an all-out war of positions, which has become a constant feature of political debate after the revolution has cast its long shadow on the cultural scene, in which everything came to be valued, attacked, or embraced depending on its perceived affinity with the revolution or the counterrevolution led by the remnants of the old regime. Not infrequently, concerts have been cancelled, theatrical performances interrupted, screenings picketed, and artists attacked, or, at times, arrested on the spot. The Ministry of Culture itself has often succumbed to popular opinion: for example, it extended and then withdrew an invitation to Lotfi Bouchnak to perform in the opening ceremony of the 2011 Carthage Festival because of his association with Ben Ali's regime in the (still fresh) collective memory of Tunisians. Bouchnak's name appeared on a petition signed by many public figures—including, lawyers, businesspeople, artists, journalists, athletes, doctors, and university professors—calling on Ben Ali to run for re-election in 2014. Quite suggestively, Bouchnak was replaced at the festival by El Général, along with a host of other rappers, singers, and musical troupes associated with the "Revolution of Freedom and Dignity."[1]

The value of artists and public intellectuals has come to be routinely reassessed in post-revolutionary Tunisia in relation to the nature and degree of their past association (if any) with Ben Ali's regime, a process that was made easier after bloggers and cyberactivists published several lists of artists and public figures who allegedly supported Ben Ali in his 2014 re-election bid. These lists included the names of iconic filmmakers Moufida Tlatli and Abdellatif Ben Ammar, actress Hind Sabri and actor Hichem Rostom, as well as several famous singers, such as Latifa al-Arfaoui, Nabiha Karaouli, Amina Fakhit, Sonia M'barek, and Saber Reba'i, in addition to Bouchnak. Some of these local celebrities might not have chosen to be on the list of signatories, but may have been named by Ben Ali's entourage and included on the list without their consent. Even though they may not be held in public opinion as guilty of explicit involvement with Ben Ali's regime, they are still subject to the tacit implication that they have been complicit in the regime's search for longevity.

While many artists, especially popular singers, who thrived under the Ben Ali regime experienced a rude awakening, or a fall from grace of sorts, after the events of 17 December 2010 and 14 January 2011, others, who had previously opposed Ben Ali, and were consequently forced to disappear from public view, were catapulted to instantaneous, albeit long overdue, fame. Many of those whose reputations declined in the wake of January 2011 due to perceived connections to the regime, have attempted to hitch their wagons to the train of revolution and have managed to redeem themselves, at least partially. Those who enjoyed overnight fame, or belated acknowledgment of their revolutionary credentials, found themselves suddenly caught in the polarizing political atmosphere of post-revolutionary Tunisia. Often, their political views, or public stances on current events, have made them targets of blame and hate speech on Facebook and other social networking forums, as well as in the public sphere.

With the post-revolutionary overdose of political debates raging in public and virtual spaces, the unprecedented proliferation of political parties, the relentless wars of positions and the adhocracies of political alliances, the current Tunisian cultural sphere risks becoming further captive to political events. The countrywide unity that brought together thousands of Tunisians in mass demonstrations against Ben Ali's regime has now largely given way to disunity and divisiveness along ideological lines and party politics. While Islamists, secularists, leftists, Arab nationalists, and Salafists, among others, have all made various socio-political contributions to the toppling of Ben Ali, their common histories of victimhood, resistance, and struggle have not resulted in a common agenda in post-authoritarian Tunisia. The same can be said about artists and intellectuals whose varying positions in the debates (and/or how the public viewed those positions) eventually voided the deep commonalities their pre-revolutionary struggles against Ben Ali's regime had shared. However, rediscovering these pre-revolutionary commonalities of struggle is more important than ever as some have argued that cultural debates and controversies have hindered the transition to democracy, eclipsing in the process the significant role culture previously played in the making of the Tunisian revolution.

The purpose of this chapter is to address the value of cultural politics in the gradual emergence of a dissident social imaginary. Perhaps because of the rigidity of censorship and the severity of self-censorship during the successive dictatorships of Bourguiba and Ben Ali, one of the remarkable constants of Tunisian cultural products is that much of what would count for political dissidence has been couched as forms of social or cognitive dissonance, in which the norms of social intelligibility collapse and with them all sorts of taboos. Nowhere else is this as evident as in postcolonial Tunisian films produced in the last three decades. This chapter seeks to disentangle the common genealogies of cultural resistance and dissidence that have characterized the artistic ventures of a number of filmmakers in postcolonial Tunisia. These shared genealogies seem to have been forgotten amidst the vociferous political debates that have come to characterize post-revolutionary Tunisia. This chapter excludes other forms of cultural expression (such as theater, music, and literature) in order to focus on film, one of the most vital elements of Tunisia culture.[2]

In the years that preceded the revolution, Tunisian film ran the gamut of responses to authority (be they political, religious, or social), from conformity and consent to resistance and dissent, and anything in between. In this chapter, I outline the trajectory of Tunisian film from its somewhat amateur beginnings in the 1960s to its rise in prominence in the 1980s thanks to a generation of innovative and committed filmmakers whose neo-realist artistic vision shaped today's cinematic landscape in Tunisia. The major part of this chapter is devoted to a discussion of select postcolonial dissident films, examining the critical latencies of each film along with the ways that each helped capture and articulate, at least retrospectively, Tunisians' mass discontent with the authoritarian regimes of both Bourguiba and Ben Ali. Under dictatorship, cinematic dissidence may not be publicly decoded, much less acknowledged, either because it is rhetorically ambiguous or simply because it is impermissible for viewers and film critics alike to articulate it, or perhaps to even imagine it. Nonetheless, it never ceased to exist, circulate, and occupy, along with other forms of cultural dissidence, an underground space for political critique. I argue that Tunisian cinema—along with artistic and cultural productions such as poetry, music, and theatrical performances—played a fundamental role in carving out a tradition of artistic dissidence in the history of postcolonial Tunisia. It is undeniably the power and cumulative effect of this creative critical tradition that inspired and sustained the popular uprising that has shaken the country and the entire region since 17 December 2010. In fact, the leading slogan of the uprising, "the people want to topple the regime," comes from Abul-Qasim al-Shabbi's poem "The Will to Life."

Tunisian film is undoubtedly part of this tradition of creative and discursive dissidence. It may not always be possible to measure the extent to which modern Tunisian cinema stirred political contention in public life, much less to gauge the role it played in the popular mass uprising of December 2010. But this is not necessarily undesirable. To establish causality between cinematic dissidence and social insurrection and revolt is precisely to reduce filmic representation to ideological premeditation. Not only does this remove any claim that art may have to aesthetic autonomy, but also, it ends up narrowing the idea of political agency to direct actions against, or interactions with, the state including those made by social movements or political parties. On the contrary, however, cultural politics need not be wedded to state politics, as the short-term goals of the latter are in stark contrast to the long-term visions of the former. It is important to wrest the concept of political agency away from "its imaginary coupling with the state,"[3] because the goal of cultural politics is not necessarily immediate policy or regime change, but rather the transformation of public life through the generation of a new social imaginary, a new mode of organizing social relations that is different from the status quo. These new social imaginaries are not created by individual films, but through the concatenation of multiple films, and other cultural products, over time. While a film may not result in regime change, I argue that a new social imaginary will make such a change possible.

The Emergence of Postcolonial Film

It is impossible to watch a postcolonial Tunisian film today from an exclusively pre-revolutionary perspective as the current historical climate and juncture are ever present. Besides, the value of film is not derived solely from its appropriateness to its own historical moment of production (that is, post-independence Tunisia), but also from its relevance to historical moments that are yet to come. It is inevitable, but also highly productive, that we now view postcolonial Tunisian films through the lens of revolutionary and post-revolutionary Tunisia. Through this new lens it becomes clear that several Tunisian filmmakers creatively evaded censorship, and charted a counterintuitive genealogy of rebelliousness, both scholarly and non-scholarly, to understand the provenance, scope, and significance of what happened in Tunisia and beyond since 17 December 2010.

From its early beginnings to the present, Tunisian film has relied largely on the financial support of the postcolonial state (the Ministry of Culture, to be precise), which, in turn, found in film and visual culture at large, a viable means of promoting its national image and ideological discourse. With that in mind, the Ministry of Culture founded ERTT (Tunisian Radio and Television) and SATPEC (Tunisian Production and Cinematographic Expansion Company), along with the Carthage Film Festival for Arab and African Cinema.[4] Early Tunisian films emerged from the amateur film movement and were nationalist in content and purpose, seeking to document and represent the realities of the anticolonial struggle of Tunisia against French colonialism, especially after World War II. Notable examples include Omar Khlifi's films, especially his 1966 al-Fajr (The Dawn), which was arguably the first Tunisian feature film, and Abdellatif Ben Ammar's 1973 Sejnene. Al-Fajr delved—documentary style—into the national struggle against French colonialism, while Sejnene focused on the role of the UGTT (The Tunisian General Labor Union) in the events of 1952–1954 that led up to independence. With Brahim Babai's 1972 Wa Ghadan (And Tomorrow) and Naceur Ktari's 1975 al-Sufarā' (The Ambassadors), as well as Ridha Behi's 1976 Shams al-Dibā' (Hyenas' Sun), a revisionary and counter-colonial critique of Tunisian history opened up to realist social critique of the postcolonial state and of its failed socio-economic policies. *Wa Ghadan* addressed the social problems that result from rural exodus to towns and cities, while *al-Sufarā'* addressed the challenges of racism and integration that Tunisian migrants faced in the Goutte d'Or district in Paris, France. *Shams al-Dibā'* focused on how tourism lead to neo-colonial and sociocultural problems; this was well before the economic pitfalls and social malaise of the tourist industry were exposed by Nouri Bouzid's 1992 *Bezness*. Both Behi and Bouzid, to use Kmar Kchir-Bendana's words, "mounted a critique in which the ravages of the tourist industry were perceived as acts of rape."[5]

Gradually, but steadily, Tunisian film has begun approaching the plight of postcolonial nationhood in terms of individual struggles for social recognition, political redress, and, above all, for justice and freedom of expression. This was especially true during the mid-1970s when Bourguiba consolidated power in his own hands, proclaimed himself president for life, and neutralized the role of UGTT, while crippling any existing or aspiring political opposition. Even before that, however, we can see this change in approach in films like Omar Khlifi's 1968 *Khlifa Lagra'* (*Khlifa Ringworm*), Sadok Ben Aicha's 1968 *Mokhtar*, Abderrazak Hammami's 1972 *Ummi Traki*, and, most notably, in Salma Baccar's 1976 *Fatma 1975*. Although the beginnings of this neorealist approach can be seen in these older films, it has flourished in newer films such as Nouri Bouzid's 1986 *Rih Essed* (*Man of Ashes*) and 1988 *Safa'ih min Dahab* (*Golden Horseshoes*), and consolidated itself with Moufida Tlatli's 1994 *Samt al-Qusur* (*Silences of the Palace*), Mohamed Zran's 1996 *Essaida*, Naceur Ktari's 2000 *Hulu wa murr* (*Sweet and Bitter*), Jilani Saidi's 2006 *'Urs al-Dhib* (*Tender is the Wolf*), and Fadhil Jaibi's *Junun* (*Madness*) of the same year. These latter films represent the maturing of Tunisian cinema. Whether through their exemplary attention to real-life stories, the complexity of character-development, or their aesthetic and stylistic sophistications, these films have moved Tunisian cinema toward the realm of art, as opposed to commercial and melodramatic tendencies of other national cinemas, particularly the major corpus of Egyptian cinema.[6]

It is not for nothing that the emergence of this neorealist trend of auteur filmmaking, in which much of the material for the films comes directly from the private stories of the filmmakers themselves, has occurred almost hand-in-hand with the rise of private production companies, namely Tarek Ben Ammar's Carthago Films and Ahmed Baha Eddine Attia's Cinétéléfilms. The latter came into being in order to produce Nouri Bouzid's groundbreaking *Man of Ashes* after it was turned down by Ben Ammar.[7] Attia went on to singlehandedly produce the films that would constitute the golden age of Tunisian filmmaking in the 1980s and 1990s, including Bouzid's *Golden Horseshoes*, Boughedir's *Halfaouine*, and Tlatli's *Silences*.[8] Most of the films that came after Bouzid's trailblazing *Man of Ashes* have focused on marginal and marginalized individuals—from defeated leftists, prostitutes, gravediggers, failed singers, thieves, suicide bombers, and housemaids—as if defeat and failure were the new chronotopes of the cultural politics of neorealism. As Bouzid himself propounds in his quasi-manifesto, "New Realism in Arab Cinema: The Defeat-Conscious Cinema,"

> the search for all that was novel went on, giving rise to new feelings that found expression in those new features, and which had nothing to do with the old notions of the classical hero—the foremost protagonist. The new realism took upon itself to demolish the myths which classical literature and classical cinema perpetuated.[9]

The interest in defeated and marginalized individuals is an essential component of the post-1967 reality of new realism. It should be seen less as an attack on men than an attack on patriarchy—a trend that was consolidated by a wave of female filmmakers.

While the emergence of female filmmakers (such as Salma Baccar, Nejia Ben Mabrouk, Kalthoum Bornaz, Moufida Tlatli, Nadia El Fani, and Raja Amari) has brought to the fore a variegated and peculiar focus on female characters and their lived experiences and struggles, some male filmmakers have all along approached women in their films as critical to their cinematic discourse and agenda, namely the call for the emancipation and revalorization of the individual, and for the implementation of gender equality and social justice. For example, Ali Abdelwaheb's 1969 *Um Abbes*, Rachid Ferchiou's 1971 *Yusra*, Khilifi's 1972 *Surakh* (*Screams*), and Sadok Ben Aicha's 1978 'Aridhat al-azia (*Mannequin*), or Boughedir's 1996 *Saif Halq Eloued* (*A Summer in La Goulette*), and Khaled Ghorbal's 2001 *Fatma*, Bouzid's 1997 *Bent Familia* (*Girls from a Good Family*), and 2002 'Arai's Tein (*Clay Dolls*). All visualized the individual stories of a number of heterogeneous female characters while breaking all kinds of social and religious taboos relating to gender roles, adultery, premarital sex, nudity, interfaith relations, virginity, child molestation, and child labor, among other controversial topics.

Moufida Tlatli makes a particularly relevant observation regarding some male filmmakers' use of female characters and women's struggles as indirect routes toward cinematic dissident practices: "I often wondered why it was that male directors should be so preoccupied with the question of women. Until I realized that, for them, woman was the symbol of freedom of expression, and of all kinds of liberation. It was like a litmus test for Arab society: if one could discuss the liberation of women then one could discuss other freedoms."[10] Dissidence is contagious; once you practice it somewhere, chances are you will be able to practice it elsewhere, even in the realms of the everyday or of grand politics, which was unheard of in Ben Ali's Tunisia prior to 17 December 2010. In this sense, the preoccupation of some male filmmakers with the representation and emancipation of Tunisian and Arab women challenges the existing gender norms and unleashes a process or a dynamic of social change that, while not leading directly to revolutionary events, do engender human agency. That is, they create the very possibility of critical thinking and social transformations that often precede insurrection and revolt. As Roland Bleiker observes,

> human agency is not something that exists in an a priori manner and can be measured scientifically in reference to external realities. Strictly speaking, there is no such thing as human agency, for its nature and its function are, at least in part, determined by how we think about human action and its potential to shape political and social practices.[11]

The films mentioned above, among others, constitute a continuum of visual dissidence and critique that is critical to an inclusive understanding of the cultural forces that have propelled the popular protests in the wake of Bouazizi's suicide attempt on 17 December 2010. Cultural and cinematic practices of dissent may be slow and not immediately manifested in the public sphere, but their role in the formation and transformation of societal values is crucial to the emergence of political human agency. Even the technical or stylistic innovations filmmakers introduce, their appropriation of new cinematic trends, and their rejection of traditional genres are of paramount significance, not only to formal analyses but also to cultural critiques. This is because they shake our habits of mind and sense of hermeneutic security, and point toward new modes of perception that demand the reassessment of sociopolitical relations. Nouri Bouzid recalls how his generation of filmmakers rose up against the old style of Egyptian cinema that once dominated the market, shaping societal emotions, morals, and tastes:

> We went to war against censorship, which was another thing that divided old and new. We declared war on the old emotions. Hitherto the idea had been to make people weep at fate with all the simple, melodramatic tricks. We were fed up with that cinema and wanted to go the other way. So we waged war on the aesthetic and all the models on which that cinema was based. We sometimes went so far as to reject plot and anecdote, considering that it was too easy to tell a story.[12]

The "story" did not disappear completely in these new genres, but it no longer follows a developmental, linear narrative. It is disentangled from narrative fragments, symbols, flashbacks, and other artistic and technical tools. As Bouzid further clarifies, "new realism, then, is not a form, but a specific content that has a form; it is concerned with reality—a new reality and, hence, the newness of its form."[13]

The following section focuses on a few films that I believe to be reasonably representative of the diverse but cohesive neorealist venture of postcolonial Tunisian cinema: Nouri Bouzid's *Man of Ashes* and *Golden Horseshoes*; Férid Boughedir's *Halfaouine*; Moufida Tlatli's *The Silences of the Palace*; Mahamed Zran's *Essaïda* and Moncef Dhouib's *The TV's Coming*. I argue that these films chart a subtle genealogy of dissent from the normative representations of "Tunisian-ness" (*tunisianité*) in mainstream media, history, and state rhetoric. The crucial importance of these films lies in their ability to challenge the sociocultural status quo, and form the critical basis for challenging the governmental and political state apparatus. The obsession with the female/male body in Tunisian cinema almost always bespeaks an allegorical obsession with the body politic. In other words, regardless of whether or not these films criticize the successive dictatorships of Bourguiba and Ben Ali directly, or precipitate protests or acts of civil disobedience, it is the role they play in the gradual rethinking of social values—of gender boundaries, family ties, and national identity in an increasingly globalized capitalist economy—that should be appreciated as an integral first step toward wider political dissent.

Moufida Tlatli's 1994 *The Silences of the Palace* (صمت القصور)

Set in Beylical Tunisia (the Hussein Dynasty of Beys 1705–1957), which was technically part of the Ottoman Empire but in reality operated as a French protectorate, *Silences* travels back and forth (through the cinematic economy of the flashback) between Tunisia on the eve of independence and the postcolonial Tunisia of ten years later. It acts to compare and contrast the fate of the nation and that of its male and female subjects, particularly Alia, the protagonist. The aim of *Silences* is not only to reclaim the lived experiences and expose the unspoken sufferings of women servants (who were practically slaves) under the Beys,[14] but also to assess the extent to which the independence of Tunisia from French colonialism intersected with their emancipation from patriarchal bondage.

In the film, the fervent and enlightened nationalist Lotfi (played by Sami Bouajila) tries to assure the young Alia (Hend Sabri) of this promissory future before she elopes with him on the night her mother dies while trying to abort the child resulting from the recent rape by the evil Bey character, Si Bechir (Hichem Rostom). "You're as indecisive as our country. One word thrills you, the next scares you," Lotfi reproaches the young Alia before reassuring her that "Things are going to change. A new future awaits us. You will be a great singer. Your voice will enchant everyone."

In the same way that many are now questioning whether any significant changes have resulted from the 14 January 2011 popular revolution in Tunisia, the adult Alia (Ghalia Lacroix) questions Tunisian society of the 1960s, only to realize that postcolonial Tunisia did not offer her a fate any different from that of her mother's. In the end, Lotfi's post-independence behavior proved to be more conditioned by the same patriarchal impulses that sealed Alia's fate as an illegitimate child than by his idealistic vision of a successful Alia and a free Tunisia uninhibited by the past.

After presenting the viewer with a series of extended flashbacks that oscillate comparatively between past and present to tell Alia's backstory, the film ends with Alia finally comprehending the extremity of her mother's suffering and addressing herself to the latter in a moving inner monologue, expressive of both Alia's entrapment and defiance:

> I thought Lotfi would save me; I have not been saved. Like you, I've suffered, I've sweated. Like you, I've lived in sin. My life has been a series of abortions. I could never express myself; my songs were stillborn. And even the child inside me Lotfi wants me to abort. This child, however, I feel has taken root in me; I feel it bringing me back to life, brining me back to you. I hope it will be a girl. I'll call her Khedija.

Alia's decision to keep the baby can be seen as a signal of a better and more fruitful future different from the abortive past she had. At the same time, it is a future past in the sense that it is ultimately a reenactment of her mother's fate to bring up her child as illegitimate. Her choice to disobey Lotfi, however, is not something that her mother could have possibly chosen, let alone exercised. Here, it becomes clear that Alia's childhood rebelliousness against her mother's submission to the Beys served her well in her subsequent rebelliousness against Lotfi. Additionally, her courage to break the wall of silence regarding the anti-colonial protests that were going on outside the palace and sing the forbidden national anthem at a party is a vindication of both national and female self-determination.

This scene, which constitutes the film's finale, elevates Alia to a powerful yet vulnerable position: at the same time that she asserts her own voice and the voice of a nation in the throes of an anti-colonial war, her audience deserts her for fear of complicity, and her mother passes away in a shadowy room in the palace following a failed self-performed abortion. This is arguably the important lesson of the film, and one that is of particular relevance to post-revolutionary Tunisia: the power and responsibility to speak up—when few are able—should necessarily override the fear of being left alone and exposed. This scene therefore acts as an economic foil to a previous, evocative scene in which Alia is portrayed (as if caught in a nightmare) screaming hysterically and running toward the open gates of the palace after she witnessed her mother being raped by Si Bechir. The closer she gets to the gates, the faster the doors shut in front her, locking her in—her screams inaudible and drowning in the crushing silence of the impervious night.

While the film is titled *Silences of the Palace*, its ultimate goal is not only to show how agentive silence might be by virtue of being endured by the women servants thanks to their communal solidarity, but also to point toward the inevitability of breaking that contract of silence. Khalti Hadda evokes this contract by saying, "We are taught one rule in the palace: Silence." The image of Alia's muted screams remain, however, a poetic epitaph to generations of Tunisian women whose voices were forever lost in the clatter of nationalist discourse, their stories of pain and suffering never seeing the light of day. The image of the muted scream also raises the question of whether such past pain can be acknowledged belatedly, even if it cannot be verified. If Alia's scream cannot be heard, the question it alludes to is not only whether her suffering can be acknowledged, but also whether it actually happened.

The challenge for *Silences* is to reclaim and give voice to that silent scream. The poetic significance of the image of the muted scream derives from the fact that it is performative of the very question that haunts the ethical and aesthetic endeavors of the entire film: how much pain has gone into the making of the Tunisian postcolonial nationalist discourse, and how much of it has gone unacknowledged, either because it did not count or because there were no available means of counting and quantifying it? The slow-paced motion of the camera, the impeccable *mise-en-scène*, the slow rhythm of the film and accomplished editing, as well as the measured deployment of close-up scenes and long shots, might all be seen as aesthetic techniques typical of art film, but in *Silences of the Palace* they are also thematic pursuits, mapping and signifying in minute detail the unquantifiable silences that seal the fate of the women inside the palace and simultaneously inside their own bodies (which they can neither own nor disown). *Silences* delivered a lasting lesson: that silence about (sexual or political) abuse does nothing to help overcome it. This lesson may have informed some of the thousands of Tunisians who took to the streets after 17 December to break the wall of fear and media silence, and to protest against corruption, cronyism, and the travesty of human rights.

Nouri Bouzid's 1986 *Man of Ashes* (ريح السّد) and 1988 *Golden Horseshoes* (صفايح ذهب)

Film plays the same role for the director Tlatli that music plays for the character Alia: a means of expression and empowerment. Alia's scream after she witnesses Si Bechir rape her mother is muted not because it is not a genuine scream, but because in order for a scream to be a scream it needs to be heard and acknowledged by an empathic witness. The muted scream aims to put the viewer on the alert for any signs of injustices that threaten to go unnoticed due to a lack of vigilance and competence on the part of society rather than due to a lack of expression on the part of the scream's originator. The organizing narrative principle in *Silences* is a question: Does a scream count if it falls on deaf ears, or is not heard? What counts as a scream and what counts as less than a scream? This very same set of questions has also been broached by Nouri Bouzid in his directorial début, *Man of Ashes*, as the protagonist of the film searches in vain for an empathic person to listen to the story of his childhood rape by his master carpenter. Like *Silences*, *Man of Ashes* seeks to reclaim and visualize the experience of invisible pain and suffering, and to ponder its potential to transform families and social groups within a community that is itself struggling to come to terms with the changes it has undergone in the transition from colonial to postcolonial times.

The film not only reproduces the dismal, delayed effects of unwitnessed suffering, but also serves as the empathetic witness, infusing the individual, secret traumas of the protagonists with a breath of realism and, above all, with the dignity of recognition.[15] *Man of Ashes* chronicles the experiences of two childhood friends, Hachemi (played by Imad Maalal) and Farfat (played by Khaled Ksouri). The former is soon to be married, while the latter is kicked out of his father's house due to public rumors, gossip, and street graffiti calling his manhood into question. The viewer learns that Hachemi and Farfat were molested as young apprentices by their carpentry mentor, Ameur (Mustafa Adouani), and that the two grew up indelibly marked by this secret trauma. As the tragic episode comes back to haunt them, they find themselves frantically scrambling for a final exit becoming obsessed and anxious over their virility, masculinity, and manhood within an allegedly heterosexual community they can neither desert nor be reintegrated into.

Bouzid shrewdly broaches the question of homosexuality in Tunisia, and in the entire Arab Muslim world, through the crime of child molestation. The film not only exposes the naturalized hypocrisy and moral vagaries of a society in which homosexual panic overrides outrage over pederasty, but also distinguishes unequivocally between masculinity and manhood, on the one hand, and between homosociality and homosexuality, on the other. The bond between Hachemi and Farfat is homosocial and not homosexual. Bouzid raises the question of homosexuality not only to challenge sexual heteronormativity, but also to underscore the extent to which homosexual panic has come to undermine homosocial bonds in Arab societies. This is illustrated in the brothel scene at the end of the film, when homosocial desire gives way to homosexual panic. This, in turn, gives way to the reassertion of normative heterosexuality, best illustrated by the rivalry between Farfat and Azaiez (Mohamed Dhrif) to sleep with one of the two prostitutes.

While Tlatli's film spans colonial and postcolonial times, Bouzid's film situates itself squarely in postcolonial Tunisia and in the post-1967 Arab world, where the culture of defeatism became rampant. Bouzid avers that he wanted to discern "what makes up our present situation of crisis, the bankruptcy of our society. Thus, my first film [Man of Ashes] addresses childhood, not exactly mine but rather my generation's, how we were 'broken' from the beginning, how we suffered from adult violence."[16] While Bouzid might be referring here to the inaugurating, constitutive, and inscriptional violence that accompanies our introduction to a sociality that prefigures our existence, his remarks take on a specific historical and political dimension in the context of Man of Ashes. Without diminishing the importance of the political allegory of French colonial and neocolonial rape, or of Israel's rape of Arab lands following the Six-Day War of 1967 (both of which are at the origin of the persisting malaise of postcolonial nationhood and the agony of Arab nationalism), Bouzid's film is concerned with the immediate material and psychological effects of these wider historical and societal crises as they become manifest—in a rather condensed and indirect form—in individual histories.

However, one cannot understand the gravity of this individual trauma without situating it firstly in the context of Tunisia, secondly in the context of the Arab world, and perhaps thirdly in the wider context of the Third World or Global South. Insofar as Tunisia is concerned, Habib Bourguiba's personification of the neopatriarchal cult of personhood informs, what I have called in an article titled "Bourguiba's Sons," the "melancholite proclivity of Tunisian men, that is, their fantasy of patriarchal omnipotence which goes hand-in-hand with their cultivation of modernity."[17]

Bourguiba's autocratic rule was informed by the history of French colonialism as well as by the trials of Arab nationalism against colonial Zionism and Euro-American imperialism. Both Bourguiba and sons are belated to a historical condition that contributed to their de-formation and continues to exert immense psychic pressure on their present and future survival. The importance of Bouzid's *Man of Ashes* is the severity of its critique of the allegorical link between patriarchal manhood and Bourguiba's brand of Tunisian nationhood. Both Hachemi and Farfat renounce any possible identification with their biological fathers and their mentor-turned-molester who boasts of having initiated them, both sexually and professionally. For Hachemi, the only remaining model of manhood is Monsieur Lévy, an elderly Tunisian Jew, but he dies before he can listen to Hachemi's secret trauma. When, at the end of the film, Hachemi seeks but is not granted refuge in a brothel run by Sejra, this demonstrates the ways in which the interplay of identifications recasts the nets of paternity, fatherhood, motherhood, and manhood, insofar as it is in excess of the empty rhetoric of men and masculinity (which are almost entirely dissociated from normative patriarchal expectations throughout the film).

In this respect, the opening scene of a slaughtered red cockerel, flapping its wings and gasping for its last breath is not an allegorical gesticulation toward emasculation, but rather an animating trope of the traumatic predicament of manhood. The slaughtered red cockerel, a symbol of virility and masculinity, does not so much conjure up the fear of castration as it does the imperative to separate virility and masculinity from manhood. From the outset, the film depicts what might have been a castrating historical situation of colonial rape or child molestation in order to prod the viewer to rethink manhood beyond the fallacy of linking it to virility and masculinity. The opening scene of the slaughtered red cockerel is in tune with Bouzid's overarching goal of examining how Hachemi and Farfat's generation was penetrated by adult violence, and its enduring psychic demarcations, in the very same manner that Palestine was raped and dispossessed by Israel following the 1967 Six-Day War. More precisely, Bouzid is interested in the privatized experience of defeat that is at once structural (pertaining to being human) and historical (pertaining to being Arab in this particular historical juncture). Bouzid argues,

> What interests me in this business of defeat is the idea that the conflict is internal. Not only internal, the conflict is borne by every individual and it cannot be

settled except by each individual. *The Man of Ashes* was a notable film in this respect, it was almost a key film, and that continued with *The Golden Horseshoes*. The first film speaks of the destruction and rape of a child; the second speaks of another form of destruction and rape of an adult.[18]

Specifically, *Golden Horseshoes* retells Bouzid's own experience of torture during his imprisonment of more than five years (1973–1979) for his political involvement in the leftist movement Perspectives, Bouzid's film, which was released shortly after Bourguiba's removal from power in 1987, is a bold indictment of the dictator's clampdown on leftists and of his abuse of human rights by systematically repressing, torturing, and "disappearing" his political opponents. Like the carpenter-father in *Man of Ashes*, Bourguiba saw himself as the father of Tunisia and Tunisians, a father who would not hesitate to sacrifice (in an Abraham-like fashion) some of his sons. Both of Bouzid's films aspire to transform this sacrificial relationship to the father of the nation (and to all the powers that be) into an oedipal, and therefore, rebellious confrontation. His revisionary approach to Tunisia's, and the Arab world's, postcolonial history through the lens of defeat should not only be understood as an expression of discontent, but also as an allegorical conjuration of a future free from injustice.

As Jeffrey Ruoff rightly suggests, "While Bouzid's cinema is conscious of defeat, it is not defeatist."[19] The protagonists of *Man of Ashes* do finally discern and disentangle themselves from their past trauma, and, with the complicity of Hachemi, Farfat stabs Ameur, their childhood molester, in the groin. This symbolic act, with which the film ends, does not so much condone revenge as condemn patriarchal, postcolonial, and neo-colonial rape. By staging broken and defeated individuals for Tunisian audiences, Bouzid not only makes it possible for viewers to identify with and distance themselves from those individuals on the screen, but also—and simultaneously—offers them an opportunity to immunize themselves against the psychology of defeat and the state apparatuses that perpetuate it. In the final analysis, the cinematic tendency to grapple with and visualize the experience of defeat indirectly becomes the basis for fostering strategies of empowerment.[20]

Toward the end of *Man of Ashes*, Farfat kills Ameur, exacting long overdue vengeance on the man who "initiated" him sexually and professionally. Interestingly, while the plan to kill Ameur was premeditated, it only developed following Farfat's sexual encounter with one of the prostitutes in the brothel. After raising the question of homosexuality, the film seems to settle for normative heterosexual practice as the midwife to Farfat's manhood, revenge, and freedom from the trammels of the past. Farfat has, at last, become what he wanted to be at the beginning of the film: "a rooftop bird." In the film's finale, he is portrayed running from the police, jumping in front of a moving train, and hopping across rooftops, even as the graffiti that called his manhood into question is being erased. While the film ends with Farfat's ultimate conformity to a conservative and patriarchal apparatus of manhood, its goal is to expose and critique it rather than to reenact and reinscribe it. The same can be said about Boughedir's *Halfaouine* where the rituals of becoming a man in a patriarchal society are unravelled in greater detail and in a far lighter register than in *Man of Ashes*.

Férid Boughedir's 1990 *Halfaouine: Boy of the Terraces* (عصفور السطح)

Halfaouine is the story of Noura (Selim Boughedir), a boy going through the trials of puberty and trying to reconcile the demands of his body with those of the social body, and vice versa. Not infrequently, he gets confused about what he wants and what is demanded from him by others, and thus he finds himself attempting to reconcile clashing desires and needs. For instance, his impatience to join the men's club is matched only by his eagerness to retain the privileges of childhood, namely accompanying his mother to the women's hammam to gaze at local beauties and satisfy his growing sexual curiosity. Boughedir assembles an inventory of the different steps involved in Noura's becoming a man, which include circumcision, banishment from the women's hammam, and, above all, sex. Unsurprisingly, Noura's first sexual experience with an orphaned servant-girl leads immediately to his revolt against his father, Si Azzouz (Mustapha Adouani), signaling his triumphant resolution of the oedipal struggle, mastery of his fear of castration, and, ultimately, his ascension to manhood through his newly demonstrated virility.

The importance of *Halfaouine* from a post-revolutionary perspective lies not only in Noura's ability to break through the spatial and gendered boundaries that regiment the private and the public (which is never more to be desired than in the political life of a police state in which secrecy is the essence of governance), but also in his exposure to political dissidence as an indispensable component of responsible manhood. Noura witnesses the arrest of Salih (Mohammed Driss), an unmarried cobbler, playwright, musician, and public opponent of Bourguiba's dictatorship, which was considered obsolete in the 1980s (the decade in which the film is set) when his health deteriorated and his neurotic obsession with power bordered on psychosis. Notably, the scene in which Noura asks Salih, "When does one become a man?" is followed immediately by the scene in which Noura helps Salih stand on an overturned bucket to cross out graffiti that says, "Our Leader's idea is all that matters." They write above it instead, "Our idea is all that matters and without a Leader," an apt and prophetic qualification of the Tunisian revolution.

Mahamed Zran's 1996 *Essaïda* (السّيـدة)

Zran's directorial debut, *Essaïda*, delves into the living conditions of the working-class neighborhood of Essaïda, one of the shanty towns surrounding Tunis, to expose the sociopolitical realities of Tunisia in the mid-1990s. This is the same era during which Tunisia signed an association agreement with the European Union, ushering the country into the global economy. The neoliberal restructuring of the economy that resulted, however, served to aggravate, rather than resolve, unemployment, and fostered a culture of corruption, crime, and cronyism that negatively affected all Tunisians except for a small number of elite who benefited from the new structure. The film opens with a chance encounter in downtown Tunis between Amine (Hichem Rostom), a painter in search of a source of inspiration, and Nidal (Chadli Bouzayen), a poor youth begging for money. Nidal's gaze, which typifies Essaïda's (and Tunisia's) many stories of poverty, pain, and suffering, captivates the attention of Amine so much that he offers to pay Nidal to sit for him to paint his portrait. Eventually, Amine moves on to live in Essaïda to experience life in a crowded neighborhood where poverty, crime, and unemployment prevail. As if his immersion into the world of Nidal and Essaïda would not be complete simply by relocating there, Amine breaks up with his fiancée Sonia (Myriam Amarouchene), who drives a fancy car and still lives in Carthage, a town insulated from the everyday realities of most Tunisians, and where Amine used to live with Sonia.

As a filmmaker, Zran finds in the character of Amine, the artist and painter, someone capable of expressing through his portraits Zran's own cinematic preoccupations; this is especially true of Amine's final portrait of the Essaïda neighborhood, which alludes to Zran's own socialist realist portrayal of Essaïda in the film. By making Amine descend from his Carthage ivory tower, Zran is not only advocating that art should return to social reality, but is also decrying how out of touch artists, not to mention the politicians in Palace Carthage, have become with the realities of life on the margins of the capital (and of the coastal cities in the interior and southern parts of Tunisia, where the protests that led to Ben Ali's deposition started).

Zran's *Essaïda* takes us on a disturbing journey through the life of Nidal, a downtrodden teenager, chronically beaten by his father and ostracized by his peers, as he begs, steals, and, eventually, kills to make money. There is nothing special about Nidal, Zran seems to suggest; in his dreams of a better life, he represents all Tunisian youth. Nidal might be a little eccentric in his aspiration to be smuggled into the United States rather than into Italy or France (both of which he thinks are full of Arabs already), but the viewer cannot fail to recognize in his gaze the bitterness and adversity of life in Essaïda and Ben Ali's Tunisia.

This bitterness is best captured at the end of the film when Nidal is chased by the police for murdering a cab driver. He deserts his motorbike and climbs up a tall, high-voltage steel tower and screams at the crowd that pleads with him to come down, "I'm fed up with you, do you not hear me? I'm going to die here in front of you and you will all be relieved. I want to live. I'm fed up, fed up." In the end, Nidal appears to comply with his pleading father and begins descending the tower, only to accidently fall—or deliberately jump—to certain death. Zran's *Essaïda* paints a bleak vision of Ben Ali's Tunisia; this vision, needless to say, has proven prophetic in the wake of Mohammad Bouazizi's self-immolation in Sidi Bouzid. Even while the film prophesied and cautioned about Bouazizi's suicidal protest through Nidal's demise, it is tragically ironic that its full lesson was not learned then and has still not been learned in post-revolutionary Tunisia. Several young men have already committed suicide to protest against practices of the post-revolutionary interim governments, which have so far not achieved many of the goals of the revolution: easing unemployment by revitalizing the economy; offering reparations to families of the martyrs or providing medical care to the injured; bringing members of the old regime and the snipers who killed dozens of Tunisians to justice; reforming the justice and media systems; and, above all, fighting corruption, which remains the burning issue. If suicide had become a desperate form of protest for some frustrated citizens, it is because post-revolutionary leaders have not been attentive to or have failed to attend to the lessons of Zran's *Essaïda* and the cautionary implications of Nidal's fate.

Dhouib's 2006 *The TV's Coming* (التّلفزة جايّة)

Moncef Dhouib's *The TV is Coming* was released in 2006, the same year Tunisia celebrated the fiftieth anniversary of its independence from France. While a celebratory mood runs throughout the film, Dhouib's main directorial thrust is clearly to poke fun at the rosy rhetoric of state nationalism and the ways in which mainstream media of TV and radio became legislators and disseminators of a fabricated reality boasting claims of democracy, stability, and prosperity. Not even a remote village in the interior of the country by the name of El-Malga (where the film is set) is immune to this contagious flow of simulated happiness, or the enthused support to serve the powers that be in Palace Carthage. Because *The TV is Coming* is a film about how reality is manipulated, and, therefore, manufactured, when it is televised, the film positions itself as a counter-medium to the official state propaganda machine, the national station TV7 (which references 7 November 1987, the day of Ben Ali's accession to power). *The TV is Coming* juxtaposes televised "reality" (sanitized for mass consumption, both locally and globally) against lived reality (raw, and showing the brute facts of life under indigenous forms of colonialism and media silence). The film aspires to relay or portray lived realities by tearing down the walls of media silence that usually prevent their true portrayal. *The TV is Coming* positions itself therefore as a counter-narrative to official state narrative and delves into and recovers the stories of El-Malga, which had been marginalized and excluded from the mainstream national narrative. Understanding these cinematic achievements helps to shed light on the scope of the film's artistic dissidence.

The satirical plot of *The TV is Coming* is set in motion with a phone call. A top official in the capital informs Fitouri (Ammar Bouthelja), the leader of the village cultural committee, that a German television crew would be visiting the remote village within a month. Although the viewer later learns that the crew was coming to film a documentary about the deadly scorpions of North Africa and the search for a vaccine, Fitouri thinks that they will be making a documentary about the village. The entire script of the film hinges on this miscommunication, which is not revealed to viewers until the very end of the film. In the interim, the misinformed cultural committee scrambles to primp itself for the imminent visit, cinematically representing the ways official rhetoric of postcolonial Tunisia dissimulated its moral bankruptcy by projecting rosy images of stability and prosperity for both local and foreign consumption. This manufactured reality represents the actual mortal poison for which Ben Ali's Tunisia did not bother looking for a cure but let it spread throughout the country, taking innocent lives, until it experienced a rude awakening on 17 December 2010.

At the beginning of the film, a Tunisian official visits the village on National Tree Day, and is offered various bribes, which he declines to the villagers' dismay. The German crew, however, is served differently and are presented a version of Tunisian history catered to Western sensibilities and sanitized from any forms of authenticity that may offend. A Sufi group, for example, is barred from practicing its indigenous dances and trances, while the owner of a local café frequented by unemployed villagers is instructed to host fake book and newspaper readers to give a positive impression of El-Malga (and, by implication, Tunisia) to the Germans and Europeans. It is through this depiction of the town's staging a spurious façade of modernity that Moncef Dhouib's film delivers its acutely critical judgement of Ben Ali's façade of democracy.[21]

The film is saturated with jokes and comic encounters, but its ultimate goal is didactic and critical. It exposes how Tunisian officialdom was able to produce and disseminate a falsified image of the country to Tunisians and non-Tunisians alike, while unemployment, corruption, and national disillusionment were driving the country to the brink of insurrection and revolt. The satiric comic register has commonly been used by playwrights and comedians in postcolonial Tunisia to evade state censorship and to deliver sociopolitical critique. Dhouib's film is no exception. While filmmakers who use this approach risk that neither the message nor the messenger will be taken seriously, great benefit can be gained from the comic approach. For example, the comic encounters in *The TV is Coming* provide productive vantage points for the viewer that foster the development of self-reflection, and so that critical human agency may emerge. While films of this genre may not have resulted in immediate protests against the Ben Ali regime, they served to engender a collective withdrawal of consent, and, ultimately, a sustained practice of cultural dissent.

Much like the theatrical solo performances of Raouf Ben Yaghlan and Lamine Nahdi (it is worth noting that Moncef Dhouib wrote the scripts for two popular one-man shows performed by Nahdi), the humorous encounters in *The TV is Coming* are "rehearsals of an implied or imagined commitment to collaborative revolutionism as a mode of relationality which might remain unlocalizable and free from the anxieties of direct action but not entirely oblivious to the promise of a popular eruption of mass solidarity and discontent."[22] In other words, when Tunisian viewers of *The TV is Coming* laugh at the expense of authority, and momentarily release their pent-up anger, they engage in a collective act of dissidence, even from within the contours of manifest allegiance to the regime. Gradually, these dispersed, yet collective, acts of laughter insinuate themselves into public discourse and start to interfere with the dominant ideology of the façade of democracy. It is only in this sense that acted dissent on the screen can have a correlative life of its own on the streets.

Clearly, though, we gain nothing insightful about the making of sociopolitical dissidence (in postcolonial Tunisia or elsewhere in the Maghreb) by silently passing over the true spaces of cultural critique opened up by the types of cinematic discursive practices I have discussed in this chapter.

"CURATING THE MELLAH"

CULTURAL CONSERVATION, JEWISH HERITAGE TOURISM, AND NORMALIZATION DEBATES IN MOROCCO AND TUNISIA, 1960s–2017

Aomar Boum

In the midst of the Arab, Islamic, and international calls for boycott, divestment, and sanctions against Israel, a handful of Arab countries—Lebanon, Morocco, and Tunisia—have engaged in a number of projects to restore local Jewish sites and synagogues. In Lebanon, the Magen Avraham synagogue, which recently opened its doors for religious services, has been restored largely through donations from Lebanese Jews in the diaspora. However, Tunisia and Morocco remain the most celebrated countries in which the revival of Jewish heritage is not only part of the political discourse of the government, but also a key aspect of the tourism industry. While President Habib Bourguiba and King Hassan II played a major role in nurturing direct political engagement with Israel dating back to the early Arab-Israeli wars in the 1960s and 1970s, the celebration of Jewish heritage and its conservation emerged as a social trend within the Jewish diaspora as a way to rediscover Tunisian and Moroccan heritage, gaining momentum after the Oslo agreement. The rediscovery of Jewish heritage—and its underlying economic benefits—has produced varied internal social and political reactions in Tunisia and Morocco since their independence in 1956.

In this chapter, I explain the context for this political and cultural current of rediscovering and conserving Jewish heritage, and I highlight the internal political dynamics and challenges it faces today. I discuss the movement of cultural renovation and marketing of Jewish heritage in Tunisia and Morocco and its ties to the development of a Jewish cultural tourism that targets Israeli tourists of North African descent (and sometimes those of Ashkenazi descent as well). Equally important, I analyze the political and social debates about Israeli relations with Morocco and Tunisia, and Jewish-Muslim relations that have been generated by this movement of cultural preservation. Unlike Algeria, which has mostly dismissed these forms of cultural dialogue, Tunisia and Morocco have largely embraced them because of the positive connections its Jewish communities have with both countries. I argue that this movement has a philo-Semitic dimension given its focus on Jewish capital and tourism revenues rather than on a serious national debate about the place of Jews as citizens in Morocco and Tunisia. While Jews are admired as successful business owners and traders, they are socially and religiously stigmatized because of their direct or indirect links to the conflict between Israel and Palestine. Therefore, negative perceptions of Jews are seen largely through debates revolving around the appropriateness of normalizing relations with Israel, especially after the Arab uprisings. I also contend that despite the relative physical absence of Jews in Tunisia and Morocco today, they still play a role in the political economies of both countries to the extent that important sections of the tourism industries cater to Jews who trace their descent to both countries. Therefore, even with the damaging political impact of the Arab-Israeli conflict on perceptions of Jews in Morocco and Tunisia, governments are still using their countries' historical Jewish heritage to market a living Jewish culture in North African cities and villages.

On 2 May 2013, the Washington-based Cape Verde Jewish Heritage Project (CVJHP) organized a ceremony to honor a small—and close to extinct—Jewish community on the Island of Santiago in the town of Praia, the capital and largest city of Cape Verde. During the nineteenth century, many Jews from northern Morocco resettled in Praia in search of trading and commercial opportunities. With only a few Jews left in Cape Verde today, the cemetery and Jewish heritage of the community declined into oblivion. Yet, the historical connections of Cape Verde's Jewry to Morocco led the CVJHP to seek donations from King Mohammed VI who contributed a sum of $100,000 to renovate the Jewish tombs. Despite the viable historical connection between Moroccan and Cape Verdean Jewries, many observers speculated that the royal interest was "motivated by a desire to attract tourists and to curry favor with American Jews."[1]

The connections between safeguarding Jewish quarters and neighborhoods, heritage tourism, interfaith dialogue, tolerance, and normalization of relations with Israel have dominated public political discussion in Tunisia and Morocco. In the aftermath of the rise of the Tunisian Ennahda Party and Moroccan Party of Justice and Development (PJD), political and electoral gains following post-Arab Spring parliamentary elections, and in direct response to Israeli calls for the emigration of the last remaining Jews, members of Ennahda and the PJD publicly assured Jewish communities that their rights and personal security would be guaranteed by the state. Later, it was rumored that both North African Islamic governments were set to nominate René Trabelsi and Serge Berdugo to be their next ministers of tourism, replicating past nominations of Jews to ministerial posts the early decades of independence.[2]

The social and political perception of Jews as "economic saviors" is culturally grounded in a traditional philo-Semitic North African admiration of Jews and their reputation as successful economic brokers.[3] These perceptions align with the traditional belief that Jews possess "economic powers" that could revive a failing economy.[4] Accordingly, Morocco, and to lesser degree Tunisia, have been widely engaged in a process of cultural conservation and redevelopment of Jewish sites, synagogues, and cemeteries, especially since the Oslo agreement. This conservation was largely initiated to encourage—though indirectly and unofficially—Israeli tourists of North African descent to visit Morocco and Tunisia. As a result, a new brand of Jewish heritage tourism began dominating the tourism industry of Tunisia and Morocco by the mid-1990s. Individual and group tourism packages catered to descendants of Jewish communities in Europe, North America, and Israel. As an option, Jewish cultural tours of Morocco and Tunisia can take tourists to rural and urban spaces once occupied by Jews whose descendants live today outside the region. In addition to these cultural and historical walks in the Jewish neighborhood (*mellah* or *hāra*), visits to shrines, cemeteries, and Jewish religious festivals are a central part of this brand of Tunisian and Moroccan tourism.[5]

SOCIAL CURRENTS IN NORTH AFRICA

Minority Quarter and Jewish Heritage Tourism

Throughout the Middle East and North Africa, the Jewish quarters (*ḥārat al-yahūd*) of old Islamic cities have been largely emptied since Jews began emigrating and resettling outside the region. The Jewish quarters have been generally discussed in European literature as ghettos where Jews lived separate from Muslims in overcrowded conditions.[6] With European colonization, many Jews, especially merchants, moved outside the walls of the *mellah* and settled in what would later be known as the European *nouvelle ville*. Historically, the *mellah* was a secure, but vulnerable place.[7] It was a residential neighborhood that guaranteed the protection of Jews, given its location near the sultan's palace, but, at the same time, it was the first place to be targeted when there was political insecurity or natural disasters. Despite the protective dimension of the *mellah*, there was a belief that its closeness to the sultan's residential palace was intentional so that the sultan could secure shares of the monetary gains of Jewish merchants. The *mellah* was also perceived as a space for illicit activities such as prostitution, gambling, and drinking.[8] This view continues to predominate in the memory of many local Muslims to the extent that few desire to live in the *mellah* today. In this context, the Jewish character of the *mellah*, even as a geographic space, makes Muslims who live within it today the subject of social stigma. During my ethnographic work in southern Morocco, many Muslim informants expressed negative and stereotypical views of poor people who occupy some of the former Jewish houses. But how can we explain the government's push for the conservation of a relatively forbidden space? And why do North African Jews still spend their money in a market where their hosts display religious and social discomfort exacerbated by the political realities of the Palestinian conflict?

In his book, *The Pillar of Salt*, Albert Memmi remembers his childhood growing up in "the blind alley" of the Jewish neighborhood of Tunis:

> Narrow as it was, it seemed huge to me. Closed at one end by the wall of the cemetery, the other opened onto the narrow rue Tarfoune, useless and deserted. This double bottleneck that led into the heart of the noisy crowded Arab neighborhood followed two sudden turns so that it seemed to be defending a hollow silence. And we defended it, too, against the few children who ever dared venture there, until the day when a howling gang of rough and nasty boys picked this out-of-the-way place in which to play their forbidden games. We were insulted, pushed around, even beaten; and our dead end, no longer safe for us, ceased to play so important a part in our imagination for it became just another alley in this sordid city.[9]

Although Jewish-Muslim relations vary depending on regional and historical contexts, the memory of the Jewish experiences in Muslim environments is largely governed by a spatial separation conditioned by religion. In fact, life inside the *mellah* allowed Jews to engage in their social and religious traditions without any restrictions. The alley of the *mellah* was an extension of the home and the synagogue. Today, the majority of the Jewish neighborhoods throughout the Arab world are either empty or serve as residence for squatters. Their synagogues have been closed for years and left to the destructive forces of nature.[10] For example, after the ousting of Muammar Gaddafi, David Gerbi, a Libyan Jew whose family had fled after the 1967 war, returned to Tripoli and tried to reopen and renovate the Dar al-Bishi Synagogue in the old city of Tripoli. Many Muslim Libyans demonstrated against his renovation projects, and he was denied permission to restore the synagogue. These attitudes toward any Jewish presence in North African societies today reflect some of the widespread negative attitudes surrounding the Arab-Israeli conflict, and date back to the 1960s. Said Ghallab writes of what it was like growing up during that period of early conflict:

> The worst insult that a Moroccan could possibly offer was to treat someone as a Jew.... My childhood friends have remained anti-Jewish. They hide their virulent anti-Semitism by contending that the state of Israel was the creation of European imperialism.... A whole Hitlerite myth is being cultivated among the populace. The massacres of the Jews by Hitler are exalted ecstatically. It is even credited that Hitler is not dead, but alive and well, and his arrival is awaited to deliver the Arabs from Israel.[11]

Despite these negative, traditional views about Jews, Tunisian and Moroccan governments continued to make a space for Jews through political representation and/or a relative level of religious tolerance from the government. Unlike Libya and Algeria, where Jewish heritage is not the government's priority in terms of cultural preservation, Moroccan and Tunisian governments have, since the 1960s, approached Jewish heritage from a pragmatic perspective. After all, Libya and Algeria are oil states whereas the Tunisian and Moroccan economies rely heavily on tourism revenues. They have not only restored synagogues, cemeteries, and Jewish homes, but they are also turning Jewish neighborhoods into living museums targeting the market of global travelers interested in North African Jews and other Jewries. This cultural policy is meant to transform Tunisia's and Morocco's old Islamic cities, including their Jewish neighborhoods, into tourist destinations where minority quarters serve not only as world heritage sites but also as living Jewish museums.[12]

In the 1990s, Tunisia and Morocco witnessed an increase in Jewish heritage tours. Many companies based in the United States, Israel, and European countries began marketing the Jewish "spirit" of Tunisia and Morocco.[13] Israeli-Moroccan anthropologist André Levy described one of these tours, which he joined as a participant-observer in 1987:

> Like most of the trips, we began our journey shortly before Lag Ba-'Omer, the death anniversary of Rabbi Shim'on Bar-Yohai. The itinerary we followed was highly standardized, and included the following: after two days in Spain, waiting the *laissez passer*, we proceeded to travel along the south-east coast of Spain toward Algeciras, sailed to Ceuta, and then took a bus to Tangiers, Morocco....
> In tours such as these the Israeli travel agent sends along an Israeli escort, who usually does not have any formal training. He is generally someone who succeeded in recruiting several participants on condition that he act as a group escort; he receives a free ticket. The Moroccan Tourist Bureau assigns as local guide, who serves as mediator between the travelers and the local population.[14]

These tourism operators and others have turned Moroccan and Tunisian Jewish religious and cultural heritage into a commodity to be sold even as anti-Jewish and anti-Israeli sentiments have increased due to the political situation in the Middle East. Therefore, Morocco and Tunisia are faced with a similar situation seen in Eastern and Western parts of Europe where tourism operators are marketing Jewish history even as a dormant, but growing European anti-Semitism spreads among old and new generations.

"Necessary Evil": Philo-Semitism and Jewish Business

In his work, *The Whitewashing of the Yellow Badge: Anti-Semitism and Philo-Semitism in Postwar Germany*, Frank Stern debates the transformation of public opinion regarding Jews during the Allied occupation and the first four years of the Federal Republic. Stern contends that the rise of philo-Semitism should not be seen as a genuine manifestation of German acceptance of Nazi guilt or repentance for the Jewish genocide. Instead, he argues, philo-Semitism is part of a deliberate postwar German policy to establish German sovereignty through the financial and economic support of the Allies. Stern has strong reservations about Germany's genuine change of heart, arguing that current German perceptions of Jews as good business people do not dispel the marginal status of Jews or change the fact that they are considered outsiders and strangers within German society, or that there is an underlying anti-Semitic feeling among blue-collar and white-collar workers.[15] Stern actually sees a link between the traditional anti-Semitic stereotypes and this new philo-Semitic culture in Germany. Societies are free from anti-Semitism "when they [have] combatted traditional and new prejudices and helped anchor democratic values in the population."[16]

The cultural revival of European Jewish heritage in many cities that were emptied of their Jewish citizens during and after the Holocaust is part of a European tourism that targets, among other potential visitors, Jews from all over the world.[17] In the late 1990s, as the Berlin Wall fell and its historical psychological effects began to disappear, East European cities began to revisit their cultural histories, especially their Jewish chapters, as a way to come to terms with the destructive forces of the Nazi racial genocide. After the flattening of European Jewish synagogues and homes, as well as the burning of libraries, prayer books, and Torah scrolls, and the demolition of tombs, schools, and businesses, Europe had a sudden change of heart and began embracing its Jews and Jewish cultural objects. In fact, "Jewish culture—or what passes for Jewish culture, or is perceived or defined as Jewish culture—has become a visible, and sometimes highly visible, component of the popular public domain in countries where Jews themselves now are practically invisible."[18] The cultural Judaization of urban spaces and the "museumification" of synagogues and homes denote underlying economic objectives, especially as Eastern European cities faced dramatic financial challenges in the aftermath of the Soviet Union's political breakup. Hence,

> Jews and things Jewish, meanwhile, are popular attractions, even a category of commercial merchandise.... Old Jewish quarters are under development as tourist attractions, where "Jewish-style" restaurants with "Jewish-sounding" names write their signs in Hebrew or Hebrew-style letters, use Jewish motifs in their décor, and name their dishes—sometimes even dishes made from pork or nonkosher mix of meat and dairy products—after rabbis and Old Testament prophets.[19]

In her work on Jewish tourism in Poland, Erica Lehrer argues that Jewish Holocaust tourism shaped the politicization of emotion and the cultivation of shared feelings of historical belonging. Lehrer argues that these Jewish travels to Europe are influenced by "Jewish missions [which] grew with the development of tourist infrastructure and Israeli university foreign-student programs through the 1960s and 1970s, and until the late 1980s a robust industry of mission tourism consisted largely of American youth trips to Israel."[20] However these organized Jewish groups developed in a context of troubling post-war anti-Semitism that Jewish tourists rarely experience in a direct way. Instead, Jewish tourism in Europe is built upon a de-historicized anti-Semitism and an image of Europe "fossilized in the near aftermath of World War II."[21]

This interest in cemeteries and neighborhoods limits Jewish tourists' direct contact with local populations and cultures. Jack Kugelmass notes that the experiences which Jewish tourists in Poland "remember are likely to be those that enhance an already existing negative opinion."[22] While Jewish tourists in Europe travel to see the camps, North African Jews travel to Tunisia and Morocco to celebrate their religious shrines and visit family tombs. For many Jews, Tunisia and Morocco serve as nostalgic symbols of a Jewish heritage within Arab lands. By the early 1990s, and despite the second Gulf War, many Israeli tourists had already begun to enter Morocco. For these tourists, Michael Laskier writes,

> the opportunity to visit their ancestral land, sink into nostalgic childhood memories, and frequent the graves of venerated Jewish saints, known as *Saddiqim*, turned out to be a positive emotional experience. For Morocco, it became a profitable enterprise in that it also attracted Jewish tourists of Moroccan origin from France and Canada.[23]

In Tunisia and Morocco, where tourism represents a central part of both economies, considerable numbers of Jewish tourists annually visit cultural Jewish quarters that have become a key source of the regeneration of old Islamic cities such as Fez and Tunis. However, like Eastern European cities, they are haunted by Jewish destruction and alienation and a state approach to Jewish culture that is marked by the political debate over the Arab-Israel conflict.

Tunisia, Morocco and Israel: Common Interests and Hidden Relations

In 1946, about 230,000 Jews lived in Morocco and 100,000 in Tunisia, but by the early 1960s, the biggest populations of Moroccan and Tunisian Jews had emigrated to southern settlements in Israel. Today, less than 1,500 and 4,000 Jews live in Tunisia and Morocco, respectively. The majority of Moroccan Jews reside in Casablanca, while Tunisian Jews are largely in Djerba. Before French colonialism, they lived as *dhimmis*, People of the Book, enjoying Islamic legal protections in return for paying a *jizya* (tax paid by non-Muslims). By the middle of the nineteenth century, significant political changes began to take shape with regard to the status of Jews in North African societies. For example, in 1857, the Tunisian Jew Samuel Batto Sfez was sentenced to death for cursing the Prophet Muhammad. In 1863, approximately ten Jews were imprisoned in the coastal city of Safi for allegedly poisoning a Spaniard. These incidents and others led to a surge of religious violence against Jewish neighborhoods many North African cities. Jewish leaders sought the intervention of British and French Jews, culminating in the visit of financier and banker Moses Montefiore to Marrakesh in 1864. Following these events, Britain and France began to call for equal rights for all Tunisian and Moroccan subjects "without religious distinctions, and eliminating the requirement for Jews to wear distinguishing marks on their clothing and to pay *jizya*".[24]

The establishment of Alliance Israèlite Universelle schools throughout North Africa accelerated the process of political emancipation of many Jews who became protégés of European governments. With the adoption of the Crémieux Decree in 1870, which granted Algerian Jews citizenship, a spillover effect enabled Tunisian and Moroccan Jews to begin obtaining foreign passports. By the end of the nineteenth century, relations between Jews and Muslims worsened over the political relations of local Jews with France. Equally important, the rise of Zionist activities towards the turn of the twentieth century further widened the social gap and political rifts between Muslims and Jews as Tunisian and Moroccan Jews were increasingly enlisted to join the Zionist project in Palestine.

Underground migration to Israel increased in the 1950s, especially as Nasserism created fear and anxiety among many Jewish communities. Calls for economic boycotts and attacks on Jewish property impacted negatively on some communities even as the monarchy and Bourguiba tried to curb the post-independence anti-Jewish movement. In the aftermath of the Six-Day War of 1967, a crowd of Muslims caused considerable damage to the Great Synagogue of Tunis. Fortunately, they failed in their attempt to set fire to the synagogue, where a considerable number of the Jewish population had sought refuge. Habib Bourguiba called the protestors "irresponsible fanatics" who deserved death sentences, but he also warned Tunisian Jews against any involvement in the Arab-Israeli conflict. On 6 March 1965, Bourguiba delivered a peace proposal in the Old City of Jerusalem. His initiative was based on the UN General Assembly's 1947 Resolution 181, which outlined the partition of Palestine as well as the 1948 Resolution 194 that advocated for the return of Arab refugees to their homes. Bourguiba noted that Arabs would recognize the existence of Israel if Israel accepted the return of Arab refugees. During this period, Bourguiba was one of the few Arab leaders who stood against Nasser's ideological dominance and called for engaging Israel diplomatically and politically. On 10 April 1965, he addressed the question of Palestine in Tunis:

> With regard to Palestine, it is necessary to be realistic, to go beyond the stage of recrimination and jeremiads. To repeat that the existence of Israel is an injustice

195

is true, but serves no purpose. I am in the habit of speaking frankly. I have, there-fore, thrown a large stone into water.... It is true that I have perhaps offended some sensibilities, but I have only said aloud what many think in quiet. Yet [Arab leaders] are beclouded and certain regimes are not stable. They do not want to have trouble with Cairo.[25]

Unlike many Arab leaders during the early years of independence, Bourguiba's position towards Israel was nuanced. At times he called for the elimination of Israel before later advocating for a peaceful solution to the con-flict. Yet, despite this critical stance towards Israel and Zionism, he maintained a relatively positive attitude toward Jewish emigration. Bourguiba's initiative was met with harsh criticism and rebukes from representatives of Arab states in Cairo on 28 April 1965 following a meeting of Arab League. Although Morocco objected to the Arab League's critical demonization of Tunisia, Nasser denounced the Tunisian plan as a step that could harm Arab unity.

After an initial lukewarm attitude toward Bourguiba's plan, Israel began to show interest in collaborating with the Tunisian government. In addition to agricultural cooperation, tourism projects were at the forefront of their discus-sions on potential collaborations as early as the late 1960s. Muhammad Masmoudi, Tunisia's ambassador to France, played a key role in opening and maintaining diplomatic channels with Israeli officials. Bourguiba preferred that economic projects between Tunisia and Israel should be carried out through a "third party and that Israel's direct involvement should be camou-flaged."[26] Muhammad Sfar, a successful Tunisian businessman, discussed the construction of hotels in Mahdia and Tunis with Israelis in Paris.

It was clear that tourism was the most important component of Bourguiba's plan to collaborate with Israel in the mid-1960s. In his capacity as Minister of Foreign Affairs, Habib Bourguiba, Jr., Bourguiba's son, had discussions with Israeli officials in Washington, D.C. about ways to develop and improve Tunisia's growing tourism industry by learning from Israel's experience and encouraging Jewish tourists from Western countries to include Tunisia in their list of destina-tions. In June 1965, Golda Meir asked Avraham Harman, Israel's Ambassador to the United States, to encourage American Jews to support the Tunisian gov-ernment by adding Tunisia to the list of tourist destinations. As early as 1966, the United States Council of Synagogues officially made Tunisia one of its tour-ism destinations. Although the 1967 war slowed the movement of Jewish tour-ists to Tunisia, Israel and Bourguiba maintained contact, even after the PLO was driven out of Lebanon and relocated its base to Tunis in 1982.

Like Bourguiba, King Hassan II tried to project a moderate attitude toward the Arab-Israel conflict even as he battled the influence of Nasserism and

Egypt's interference in Moroccan local politics. As a result, unofficial diplomatic relations between Morocco and Israel improved in the aftermath of independence and began to include agricultural support and military intelligence. Israeli personnel active in Morocco worked under the Ministry of Interior led by first by General Mohammed Oufkir and later by Ahmed Dlimi. Disguised as Western advisors, Israelis played a key role in supporting Morocco during its 1963 border war with Algeria and in lobbying the United States for military and economic aid. In the meantime, thousands of Moroccan Jews were permitted to migrate to Israel.

Unlike Tunisia's interest in Jewish tourists in the 1960s, Morocco focused its initial attention and partnership on bringing in Israeli agriculture experts, military aid, and on improving intelligence cooperation. However, the failing economy and the rise of unemployment in the late 1980s and early 1990s would force the Moroccan government to take an approach similar to that of Tunisia. Despite the fact that Hassan II met publicly with Shimon Peres in Ifrane in July 1986, raising criticism of Israel throughout the Arab world, early meetings between Hassan II and Peres went back to 1978 before Sadat signed a peace treaty with Israel. Hassan II replaced Bourguiba as the new political mediator between Israel, the Palestinians, and other Arab officials. He relied politically on Moroccan Jews inside and outside Morocco who were benefiting from the positive image he had cultivated among Moroccan Jews in Israel, France, and Canada. Hassan II went so far as to criticize the political approaches of some individuals within the PLO and their strategies against Israel. On 24 December 1977, he gave an interview to *Al-Ahram* in which he argued:

> I belong to the school of thought of our Prophet Muhammad, who stood for dialogue and waged war only as a last resort. I proposed this to the Palestinians four years ago. If they would have responded affirmatively, we could have assisted them in this endeavor. Yet the circumstances rendered this option morally premature.[27]

Unlike Bourguiba who discussed relations with Israel through intermediaries, Hassan II was personally involved in issues pertaining to Moroccan Jews. Although he never linked their return to tourism, he encouraged Moroccan Jews living in Israel, France, and North America to visit and live in Morocco.

Several Moroccan Jews played a key role in Hassan II's attempts to seek Jewish support between 1960 and 1990. They included the former minister of communication Léon Benzaquen, David Amar, Sam Benzeraf, Robert Assaraf, Maxim Azoulay, Serge Berdugo, and André Azoulay. A few Moroccan Jews such as Abraham Serfaty, Sion Assidon, and Edmond Amran El Maleh were critical of Israel and Zionism and opposed these official partnerships. During his visit to Washington in 1978, Hassan II sought the support of key figures within the American Jewish community for the Western Saharan issue. David Amar and Robert Assaraf, leading figures within the Jewish community of Morocco, were members of the delegation. Despite early resistance from the United States, under the administration of President Jimmy Carter, to selling American weapons to Morocco in its fight against the Polisario, the Iranian revolution changed President Carter's views. As a result, the United States Congress passed an unopposed proposal to sell reconnaissance planes, F-5E fighters, and helicopters with financial support from Saudi Arabia. Morocco's unequivocal support of the Sadat-Begin initiative put the king at the forefront of American-Middle Eastern diplomacy.

Despite what this relatively positive attitude toward Moroccan Jewries meant for the international community and its support of the monarchy, the Moroccan nationalist *Istiqlal* party launched a massive anti-Jewish campaign in its Arabic and French newspapers: *al-'Alam* and *l'Opinion*. In its critique of the West and Israel, the *Istiqlal* used Jews as its central theme to denounce what it considered a worldwide conspiracy against the Islamic nations, largely led by Jews. *Al-'Alam*'s critique centred on the Moroccan government for allowing Jews to migrate freely to Israel and seize Palestinian lands. In its election campaigns prior to and after 1967, the party relied on slogans such as "voting for a Jew equals a traitor of the nation." Ahmed Reda Guedira, a supporter of Moroccan Jews and Arab-Israeli negotiations, was also denounced by the *Istiqlal* party through slogans such as: "Guedira defends Jews, Christians and drunks!"[28] The party's newspapers also wrote about how the "Jew" should be left out of post-independence Moroccan society. In fact, while serving as the minister of Islamic Affairs, Allal al-Fassi announced that "when we say Moroccan we mean Muslim. The Moroccan Jew is nothing but a *dhimmi*. From now on, no stranger can have a Moroccan nationality unless he embraces Islam first and foremost."[29] In 1964, Allal al-Fassi critiqued the political rapprochement between the government and Israel, arguing that "Morocco is a Jewish state. Morocco is governed by Jews and foreigners."[30] Because of the conservative Islamic ideological basis of the *Istiqlal*, the party was adamant about building a Moroccan society free from religious minorities, and encouraging and even forcing the conversion of Jews. This was despite the agenda contradicting the Islamic tenet of respect for religious minorities, especially Jews and Christians. The inability of the nationalist leadership to come up with a new status of the *dhimmi* within the borders of the independent nation state formed a challenge to the political parties, as well as to the government, despite the constitution's emphasis on granting citizenship to Jews living within the borders of the nation.

Under their affiliation to the royalist party Rassemblement National Indépendant (RNI), Jews were elected in 1978 as municipal representatives and to the industrial and commercial chambers. Another Jewish individual was elected from the Moroccan communist party, and in 1982 a Jewish municipal representative was elected under the Union Constitutionnelle (UC). The parliamentary elections of 1982 for the first time promoted a Moroccan Jew from the UC as representing the city of Mogador. These political changes were marked by the nomination of André Azoulay in 1992 to the position of economic advisor to the king, and Serge Berdugo as the Minister of Tourism in 1994. Advocates within the political parties, stressed the determination of the monarchy to create a positive shift in political views toward Moroccan Jews as a way to bring about future positive shifts in the general attitudes of the larger society. In Tunisia, Jews showed less interest in political participation, causing Mark Tessler and Linda Hawkins to note in the 1970s that the Jewish community of Tunisia "has no meaningful political organization and only a minimum of institutional capacity and structural unity. It is wrong to see in this a policy of harassment aimed at Jews."[31]

Nevertheless, these changes would be affected by the rise of Islamic movements that stressed the plight of the Palestinian people and emphasized the historical relationship between Moroccans and Palestinians. Like traditional nationalist parties, the Islamic parties and organizations promoted a culture of Jewish conspiracy against the Arab world and their collusion with the West to conquer Muslim lands. The Intifada of 1987–1993 and the al-Aqsa uprisings of 2000 shifted the attitudes and affiliations of young adults from traditional communist and Islamic conservative parties to newly emerging radical Salafi groups and moderate Islamic movements. The PJD emerged as a new political force in Moroccan politics. Through its newspaper, *Attajdīd*, the party advocated that the Middle East conflict was a Moroccan one and that Moroccans should be involved in supporting Palestinians against Israel and the Jews. This shift in political discourse explains why Mohammed VI has been very careful in terms of his involvement with Israel to the extent that he ordered the closure of the Israeli liaison office in Rabat on 24 October 2000.

After the Madrid Peace Conference and the signing of the Oslo Declaration of Principles on 13 September 1993, Hassan II relied heavily on the political and economic weight of André Azoulay and Serge Berdugo and their connections with Moroccan Jews in Israel, Europe, and North America. In November 1994, the liaison offices in Jerusalem and Rabat were officially opened, launching a new era of public Moroccan-Israeli relations. The establishment of postal relations facilitated economic relations, and Hassan II saw in these initiatives a way to revive the ailing Moroccan economy, especially through agricultural and industrial projects.

Out of the National Shadow: Normalization, Jewish Heritage Tourism, and Political Conflict

On 9 May 2014, the Tunisian Parliament questioned Minister of Tourism Amel Karboul and Deputy Interior Minister for Security Ridha Sfar over an incident related to tourists entering Tunisia with Israeli passports. Later, the Miami-based Norwegian Cruise Line cancelled its tours to Tunisia due to a number of its Israeli passengers being denied entry. Amel Karboul, who faced criticism during her nomination over a prior trip to Israel in 2006, resigned. Prime Minister Mehdi Jomaa resisted demands for his resignation. In Morocco, an anti-normalization bill was sponsored by the PJD, the leftist Party for Progress and Socialism, and the Party of Authenticity and Modernity to criminalize economic, cultural, and sporting relations with Israel. After local and international pressure, the bill was cancelled despite continued pressure from anti-normalization Moroccan groups.

Both cases demonstrate a dramatic public shift in Tunisian and Moroccan political views regarding Israel during the last decade. The pragmatic (yet secret) attitude toward Israel during the reigns of Bourguiba and Hassan II has been replaced by a number of vocal associations and individuals who have been critical of cultural normalization. On 18 February 2014, a group of Moroccans protested the inauguration of an exhibition on Spanish Jews in Morocco at the Spanish cultural center, the Cervantes Institute. Organized by the national committee for the support of Palestine, the demonstrators raised signs with slogans aimed at André Azoulay, King Mohammed VI's advisor, and denounced the cultural exhibit as a normalization of relations with Israel.[32] On 30 April 2014, the synagogue of Sfax in Tunisia was vandalized, joining a growing list of Jewish sites that have been attacked in the aftermath of Ben Ali's overthrow.

Despite these political attitudes that reject any form of cultural and political association with Israel and sometimes with Jews, Tunisia and Morocco are a few of the Arab countries where a public debate about Jewishness is not only allowed but also includes diverse voices. For instance, a group of young and middle-aged Moroccan Amazigh activists have publicly welcomed Jews to come to the valleys of Sous, Draa, and Tafilalt. In Sous, a political bastion of the PJD, a group of teachers and university graduates launched a Berber-Jewish friendship association. Its founders contend that their main objectives were to promote the cultural diversity of the region, disseminate social tolerance, and create economic bridges with Moroccan Jews living abroad. Against the backdrop of a national and popular movement sympathetic to Palestinian political demands, delegations of Moroccan Amazigh teachers visited Yad Vashem to participate in a weeklong educational seminar about the teaching of the Shoah. Their objective was to incorporate what they saw as the neglected subject of the Holocaust into the national school curriculum. Yet, Khalid Soufyani, the President of the Moroccan Association for the Support of Palestine, has led a fierce attack against these Berber activists and anyone who calls for establishing relations with Moroccan Jews living in Israel.

In Tunisia, *al-Jam'iya al-tūnusiya li-musānadat al-aqaliyāt*, a local association that supports minorities, has fought for the preservation of cultural rights of Tunisian Jews and the guarantee for state protection after the Arab uprisings. Yamina Thabet created the association in 2011 to fight for the rights of women, blacks, and Jews. In December 2013, Thabet organized a conference on the impact of the six-month Nazi occupation of Tunisia during World War II. Thabet has been critical of the government's silence surrounding the attacks against Jews in Djerba in the months following the ousting of Ben Ali. Despite the rising anti-Jewish sentiment in Tunisia and Morocco, Thabet is an example of growing numbers of young North African adults pushing for Jewish-Muslim dialogue within their respective countries. They also criticize the doublespeak of some political figures regarding the social status of local Jews.

In 2010, I ran into a student in the halls of the University of Qadi Ayyad in Marrakesh. When he realized that my area of research is Moroccan Jews, he told me:

> Moroccan Jews are like a valuable mortgage that cannot be afforded. Moroccans talk a lot about their Jewish subculture to outsiders and boast about their history of tolerance, yet they refuse to accept that Jews can be Moroccan citizens with full rights and obligations. Our full support and sympathy toward the Palestinian cause have blinded us hindering our acceptance of Moroccan Jews. If we believe that Moroccan Jewish history can be an economic asset worth mortgaging then we should accept their full rights. Otherwise we have to put it for sale and stop using it for our economic advantages.

In Morocco, there is a growing movement led by Muslim youth to engage this Jewish past. In December 2014, I met a few members of a youth club in Rabat known as Mimouna who were preparing to launch a cultural caravan, a 300-mile traveling roadshow about Moroccan Judaism. The club Mimouna is named after the traditional Moroccan Jewish post-Passover celebration welcoming the return of leavened bread. For Moroccan Jews, Mimouna signifies the promise of redemption and the hopeful return of the Messiah. I asked them why they care about a topic that could potentially bring them nothing but stigma and social rejection. Almost all of them highlighted how little Moroccan youth know about their history and how significant it is for their compatriots beyond the walls of university campuses to embrace Morocco's cultural diversity.

For many other Moroccans, particularly younger ones, the country's Jewish story is part of the past and has no place in post-independence society. "How could we have a club about Moroccan Jews, many of whom occupy Palestinian lands today?" one Mimouna critic in Casablanca whispered to me during a visit I made in 2010. It was an attitude I knew well from my anthropological and ethnographic research on Moroccan Jewish communities, but the social pressure on me as a professional ethnographer was minimal compared to the pressures the student members of Mimouna face. A few acknowledged their frustration and anxiety about being ostracized because of their interest in learning about Moroccan Judaism, which to them is really about Moroccan history. Recently, the name of one of the Mimouna club members was listed in a public document published online by the Moroccan Observatory Against Normalization with Israel, alongside names such as André Azoulay, Driss El-Yazami, the president of the National Human Rights Council, and Berber, or Amazigh, activists, some of whom maintain contact with Israeli citizens, institutions, and other public organizations.

But when I spoke to the student members of Mimouna, I was surprised to find that their interest in the history of Jewish-Muslim relations also emerged from their own lives. The majority were born and raised in Casablanca, Rabat, Marrakech, or Fez and knew of their hometowns' complex histories. Elmehdi Boudra, the co-founder of the Mimouna club—who later earned a master's degree in coexistence and conflict from Brandeis—talked to me about how growing up in Casablanca, he never knew about the longstanding relations between Jews and Muslims in the old city. Boudra was also inspired by one of the group's early mentors, Simon Lévy, a renowned linguist of Judeo-Arabic and Judeo-Spanish, political dissident, and former director of the Jewish

Museum of Casablanca. Lévy also played a major role in Moroccan post-independence politics as one of the leading figures of the Party of Progress and Socialism founded by Ali Ya'ta.

Conclusion

With tourism revenues becoming a pivotal part of the Moroccan and Tunisian economies, Jewish cultural heritage is increasingly seen as an integral part of their national histories. This shift began as a private endeavor of a few Tunisian and Moroccan Jews, along with Jews from other countries. When the Tunisian and Moroccan governments recognized that the two countries might be able to capitalize on their Jewish culture by marketing its dialogue and tolerance to Jews from Moroccan and Tunisian diaspora, they got their ministries of culture and tourism involved. By preserving Jewish graveyards throughout Morocco the state acknowledges the centrality of pilgrimage events (*hillulot*) to its tourism and national revenues. But the crux of the matter remains. The conservation of Jewish cemeteries will never fully succeed unless Moroccan and Tunisian Jewish history and culture are taught in the countries' schools and universities. This requires parallel legal and political dialogue about the status and rights of minorities in these states. The revival of Jewish heritage and the conservation of buildings is necessary, but without comprehensive civil and political public debates regarding Tunisian and Moroccan "Jewishness" the impact of this revival will be limited. The "curation of the Mellah," its synagogues and homes" must move beyond the conservation of walls and tombs for Jewish tourists, as a young Moroccan university student once told me during a visit to the Jewish Museum of Casablanca. Instead of simply marketing it to the outside world, the material and immaterial Jewish heritage of these countries should become part of the national collective memory and celebrated alongside Amazigh, Arab, Islamic, and African heritage. Otherwise, Jewish cemeteries, shrines, and neighborhoods will remain nothing but tourist attractions for international Jewish visitors, and a veiled reminder—to locals—of the continuing Israeli-Palestinian conflict.

NOTES

1. SOCIAL CURRENTS IN NORTH AFRICA

1. James MacDougall and Robert P. Parks, "Locating Social Analysis in the Maghrib" in *The Journal of North African Studies*, vol. 18, no. 5 (December 2013), 631–638.
2. MacDougall and Parks, *op. cit.*, 632.
3. See, for example, Michael Willis, *Politics and Power in the Maghreb: Algeria, Tunisia and Morocco from Independence to the Arab Spring* (London: Hurst, 2012); and Michel Le Gall and Kenneth Perkins, eds., *The Maghrib in Question: Essays in History and Historiography* (Austin, TX: University of Texas Press, 1997), 63.
4. Émile Durkheim, *The Rules of Sociological Method* [1895] (New York, NY: Free Press, 2013).
5. Durkheim, "Schäffle, A., Bau und Leben des socialen Körpers: Erster Band", *Revue philosophique*, 19, 1885, 84–101. For a review of various methodological approaches to the Durkheimian concept of "social fact", see George Ritzer, "A Multiple Paradigm Science" in *The American Sociologist*, vol. 10, no. 3, (August 1975), 156–167.
6. "The group is understandable and explicable solely in terms of distinctly social processes and factors, not by reference to individual psychology," in Charles K. Warriner, "Groups Are Real: A Reaffirmation" in *American Sociological Review*, vol. 21, no. 5 (October 1956), 549–554, quoted in Ritzer, *op. cit.*, 159.
7. For a broader exploration of this theme, see Asef Bayat, *Life as Politics: How Ordinary People Change the Middle East* (Stanford University Press; 2nd edition, 2013).

2. ISLAMIST PARTIES AND TRANSFORMATION IN TUNISIA AND MOROCCO

1. The authors are grateful to Fiacre Zoungni for his help on this project. Some of these issues have been explored in Francesco Cavatorta and Fabio Merone, "Post-Islamism, ideological evolution and 'la tunisianité' of the Tunisian Islamist party al-Nahda", *Journal of Political Ideologies*, 20 (2015): 27–42.

2. See Steven Heydemann, "Upgrading Authoritarianism in the Arab World," The Brookings Institution, *Analysis Paper* 13 (2007): 1–37.

3. See for instance Koenraad Bogaert, "New State Space Formation in Morocco: The Example of the Bouregreg Valley," *Urban Studies* 49 (2012): 255–270.

4. See for instance Patrick Haenni, *L'Islam de marché* (Paris: Seuil, 2005).

5. See Khalil al-Anani, "The Debacle of Orthodox Islamism," *Project of Middle East Political Science*, Briefings 24 (2014): 7–9.

6. Asef Bayat, *Making Islam Democratic: Social Movements and the Post-Islamist Turn* (Stanford: Stanford University Press, 2007). See Olivier Roy, *L'échec de l'islam politique* (Paris: Seuil, 1992).

7. See Jonathan Hill, "Islamism and Democracy in the Modern Maghreb," *Third World Quarterly* 32 (2011): 1089–1105.

8. See Francesco Cavatorta and Rikke Haugbølle Hostrup, "The End of Authoritarian Rule and the Mythology of Tunisia under Ben Ali," *Mediterranean Politics* 17 (2012): 179–195.

09. See Michael Willis, "Containing Radicalism Through the Political Process in North Africa," *Mediterranean Politics* 11 (2006): 137–150.

10. See John Entelis, "The Unchanging Politics of North Africa," *Middle East Policy* 14 (2007): 23–41.

11. See Francesco Cavatorta, "Neither Participation nor Revolution: The strategy of the *Jamiat al-Adl wal-Ihsan*," *Mediterranean Politics* 12 (2007): 379–395.

12. See Francois Burgat, "Were the Islamists Wrong-Footed by the Arab Spring?," *Project of Middle East Political Science*, Briefings 24 (2014): 24–27.

13. See for instance Nazek Jawad, "Democracy in modern Islamic thought," *British Journal of Middle Eastern Studies* 40 (2013): 324–339.

14. Fauzi Najar, "Whither the Islamic religious discourse?" *Middle East Policy* 21 (2014): 87–97; and Jean-Francois Daguzan, "L'Hiver après le printemps? La transformation arabe à l'aune des processus politico-militaires," *Maghreb-Machrek* 210 (2011).

15. See Ashraf Nabih el-Sherif, "Institutional and Ideological re-construction of the Justice and Development Party: the question of democratic Islamism in Morocco," *Middle East Journal* 66 (2012): 660–682; and Sumita Pahwa, "Secularising Islamism and Islamising democracy: the political and ideational evolution of the Egyptian Muslim Brothers 1984–2012," *Mediterranean Politics* 18 (2013): 189–206.

16. Daniel Brumberg, "Islamists and the politics of consensus," *Journal of Democracy* 13 (2002): 109–115. See Tarek Masoud, "Are they democrats? Does it matter?," *Journal of Democracy* 19 (2008): 19–24.

17. Jillian Schwedler, "Can Islamists become moderates?," *World Politics* 63 (2011): 347–376.

18. See Sarah Wilson Sokhey and Kadir Yildirim, "Economic liberalization and polit-

ical moderation: the case of anti-system parties," *Party Politics* 19 (2013): 230–255.

19. See Laura Guazzone, "Ennahda Islamists and the test of government in Tunisia," *The International Spectator* 48 (2013): 3–50; Daniela Pioppi, "Playing with fire. The Muslim Brotherhood and the Egyptian Leviathan," *The International Spectator* 48 (2013): 51–68; and Eberhard Kienle, "Nouveaux regimes, vieilles politiques? Réponses islamistes aux défis économiques et sociaux," *Critique Internationale* 61 (2013).

20. See for instance Anne Wolf, "An Islamist renaissance? Religion and politics in post-revolutionary Tunisia," *Journal of North African Studies* 18 (2013): 560–573; and Teje Hidde Donker, "Re-emerging Islamism in Tunisia: repositioning religion in politics and society," *Mediterranean Politics* 18 (2013): 207–224.

21. See Muqtedar Khan, "Islam, Democracy and Islamism after the Counterrevolution in Egypt," *Middle East Policy* 21 (2014): 75–86; and Elizabeth Iskander Monier and Annette Ranko, "The fall of the Muslim Brotherhood: implications for Egypt," *Middle East Policy* 20 (2013): 111–123.

22. See for instance Stefano Torelli, Fabio Merone, and Francesco Cavatorta, "Salafism in Tunisia: challenges and opportunities for democratization," *Middle East Policy* 19 (2012): 140–154; Khalil al-Anani and Maszlee Malik, "Pious way to politics: the rise of political Salafism in post-Mubarak Egypt," *Digest of Middle East Studies* 22 (2013); Monica Marks, "Youth politics and Tunisian Salafism: Understanding the Jihadi current," *Mediterranean Politics* 18 (2013): 104–111; Stéphane Lacroix, "Sheikhs and Politicians: Inside the new Egyptian Salafism", Policy Briefings, Brookings Doha Center, June 2012. Available online: http://www.brookings.edu/research/papers/2012/06/07-egyptian-salafism-lacroix; (accessed 1 December 2017). Bjorn Olav Utvik, "The Ikhwanization of the Salafis: piety in the politics of Egypt and Kuwait", *Middle East Critique* 23 (2014): 5–27.

23. Quintan Wiktorowicz, "Anatomy of the Salafi movement," *Studies in Conflict and Terrorism* 29 (2006): 207–239.

24. Ewan Stein, "Studying Islamism after the Arab Spring," *Mediterranean Politics* 19 (2014): 149–152.

25. "Rethinking Islamist Politics," *Project of Middle East Political Science*, Briefings 24 (2014): 3–57.

26. Francesco Cavatorta and Emanuela Dalmasso, "Democracy, civil liberties and the role of religion after the Arab Awakening. Constitutional reforms in Tunisia and Morocco," *Mediterranean Politics* 18 (2013): 225–241.

27. Matthew Buehler, "The Threat to 'un-moderate': Moroccan Islamists and the Arab Spring", *Middle East Law and Governance* 5 (2013): 1–27.

28. Roy, op. cit.

29. Fawaz Gerges, "The Islamist moment: from Islamic state to civil Islam?" *Political Science Quarterly* 128 (2013): 389–426.

30. Alaya Allani, "The Islamists in Tunisia between Confrontation and Participation: 1980–2008," *Journal of North African Studies* 14 (2009): 257–272.

31. Emanuela Dalmasso, "Surfing the democratic tsunami in Morocco: apolitical society and the reconfiguration of a sustainable authoritarian regime," *Mediterranean Politics* 17 (2012): 217–232.

32. Bruce Maddy-Weitzman, "Historic departure or temporary marriage? The Left-Islamist alliance in Tunisia", *Dynamics of Asymmetric Conflict* 5 (2012): 196–207.

33. Bruce Lawrence, "The Islamist Appeal to Quranic Authority: The Case of Malik Bennabi," *Project of Middle East Political Science*, Briefings 24 (2014): 31–33.

34. See for instance Malek Bennabi, *Vocation de l'Islam* (Beirut: Dar Albouraq, 2006).

35. Abdelouahad Motaouakal, *al-Adl al-Ihsan: an explanation of its rise and its strategy for social and political reform in Morocco*, PhD Dissertation, Institute for Arab and Islamic Studies, University of Exeter, 2014. Unpublished.

36. See Séverine Labat, *Les Islamistes Algériens: Entre les urnes et les maquis* (Paris: Editions Le Seuil, 1995).

37. Peter Mandaville, "Is the post-Islamism thesis still valid?," *Project of Middle East Political Science*, Briefings 24 (2014): 33–36.

38. See for instance Michael Laver and Ben Hunt (1992) *Policy and Party Competition* (NY: Routledge, 1992); Michael Laver, Kenneth Benoit, and John Garry, "Estimating the Policy Positions of Political Actors Using Words as Data," *American Political Science Review* 97 (2003): 311–331; Ian Budge, Hans-Dieter Klingemann, Andrea Volkens, Judith Bara, Eric Tannenbaum, Richard Fording, Derek Hearl, Hee Min Kim, Michael McDonald, and Silvia Mendes, *Mapping Policy Preferences: Parties, Electors and Governments: 1945–1998: Estimates for Parties, Electors and Governments 1945–1998* (Oxford: Oxford University Press, 2001); Ken Benoit and Kenneth Laver, *Party Policy in Modern Democracies* (London: Routledge, 2006); Ken Benoit and Nina Wiesehomeier, "Expert Judgments" in Susanne Pickel, Gert Pickel, Hans-Joachim Lauth, and Detlef Jahn (eds) *Neuere Entwicklungen und Anwendungen auf dem Gebiet der Methoden der vergleichenden Politik- und Sozialwissenschaft* (Wiesbaden: VS Verlag, 2011).

39. Mandaville, op. cit., 34.

40. Francesco Cavatorta and Rikke Haugbølle Hostrup, "Beyond Ghannouchi: Islamism and social change in Tunisia," *Middle East Report* 262 (2012): 20–25.

41. Personal interview with N., co-founder of a Quranic school in Tunis. Interview held in Tunis, October 2011.

42. Haenni, op. cit.

43. See Francesco Cavatorta and Fabio Merone, "Moderation through exclusion? The journey of the Tunisian Ennahda from fundamentalist to conservative party," *Democratization* 20 (2013): 857–875; and Fabio Merone, "Enduring class struggle in Tunisia: the fight for identity beyond Political Islam," *British Journal of Middle Eastern Studies* 42 (2015): 74–87.

44. Roel Meijer, "Introduction," in *Global Salafism*, ed. Roel Meijer (London: Hurst, 2009).

45. Joas Wagemakers, "A Purist Jihadi-Salafi: The Ideology of Abu Muhammad al-Maqdisi," *British Journal of Middle Eastern Studies* 36 (2009): 281–297.

46. Mohammed Masbah, "Moving towards political participation. The moderation of Moroccan Salafis since the Arab Spring," SWP Comments (2013). Available at: http://www.swp-berlin.org/fileadmin/contents/products/comments/2013 C01_msb.pdf.

47. Isabelle Werenfels, "Beyond authoritarian upgrading: the reemergence of Sufi orders in Maghrebi politics," *Journal of North African Studies* (2013). DOI: 10.1080/13629387.2013.858036.

48. Roel Meijer, 'Conclusion' in Francesco Cavatorta and Fabio Merone (eds.) *Salafism after the Arab Awakening* (London: Hurst, 2015).

3. SUFISM AND SALAFISM IN THE MAGHREB: POLITICAL IMPLICATIONS

1. Fabio Merone and Francesco Cavatorta, "Salafist movement and sheikh-ism in the Tunisian Democratic Transition," *Middle East Law and Governance* 5 (2013): 308–330; Stefano M. Torelli, Fabio Merone, and Francesco Cavatorta, "Salafism in Tunisia: Challenges and Opportunities for Democratization," *Middle East Policy* Vol. XIX, No. 4 (Winter 2012): 140–153. See also, Quintan Wiktorowicz, "Anatomy of the Salafi Movement," *Studies in Conflict and Terrorism* 29 (2006): 207–39, http://www.cerium.ca/IMG/pdf/WIKTOROWICZ_2006Anatomy_of_the_Salafi_Movement.pdf, Haim Malka and William Lawrence, "Jihadi-Salafism's Next Generation," Center for Strategic and International Studies, Middle East Program, Analysis Paper, October 2103, https://csis.org/files/publication/131011_MalkaLawrence_JihadiSalafism_Web.pdf, accessed on 6 April 2014.

2. A. M. Mohamed Mackeen, "The Early History of Sufism in the Maghrib prior to Al-Shadhili," *Journal of the American Oriental Society*, 91:3 (July–Sept. 1971), 401.

3. Mohamed Arkoun, "Two Mediators of Medieval Thought," available at http://unesdoc.unesco.org/images/0007/000704/070484eo.pdf, accessed 6 March 2014.

4. See, for example, Jamil Abun-Nasr, *The Tijaniyya* (Oxford: Oxford University Press, 1965), 2–3.

5. F-E de Neveu, *Les Khouan: ordres religieux chez les musulmans d'Algérie* (1846), 160–161; Ahmad bin Khalid al-Nasiri, *Kitab al-istiqsa'* (1956), ix., 17–24.

6. Jamil N. Abun-Nasr, *Muslim Communities of Grace* (London: Hurst, 2007), 104.

7. Robert Brunschvig, *La berbérie orientale sous les Hafsides des origines à la fin du XVe siècle, Vol. II* (Paris: 1940 and 1947), 322–3.

8. Brunschvig, *La berbérie orientale sous les Hafsides*, 328–9.

9. Jamil M. Abun-Nasr, *A History of the Maghrib in the Islamic Period* (Cambridge: Cambridge University Press, 1987), 206–7.

10. Louis Rinn, *Marbouts et Khouan* (1884), 202–16.

11. Ali Harazem Berrada, *Jawahir al-Ma'ani wa Bulugh al-Amani fi Fayd Sidi 'Abass Tijani*, Vol. I, 22; Muhammad Ibn Mashri, *Al-Jami' Lima Iftaraqa min Durar al-'Ulum al-Faidah min Bihar al-Qutb al-Maktum*, Vol. I, 48.

12. Abun-Nasr, *Muslim Communities of Grace*, 149–50.

13. Mohamed El-Mansour, *Morocco in the Reign of Mawlay Sulayman* (Wisbech: Middle East & North Africa Press, 1990), 172.

14. Abun-Nasr, *Muslim Communities of Grace*, 152.

15. Abun-Nasr, *The Tijaniyya*, 83.

16. Ibid., 83.

17. Ibid., 103.

18. E. E. Evans-Pritchard, *The Sanusi of Cyrenaica* (Oxford: Oxford University Press, 1949), 11; Ahmad Harzallah, *Special Mission Program, The Al-Tijaniyya Zawiya*, www.alarabiya.net/programs/2007/02/03.

19. Abun-Nasr, *Muslim Communities of Grace*, 158.

20. Knut S. Vikor, *Sufi and Scholar of the Desert Edge: Muhammad b. Ali al-Sanusi and his Brotherhood* (London: Hurst, 1995), 61–8, 73–98.

21. Abun-Nasr, *Muslim Communities of Grace*, 159–60.

22. Evans-Pritchard, *The Sanusi of Cyrenaica*, 70.

23. Ibid., 62–89; Jean-Louis Triaud, *La légende noire de la Sanusiyya: Une confrérie musulane saharienne sous le regard francais, 1840–1930* (Paris: Éditions de la Maison des sciences de l'homme, 1995), 25.

24. Evans-Pritchard, *The Sanusi of Cyrenaica*, 93–96.

25. Ibid., 195–212.

26. Khalid Bekkaoui and Ricardo René Larémont, "Moroccan Youth Go Sufi," *Journal of the Middle East and Africa* (2011) 2: 31–46

27. Albert Hourani, *Arabic Thought in the Liberal Age, 1798–1939* (Oxford: Oxford University Press, 1970), 150, 232.

28. Ibid., 225–6.

29. Muhammad Abduh, in *Waqa'i al-Misriyya*; Muhammad Abduh, *Risalat al-taw-hid*; Muhammad Abduh, *Al-Manar*, 439; David Commins, "Religious Reformers and Arabists in Damascus, 1885–1974," *International Journal of Middle East Studies* 18 (1986): 405–25.

30. Ricardo René Larémont, *Islam and the Politics of Resistance in Algeria, 1783–1992* (Trenton: Africa World Press, 2000), 80–88.

31. Abun-Nasr, *Tijaniyya*, 178–80.

32. John P. Halstead, *Rebirth of a Nation: The Origins and Rise of Moroccan Nationalism* (Cambridge, MA: Harvard University Press, 1969), 122–3; Abun-Nasr, *Tijaniyya*, 24–25.

33. Allal al-Fasi, *al-Harakat al-Istiqlaliyyah fi al-Magrhib al-Arabi* (Tanja: Abd al-Salam Jasus, 1948), 134–135.

34. Abd al-Aziz bin Abdullah, "Limadha Riayat al-Dawla al-Alawiyya li al-Tariqa al-

Tijaniyya," in *Nidwat al-Turuq al-Sufiyya, Dawrat al-Tariqa al-Tijaniyya* (Fes: 1985).

35. Khalid Bekkaoui and Ricardo René Larémont, "Moroccan Youth Go Sufi," *Journal of the Middle East and Africa*, 33.

36. Ibid., 33–34

37. Mahmoud Habboush, "'Moroccan Youth Rediscover Sufi Heritage,'" *The National* (Abu Dhabi), 12 September 2009.

38. Hamidi Khemissi, Ricardo René Larémont, and Taybi Taj Eddine, "Sufism, Salafism, and state policy towards religion in Algeria: a survey of Algerian youth," *Journal of North African Studies*, 17:3 (2012): 547–558.

39. Quintan Wiktorowicz, "Anatomy of the Salafi Movement," *Studies in Conflict and Terrorism* 29 (2006): 207–39, http://www.cerium.ca/IMG/pdf/WIKTO-ROWICZ_2006_Anatomy_of_the_Salafi_Movement.pdf, Haim Malka and William Lawrence, "Jihadi-Salafism's Next Generation," Center for Strategic and International Studies, Middle East Program, Analysis Paper, October 2013, https://csis.org/files/publication/131011_MalkaLawrence_JihadiSalafism_Web.pdf, accessed on 6 April 2014.

40. International Crisis Group, "Tunisia: Violence and the Salafi Challenge", https://www.crisisgroup.org/middle-east-north-africa/north-africa/tunisia/tunisia-violence-and-salafi-challenge, accessed on 6 April 2014.

41. Ibid.

42. Omar Ashour, "Libyan Islamists Unpacked: Rise, Transformation, and Future," *Brookings Doha Center Policy Briefing*, May 2012, http://www.brookings.edu/~/media/research/files/papers/2012/5/02%20libya%20ashour/omar%20ashour%20policy%20briefing%20english, accessed on 6 April 2014.

43. Ibid.

44. Ibid.

45. "Morocco's Salafis Encouraged to Integrate," *The North Africa Post*, 2 April 2014, http://northafricapost.com/5363-moroccos-salafis-encouraged-to-integrate.html, accessed on 6 April 2014.

46. Mohammed Masbah, "The Moderation of Moroccan Salafis since the Beginning of the Arab Spring," http://www.academia.edu/2471810/The_Moderation_of_Moroccan_Salafis_since_the_Beginning_of_the_Arab_Spring, accessed 6 April 2014.

47. Tarek Osman, "Salafism's March through North Africa," *The Cairo Review of Global Affairs*, 5 April 2014, http://www.aucegypt.edu/gapp/cairoreview/pages/articleDetails.aspx?aid=354, accessed on 5 April 2014.

4. LABOR PROTEST IN MOROCCO: STRIKES, CONCESSIONS, AND THE ARAB SPRING

1. For Tunisia, see: Sami Zemni, "From Socio-Economic Protest to National Revolt:

The Labour Origins of the Tunisian Revolution," in *The Making of the Tunisian Revolution*, ed. Nouri Gana (Edinburgh: Edinburgh University Press, 2013), 127–146; Laryssa Chomiak and John P. Entelis, "The Making of North Africa's Intifadas," 259 *Middle East Report* (2011): 1–4.

2. For Egypt, see: Marie Duboc, "Challenging the Trade Union, Reclaiming the Nation: The Politics of Labour Protest in Egypt, 2006–2011," in Mehran Kamrava, ed. *Beyond the Arab Spring: The Evolving Ruling Bargain in the Middle East* (London: Hurst, 2014), 223–248; Hesham Sallam, "Striking Back at Egyptian Workers," 259 *Middle East Report* (2011): 1–4; Joel Beinin, "Workers, Trade Unions, and Egypt's Political Future," *Middle East Research and Information Project* (2013): 1–4; Joel Beinin, "Egyptian Workers After June 30," *Middle East Research and Information Project* (23/8/2013): 1–3; Dina Bishara, "The Power of Workers in Egypt's 2011 Uprising," in *The Arab Spring in Egypt: Revolution and Beyond*, eds. Bahgat Korany and Rabab El-Mahdi (Cairo: American University of Cairo Press, 2012), 83–103.

3. Eric Hobsbawm, "The Labour Aristocracy in Nineteenth-Century Britain," in *Labouring Men* (New York: Basic Books, 1964).

4. Charles Post, "Exploring Working-Class Consciousness: A Critique of the Theory of the 'Labour-Aristocracy'," *Historical Materialism* 18 (2010): 7–10.

5. Mehran Kamrava, *The Modern Middle East: A Political History Since the First World War* (Berkeley: University of California Press, 2005), 213–214.

6. On the rural nobility, see: Rémy Leveau, *Le Fellah Marocain: Défenseur du Trône* (Paris: Presses de la Fondation Nationale des Sciences Politiques, 1976).

7. Sidney Tarrow, *Power in Movement: Social Movements and Contentions Politics* (New York: Cambridge University Press, 2011).

8. For overviews of the youth movement, see: Driss Maghraoui "Constitutional Reforms in Morocco: between Consensus and Subaltern Politics," *The Journal of North African Studies* 16 (2011): 680–687. Also, see: Emanuela Dalmasso, "Surfing the Democratic Tsunami in Morocco: Apolitical Society and the Reconfiguration of a Sustainable Authoritarian Regime," 17 *Mediterranean Politics*: 219–220.

9. See: Marc Lynch, "Political Science and the New Arab Public Sphere," *Foreign Policy*. (12 June 2012), http://www.foreignpolicy.com/posts/2012/06/12/political_science_and_the_new_arab_public_sphere; Philip N. Howard and Muzammil M. Hussain, "The Role of Digital Media," 22.3 *Journal of Democracy* (2011): 35–48.

10. Abd al-Jaleel Abu al-Jad, *Al-naqabaat Bilmaghrib* [*Unions in Morocco*] (Casablanca: Ouragan Communication, 2008), 20–21.

11. Ibid.

12. Eqbal Ahmad, "Trade Unionism," in *State and Society in Independent North Africa*, ed. Leon Carl Brown (Baltimore: The Middle East Institute, 1966), 174–176. Also, see: Douglas Ashford, "Labor Politics in a New Nation," *The Western Political Quarterly* 13 (1960): 312–331.

13. J. Salazar, "Mohamed V: The Tangiers Speech," *African Yearbook of Rhetoric* 2.3 (2001), 23.

14. Daniel Zisenwine, *The Emergence of Nationalist Politics in Morocco: The Rise of the Independence Party and the Struggle Against Colonialism after World War II* (New York: I.B. Tauris, 2010), 206–208.

15. Clement Henry Moore, *Politics in North Africa: Algeria, Morocco, and Tunisia* (Boston: Little Brown and Company, 1970), 193.

16. Ibid., 175–194.

17. Stuart H. Schaar, "The Failure of Multi-Party Politics in Morocco: A Historian's View," Middle East Studies Association conference (1969): 11–12.

18. John Waterbury, *Commander of the Faithful* (London: Weidenfeld and Nicolson, 1970), 226–228.

19. Ibid., 184.

20. Articles 8 and 9 of the 1962 Moroccan Constitution protect workers' rights to organize in labor syndicates, specifying that they have full authority to "contribute to the defence and promotion of the socio-economic rights and interests of the sector they represent." These articles also protect workers' rights to collectively bargain and organize in the workplace.

21. Frank H. Braun, "Anatomy of Palace Revolution That Failed," *International Journal of Middle East Studies* 9 (1978): 65; Mehran Kamrava, "Military Professionalization and Civil-Military Relations in the Middle East," *Political Science Quarterly* 1 (2000): 90.

22. Abdellatif Moutadayene, "Economic Crisis and Democratization in Morocco," *The Journal of North African Studies*, 6.3 (2001): 72.

23. John Pierre Entelis, *Culture and Counterculture in Moroccan Politics* (New York: Westview Press, 1989): 92–93.

24. Ibid., 93.

25. African Development Bank Group, "Morocco: Consolidation of the 1992–1994 Structural Adjustment Programme," Operation Evaluation Department (March 1990): 10.

26. Guilain P. Denoeux, "Morocco's Economic Prospects: Daunting Challenges Ahead," *Middle East Policy* 2 (2001): 69.

27. Ibid., 75–77.

28. Jawad Ghasaal, "al-hiwaar al-ijtima'ai yatajhu nahou al-baab al-masdoud," *at-Tajdid* 1430 (15/7/2009): 3.

29. Emperador Badimon Montserrat and Koenraad Bogaert, "Imagining the State through Social Protests: State Reformation and Unemployed Graduates Mobilizations in Morocco," *Mediterranean Politics* 16 (2011): 241–259.

30. "al-muaarad al-bashariyya biljamaa'aat al-mahaliyya takhuth 73% min nafaeaat al-tasiyr," *at-Tajdid* 1430 (15/7/2009): 3.

31. Ghasaal, "al-hiwar al-ijtim'ai," 3.

32. "al-ithiaad al-watani liḷshugal bilmaghreb yuqaadi al-wazir al-aoual wa wazir al-ta'alim," *al-massae* 1310 (12/9/2010): 4.

33. Ismaa'ail Rawahi, "Tajmid al-hisaab al-banki liniqaabat al-itihaad al-watani lilshugal," *as-Sabah* 3285 (2/11/2011): 8.

34. Youssef Esskat, "fadrilayioun yutaaliboun al-itihaad biraf'a al-yad 'an markazitihim," *as-Sabah* 3381 (24/2/2011): 3.

35. Ihssane Elhafidi, "siyaraat al-is'aaf wa al-amin lifad ijtimaa'a niqaabat al-itihaad," *as-Sabah* 3355 (25/2/2011): 3.

36. Francesco Cavatorta and Rikke Hostrup Haugbølle, "The End of Authoritarian Rule and the Mythology of Tunisia under Ben Ali," *Mediterranean Politics* 17 (2012): 186–187.

37. Eric Gobe, "The Gafsa Mining Basin between Riots and a Social Movement: Meaning and Significance of a Protest Movement in Ben Ali's Tunisia," *Institut de Recherches et d'Etudes sur le Monde Arabe et Musuluman* (2011): 11–20.

38. Jason Brownlee, *Democracy Prevention: The Politics of the U.S.-Egyptian Alliance* (New York: Cambridge University Press, 2012), 127–128.

39. Ibid.

40. "irtifaa'a 'adad al-idrabaat fi sinah 2010 binisbah 8 fi al-miah muqaarinah bisinah," *al-massae* 1285 (11/08/2010): 8.

41. Ibid.

42. *Telquel*. "Grève: guerre des chiffres et des mots," *Telquel* (6–12/10/2010): 8.

43. Ibid.

44. Jamal Bourfisi, "Mezouar: al-hakouma layst must'ada lilraf'a al-ujour," *as-Sabah* 3322 (17/12/2010): 1.

45. Khalid al-Suti, "al-niqaabi Mohamed Yatime yuhamal al-hakouma masoul al-idrabaat wa al-ihjiqaan al-ijtimaa'ai," *at-tajdid* 2565 (01/28–30/2011): 3.

46. "niqabaat kafathat idrabaat wataniyyah fi al-t'aliym wa al-sahah wa al-damaan al-ijtimaa'ai wa al-qataa'aaat aukhrah," *as-Sabah* 3369 (02/10/2011): 1.

47. Hajar al-Maghli, "nijah al-idrabaat bilwathifah al-'aumumiha faaq 80 fi al-miah," *as-Sabah* 3369 (02/10/2011): 5.

48. Ihssane Elhafidi, ""niqaabat al-phosophat taftah malaf al-taghtiyya al-sahaiyya bilqataa'a," *as-Sabah* 3358 (1/28/2011): 4.

49. "niqaba maaliyya talouh bilidraab limudat 48 saa'aa," *al-masasae* 1354 (1/29–30/2011): 3.

50. Ihssane Elhafidi, "al-wazir al-aoual yatadakhal liwaqif al-ihtiqaan al-ijtimaa'ai," *as-Sabah* 3367 (2/8/2011): 2.

51. Youssef Akdim et. al. "Ça ne fait que commencer..." *Telquel* 462 (02/26/2011): 19.

52. Youssef Ait Akdim, "La Paix Sociale à tout prix," *Telquel* 461 (02/19–25/2011): 30.

53. Mohammed Belqaasim, "tasaa'ad al-ihtijaajaat al-ijtimaaiyya bilrabat," *at-tajdid* 2604 (25–27 March 2011): 3.

54. Khalid al-Suti, "nisaa wa rijaal al-t'alim yandadoun biltadakhalaat al-aminiyyah," *at-Tajdid* 2608 (03/31/2011): 1.

55. Rachid Jarmouni, "dafaa'an 'an karaamat nissa wa rijaal al-t'atim," *at-Tajdid* 2606 (03/29/2011): 7.

56. al-Sadiq Boukazoul, "naqabaat bisouk al-jumla tad'aou ila idraab khilal maars," 3382 (2/15/2011) *as-Sabah*: 5.

57. Mohamed Yatim, "al-itihad al-watani lilshugal bilmaghreb yahthur min al-rajou'a bilhiwar al-ijtima'ai," 2609 (4/1–3/2011): 3.

58. H. Dades, "Ça bloque sur les augmentations de salaires, les retraites..." *Le Reporter* (04/14/2011): 28–29.

59. M. Bin Sidi and A. Bin'abaad, "al-hiwar al-ijtimaa'ai yantaliq wa al-amoui ya-qaata,'" *maghreb al-youm* (04/08–14/2001): 16.

60. Murad Thaabi, "insihaab wafd al-itihaad al-watani lilshugal bilmaghreb min jalisat al-hiwaar al-ijtimaa'ai bisubub khalifaat bayna al-niqabaat wa al-hakouma," *al-massae* 1414 (04/09–10/2011): 3.

61. Hajar al-Maghli, "insihaab al-itihad al-watani lilshugal min lhiwar al-ijtima'ai," *as-sabah* 3420 (11/4/2011): 2.

62. Dades, "Ça bloque sur les augmentations de salaires, les retraites..."

63. Siham Ali, "Morocco Launches Labor Talks," *Maghrabia.com* (4/15/2011), http://magharebia.com/en_GB/articles/awi/features/2011/04/15/feature-03.

64. Hajar al-Maghli, "thlaath markaziyaat niqaabiyyah tarf'a saqif al-mutaalib," *as-Sabah* 3427 (4/19/2011): 5.

65. Souhail Karam, "Moroccan Unions Win Wage Hikes as Protests Grow," *Reuters.com*, http://www.reuters.com/article/2011/04/26/us-morocco-protests-wages-idUSTRE73P7A120110426 Accessed 1 December 2017.

66. See: Francesco Cavatorta, "'Divided they Stand, divided they fail': Opposition Politics n Morocco," *Democratization*, 16 (2009): 137–139. Also, Marina Ottaway and Meredith Riley, "Morocco: From Top-down Reform to Democratic Transition?" 71 *Carnegie Papers* (2006): 7–9.

67. Steven Heydemann, "Upgrading Authoritarianism in the Arab World," 13 *Brookings Institution* (2007), 5–7.

68. Janine A. Clark and Amy E. Yong, "Islamism and Family Law Reform in Morocco and Jordan," *Mediterranean Politics* 13 (2008): 344–346.

69. Reda Dalil, "Les Fous du Phosphate," *Le Temps* (11/23/2011): 19–21.

5. THE AMAZIGH MOVEMENT IN A CHANGING NORTH AFRICA

1. Maxime Ait Kaki, *De la question berbère au dilemme kabyle à l'aube du XXIème siècle* (Paris: Harmattan, 2004).

2. Equally, the reference to the Prague Spring implicitly connects the events in North Africa to earlier student-led popular demonstrations against authoritarian rule in Serbia and the Ukraine, more generally indicating the artificiality of national or continental borders in analyzing contemporary social movements.

p. [74] NOTES

3. *Amazigh* (pl. *Imazighen*) loosely translated as "free man," is the preferred ethnonym of ethno-political activists and is increasingly recognized by state institutions, particularly in Algeria and Morocco. The term originally distinguished those tribesmen with full political and territorial status from a set of other, mostly Berber/Tamazight-speaking local groups, including Sharifian and maraboutic lineages, as well as those of enslaved or enserfed status. Abdellah Hammoudi, among others, describes these distinctions (many of which exist today) as having constituted a "caste" system of rights, privileges, and prohibitions that was in operation at least through colonial times, and which to a certain extent mapped onto a racial ideology that historically equated blackness with enslavibility. Abdellah Hammoudi, "Segmentarité, stratification sociale, pouvoir politique, et sainteté: Réflexions sur les thèses de Gellner," *Hespéris-Tamuda* 15 (1974). See Chouki El Hamel, *Black Morocco: A History of Slavery, Race, and Islam* (Cambridge: University of Cambridge Press, 2012). As I discuss below, "Amazigh" was generalized by diasporic activists in the late 1960s to replace "Berber," a word that derives from the Greek *barbaros* meant to designate outsiders speaking an incomprehensible language, and which, through the Arabic, had been adopted into the European colonial and scholarly idiom. At least until the last decade, the term "Amazigh" was primarily used by urban activists and was broadly unknown as a more general ethnonym by the majority of Berber speakers living along the rural periphery, who used more local terms of reference and address (e.g. *Ashelhi* for a southern Moroccan who speaks *Tashelhit*). See David Crawford and Katherine Hoffman, "Essentially Amazigh: Urban Berbers and the Global Village," in *The Arab-African Islamic Worlds: Interdisciplinary Studies*, ed. Kevin Lacey and Ralph Coury (New York: Peter Lang, 2000). While "Berber" today is rejected and reviled by many Moroccan activists for its primitivist connotations, it remains part of the Algerian Kabyle activist Francophone nomenclature as well as dominant within the scholarly literature. In this essay, I retain "Berber" to reference broader questions of language and culture and reserve "Amazigh" for political groups, projects, and movements.

4. While most North Africans have both Berber and Arab ancestors, current Berber speakers make up an estimated 25 per cent and 40 per cent of Algeria's and Morocco's populations, respectively. Up to 10 per cent of Libyans speak Berber, mostly concentrated in the Jebel (Idrar) Nafusa region in the northwest of the country. Tunisian Berber speakers, by contrast, only constitute about 1 % of the population, primarily located in the country's south and on the island of Djerba. Michael Brett and Elizabeth Fentress, *The Berbers* (Oxford: Blackwell, 1997), 276–7. Estimates of the number of Tuareg across southern Algeria, southwestern Libya, and the Sahel (Niger, Mali, Burkina Faso) vary widely but likely amount to upwards of one million speakers of Tamasheq and related dialects. And about 20,000 Berber speakers reside in the Siwa oasis in Egypt. Additionally, there are probably another four million Berber speakers and their children in the diaspora, mostly in France, but also with sizeable

216

populations in Belgium, Netherlands, Spain, Italy, and North America (especially Quebec). Population estimates are decidedly political and hotly contested by activists and state representatives.

5. For general studies of Amazigh activism, see Maxime Ait Kaki, *De la question berbère au dilemme kabyle à l'aube du XXIème siècle* (Paris: Harmattan, 2004), author's English translation form original French text; Brett and Fentress, *The Berbers*, 271–282; Salem Chaker, *Berbères aujourd'hui* (Paris: Harmattan, 1998); David Crawford, "Royal Interest in Amazigh Culture: The Politics and Potential of Morocco's Imazighen," in *Nationalism and Minority Identities in Islamic Societies*, ed. Maya Shatzmiller (Montreal: McGill University Press, 2005); Crawford and Hoffman, "Essentially Amazigh"; Terhi Lehtinen, *Nation à la marge de l'Etat: la construction identitaire du Mouvement Culturel Amazigh au Maroc et au-delà des frontières étatiques*. Thèse de troisième cycle (Paris: Ecole des Hautes Etudes en Sciences Sociales, 2003); Bruce Maddy-Weitzman, *The Berber Identity Movement and the Challenge to North African Societies* (Austin: University of Texas Press 2011); Stéphanie Pouessel, *Les Identités amazighes au Maroc* (Paris: Editions Non-Lieu, 2010); Hassan Rachik, ed., *Usages de l'identité Amazigh au Maroc* (Casablanca: Tarik, 2006); and Paul A. Silverstein, "Martyrs and Patriots: Ethnic, National, and Transnational Dimensions of Kabyle Politics," *Journal of North African Studies* 8 (1) (2003).

6. Women have taken active roles in Amazigh politics, particularly on university campuses, and some—like Maryam Demnati, Amina Ibno-Cheikh, Malika Matoub, and Khalida (Messaoudi) Toumi—have become outspoken international advocates for Berber language, culture, and self-determination. But most have worked behind the scenes in education and outreach, administering the cultural and socio-economic development associations through which Amazigh activists connect with broader populations. As will be noted later, women, upheld as the sanctified guardians of tradition, have also become iconic performers of an emergent artistic canon, a tradition of public spectacle that goes back at least to Taos Amrouche who performed Kabyle folksongs set to Western art music for post-war European audiences. Cynthia Becker, *Amazigh Arts in Morocco: Women Shaping Berber Identity* (Austin: University of Texas Press, 2006); Jane Goodman, *Berber Culture on the World Stage* (Bloomington: Indiana University Press, 2005). These avenues notwithstanding, the Amazigh movement, broadly speaking, remains largely masculinist in its mode of political engagement, particularly in its models of militancy and martyrdom.

7. To speak of an "Amazigh movement" in the singular is obviously an abstraction, a heuristic label given to a panoply of individual and collective efforts across North Africa and the diaspora since the late 1960s, efforts in the name of Berber language (Tamazight) and culture (*idles*), or more broadly on behalf of the Berber-speaking people (Imazighen). Various efforts to coordinate and federate such actions, as will be discussed below, have been fraught with internecine disagreements and divides over political ideology and tactics, over the scale of intervention, and over the

compatibility of Amazigh claims with secularist and Islamist political agendas. Many Berber-speaking men and women who might otherwise identify as "Berber" or even "Amazigh" do not affiliate with Amazigh associations or political parties, and indeed those of Berber heritage can be found across the North African political spectrum, even espousing Arab nationalist or Islamist ideologies that some Amazigh activists would find anathema.

8. On the vagaries of colonial Berber ethnology and policies in North Africa, see Charles-Robert Ageron, "La France a-t-elle eu une politique kabyle," *Revue Historique* 223–224 (1960); Edmund Burke III, "The Image of the Moroccan State in French Ethnological Literature," in *Arabs and Berbers: From Tribe to Nation in North Africa*, ed. Ernest Gellner and Charles Micaud (London: Duckworth, 1972); Goodman, *Berber Culture*; Gilles Lafuente, *La Politique berbère de la France et le nationalisme marocain* (Paris: Harmattan, 1999); Patricia Lorcin, *Imperial Identities: Stereotyping, Prejudice and Race in Colonial Algeria* (London: I.B. Tauris, 1995); Philippe Lucas and Jean-Claude Vatin, *L'Algérie des anthropologues* (Paris: François Maspero, 1975); and Paul A. Silverstein, "The Kabyle Myth: The Production of Ethnicity in Colonial Algeria," in *From the Margins: Historical Anthropology and Its Futures*, ed. Brian Keith Axel (Durham: Duke University Press, 2002).

9. Kenneth Brown, "The Impact of the Dahir Berbère in Salé," in *Arabs and Berbers: From Tribe to Nation in North Africa*, ed. Ernest Gellner and Charles Micaud (Lexington: Lexington Books, 1972); Jonathan Wyrtzen, "Performing the Nation in Anti-Colonial Protest in Interwar Morocco," *Nations and Nationalism* 19 (4) (2013).

10. Jean-Louis Duclos, "The Berbers and the Rise of Moroccan Nationalism," in *Arabs and Berbers: From Tribe to Nation in North Africa*, ed. Ernest Gellner and Charles Micaud (London: Duckworth, 1972); James McDougall, *History and the Culture of Nationalism in Algeria* (Cambridge: Cambridge University Press, 2006).

11. Rémy Leveau, *Le Fellah marocain, défenseur du trône* (Paris: Presses de la Fondation Nationale des Sciences Politiques, 1976).

12. John Waterbury, *The Commander of the Faithful: The Moroccan Political Elite* (London: Weidenfeld and Nicholson, 1970), 239–43; Susan Slyomovics, "Self-Determination as Self-Definition: The Case of Morocco," in *Negotiating Self-Determination*, ed. Hurst Hannum and Eileen Babbitt (Lanham, MD: Lexington Books, 2005), 145.

13. See Mehdi Bennouna, *Héros sans gloire: Echec d'une révolution, 1963–1973* (Casablanca: Tarik, 2002).

14. For a sensitive portrayal of this period in Morocco, known as the "years of lead" and its contemporary legacy, see Susan Slyomovics, *The Performance of Human Rights in Morocco* (Philadelphia: University of Pennsylvania Press, 2005).

15. Indeed, the military in particular has served as an important vehicle for social

mobility open to rural Berber speakers, and in a number of cases, local residents have close kinship ties to fighters on both sides of confrontations. This pattern similarly occurred during the anti-colonial uprisings of the 1950s, as well as during the Algerian "civil war" of the 1990s. See Benjamin Stora, *L'Algérie en 1995: La Guerre, l'histoire, la politique* (Paris: Michalon, 1995).

16. Cynthia Becker, *Amazigh Arts*; Aomar Boum, "Dancing for the Moroccan State: Ethnic Folk Dances and the Production of National Hybridity," in *North African Mosaic: A Cultural Reappraisal of Ethnic and Religious Minorities*, ed. Nabil Boudraa and Joseph Krause (Newcastle: Cambridge Scholars Press, 2007).

17. James McDougall, "Myth and Counter-Myth: 'The Berber' as National Signifier in Algerian Historiographies," *Radical History Review* 86 (2003).

18. Pouessel, *Identités amazighes*, 102.

19. *Ibid.*, 108.

20. Fadhma Aït Mansour Amrouche (1882–1967) was a Kabyle poet and singer whose works were transcribed and publicly performed by her children Jean and Taos Amrouche. Raised and educated in a Catholic mission, she raised her own children bi-culturally first in Kabylia, and later in Tunisia and France. Her memoir, *Histoire de ma vie* (1968), was published posthumously by her children.

21. See Becker, *Amazigh Arts* and Goodman, *Berber Culture* for sustained analyses of the processes by which Berber culture was differently entextualized and materialized into literature, folksong, and artistic crafts to be marketed to and performed for Berber and non-Berber audiences since the colonial period. For an extended discussion of the ABERC and parallel Berberist developments within the Kabyle diaspora in France, see Karima Direche-Slimani, *Histoire de l'émigration kabyle en France au XXe siècle* (Paris: Harmattan, 1997).

22. Ait Kaki, *De la question berbère*, 85. Paul A. Silverstein, "Stadium Politics: Sport, Islam, and Amazigh Consciousness in France and North Africa," in *With God on their Side: Sport in the Service of Religion*, ed. Tara Magdalinski and Timothy Chandler (London: Routledge, 2002).

23. Ait Kaki, *De la question berbère*, 84–100; Goodman, *Berber Culture*, 29–48; Maddy-Weitzman, *Berber Identity Movement*, 79–84. For an alternative interpretation of the uprising that emphasizes its elite dimensions, see Hugh Roberts, "Towards an Understanding of the Kabyle Question in Contemporary Algeria," *The Maghreb Review* 5–6 (1980), and "The Unforeseen Development of the Kabyle Question in Contemporary Algeria," *Government and Opposition* 17 (3) (1982).

24. Silverstein, "Martyrs and Patriots."

25. Ait Kaki, *De la question berbère*, 94.

26. These events also contributed to Kabylia's hegemony as a center of and model for Amazigh militancy in Algeria and beyond, at the expense in particular of parallel articulations of Berberness and regional specificity by Shawiya in the Aurès mountains and among Ibadi Berbers in the Mzab. For the case of the Shawiya, see Fanny

Colonna, *Les Versets de l'invincibilité: Permanence et changements religieu dans l'Algérie contemporaine* (Paris: Presses de Sciences Po, 1995); and Maddy-Weitzman, *Berber Identity Movement*, 195–197. For a discussion of the predominance of the Kabyle model for Amazigh activists elsewhere, see Paul A. Silverstein, "The Pitfalls of Transnational Consciousness: Amazigh Activism as a Scalar Dilemma," *Journal of North African Studies* 18 (5) (2013).

27. In 2008, the constitution was further amended to note that "Tamazight is also a national language. The State shall work for its promotion and its development in all its linguistic varieties in use throughout the national territory." But the officialization of the language and its equal introduction into the media, school system, and state administration remains an object of sustained activist struggle.

28. Crawford, "Royal Interest."

29. For an extended history of the Berber Manifesto and the IRCAM, see Maddy-Weitzman, *Berber Identity Movement*, 159–172; and Paul Silverstein and David Crawford, "Amazigh Activism and the Moroccan State," *Middle East Report* 233 (2004). The adoption of a modified Tifinagh for the transcription of Tamazight was strongly debated, particularly as the Latin script was broadly in use in Algeria and France, and previous efforts at transliteration in Morocco, particularly by the AMREC, had been in Arabic. The eventual choice for Tifinagh was understood as a compromise between Islamist and secularist movements within and outside the IRCAM. See Pouessel, *Identités amazighes*, 147–154.

30. On the "patriot" groups and the broader counter-insurgency warfare being fought by the Algerian military state at the expense of the broader citizenry's security, see Jacob Mundy, *Imaginative Geographies of Algerian Violence* (Stanford: Stanford University Press, 2015).

31. Ait Kaki, *De la question berbère*, 159–70; Silverstein, "Martyrs and Patriots."

32. A popular conspiracy theory actually pointed the finger at a prominent RCD deputy as partially responsible for Matoub's death. See Ait Kaki, *De la question berbère*, 152–154, and Paul A. Silverstein, "An Excess of Truth: Violence, Conspiracy Theory, and the Algerian Civil War," *Anthropological Quarterly* 75 (4) (2002).

33. The text is at: http://www.makabylie.info/?article62, accessed 9 November 2015. See Ait Kaki, *De la question berbère*.

34. Maddy-Weitzman, *Berber Identity Movement*, 188–90. When visited in summer 2014, the website of the "provisional government," http://www.anavad.org/, was notable for its iconography, particularly a logo-map of Kabylia that recognizes no distinctions between the official provinces of Tizi-Ouzou and Bejaïa, and was coloured in the blue, green, and yellow of the Amazigh flag, with a red Tifinagh zed (*aza*, the iconographic representation of Amazigh freedom) in its center. By autumn 2015, the website simply featured a video of the Kabyle "national anthem" played/sung over an image of a young man holding up a Kabyle "national flag" (different from the Amazigh flag) over a view of the Djurdjura mountain range.

The information and updates formerly contained on the website had been transferred to a Facebook page.
35. Pouessel, *Identités amazighes*, 57–66.
36. Silverstein, "Pitfalls."
37. Slyomovics, "Self-Determination," 149.
38. Paul A. Silverstein, "The Local Dimensions of Transnational Berberism: Racial Politics, Land Rights, and Cultural Activism in Southeastern Morocco," in *Berbers and Others*, ed. Katherine Hoffman and Susan Gilson Miller (Bloomington: Indiana University Press, 2010).
39. Paul Silverstein, "States of Fragmentation in North Africa," *Middle East Report* 237 (2005).
40. Mohammed Adergal and Romain Simenel. "La construction de l'autochtonie au Maroc: des tribus indigènes aux paysans amazighs," *Espace, Populations, Sociétés* 1 (2012); Stéphanie Pouessel, "Du village au 'village-global': Émergence et construction d'une revendication autochtone berbère au Maroc," *Autrepart* 38 (2006).
41. Silverstein, "Local Dimensions."
42. Dider Le Saout, "La radicalisation de la revendication amazighe au Maroc. Le sud-est comme imaginaire militant," *L'Année du Maghreb* 5 (2009); Pouessel, *Identités amazighes*, 65.
43. The English-language text of the constitution is available at http://www.maroc.ma/en/content/constitution, accessed 9 November 2015.
44. On the question of regionalization in relationship to Amazigh activism, see David McMurray, "Center-Periphery Relations in Morocco," *Middle East Report* 272 (2014).
45. On the 20 February movement and the new constitution, see Thierry Desrues, "Le Mouvement du 20 février et le régime marocain: contestation, revision constitutionelle et élections," *L'Année du Maghreb* 8 (2012); Paul Silverstein, "Weighing Morocco's New Constitution," *Middle East Report Online*, http://www.merip.org/mero/mero070511 (2011); Susan Slyomovics, "100 Days of the 2011 Moroccan Constitution," *Jadaliyya*, http://www.jadaliyya.com/pages/index/2023/100-days-of-the-2011-moroccan-constitution (2011); and Frédéric Vairel, "'Qu'avez-vous fait de vos vingt ans?' Militantismes marocains du 23-mars (1965) au 20 février (2011)," *L'Année du Maghreb* 8 (2012). The precedent for the M20F is arguably the human rights movement that has proliferated in Morocco since the 1990s but which has similarly fragmented repeatedly along ideological and regional lines.
46. Bruce Maddy-Weitzman, "Morocco's Berbers and Israel," *Middle East Quarterly* 18(1) (2011); Paul A. Silverstein, "Masquerade Politics: Race, Islam, and the Scales of Amazigh Activism in Southeastern Morocco," *Nations and Nationalism* 17 (1) (2011).
47. Samir Ben-Layashi, "Secularism in Moroccan Amazigh Discourse," *Journal of*

North African Studies 12 (2) (2007). Most Berber speakers, and even Berber activists, do not necessarily avow secularist positions, displaying a wide range of religious piety and practice. That said, a discourse of *laïcité* remains part of the official discourse of a number of Amazigh associations and political movements in Kabylia and the diaspora has been espoused by a number of publicly present Moroccan activists based primarily in Rabat.

48. Ait Kaki, *De la question berbère*, 269–86.
49. Pouessel, *Identités amazighes*, 183.
50. Ernest Gellner, *Saints of the Atlas* (London: Weidenfeld and Nicolson, 1969). This logic is also behind the leff system of checkerboard confederations that Robert Montagne identifies as an historical feature of political life in the western High Atlas. Robert Montagne, *The Berbers: Their Social and Political Organisation* (London: Routledge, 1973 [1947]). See Silverstein, "Martyrs and Patriots."
51. Ait Kaki, *De la question berbère*, 231–3.
52. Abdelhamid Larguèche, "L'histoire à l'épreuve du patrimoine," *L'Année du Maghreb* 4 (2008).
53. Stéphanie Pouessel, "Les marges renaissantes: Amazigh, Juif, Noir. Ce que la révolution a changé dans ce 'petit pays homogène par excellence' qu'est la Tunisie," *L'Année du Maghreb* 8 (2012).
54. Youssef Sawani and Jason Pack, "Libyan Constitutionality and Sovereignty Post-Qadhafi: The Islamist, Regionalist, and Amazigh Challenges," *Journal of North African Studies* 18(4) (2013).
55. Ulf Laessing, "In Libya's West, Anger Spills into Gasfields," *Reuters*, 8 November 2013. http://www.reuters.com/article/2013/11/08/us-libya-protest-berbers-idUSBRE9A70PM20131108, accessed 9 November 2015.
56. Tim Hume, "A Rebirth of Berber Culture in Post-Gadhafi Libya," *CNN World*, 3 September 2012. http://www.cnn.com/2012/09/03/world/meast/libya-berber-amazigh-renaissance/ accessed 9 November 2015.
57. Leftist organizations, most recently under the banner of human rights or unemployed graduates (*diplomés chomeurs*), had likewise used similar methods of local and transnational coordination. The membership of these groups overlaps with that of the Amazigh movement.
58. Ait Kaki, *De la question berbère*, 300.
59. Silverstein, "Pitfalls."
60. On the question of the commodification of ethnicity, see John L. and Jean Comaroff, *Ethnicity, Inc.* (Chicago: University of Chicago Press, 2009).

6. THOU SHALT NOT SPEAK ONE LANGUAGE: SELF, SKILL, AND POLITICS IN POST-ARAB SPRING MOROCCO

1. I use the term "20 February Movement" to refer to young Moroccan activists who created online platforms similar to those that undergirded the Egyptian and

Tunisian popular upheavals. Veteran activists in the field of human rights, trade unions, the Amazigh cultural movement, left-wing political parties, and the extra-parliamentary Islamic groups of al-'Adl wa'l-Iḥsān (Justice and Spirituality) and al-Badīl al-Ḥaḍārī (The Civilized Alternative) subsequently joined this Movement. For detailed information on the 20 February Movement, see Thierry Desrues, "Le Mouvement du 20 Février et le régime marocain: Contestation, révision constitu-tionnelle et élections [The 20 February Movement and the Moroccan Regime: Contestation, Constitutional Reform and Elections]," *L'Année du Maghreb* 8 (2012): 359–389; and Irene Fernandez Molina, "The Monarchy vs. the 20 February Movement: Who Holds the Reins of Political Change in Morocco?" *Mediterranean Politics* 16 (2011): 435–441.

2. Mamfakinch, https://www.mamfakinch.com; and Lakome, https://www.lakome. com. Beyond dārija, slogans in rallies and banners made use of all of Morocco's reg-isters (including French and English) as well as Egyptian Arabic adopted by Tahrir Square protests. See Catherine Miller, "Observations concernant la présence de l'arabe marocain dans la presse marocaine arabophone des années 2009–2010 [Observations Concerning the Presence of Moroccan Arabic in the Arabophone Moroccan Press during 2009–2010]," in *De los manuscritos medievales a internet: la presencia del arabo vernáculo en las fuentes escritas* [From Medieval Manuscripts to the Internet: the Presence of Vernacular Arabic in Written Sources], ed. Mohamed Meouak, Pablo Sánchez, and Angeles Vicente (Zaragoza: Universidad de Zaragoza, 2012), 419–440.

3. "Al-mamlaka al-maghribiyya, al-dustūr 2011, al-amāna al-'āma li-l-hukūma, mudīriyyat al-ṭab'a al-rasmiyya [Kingdom of Morocco, The Constitution 2011, The General Secretariat of the Government, Directorate of Official Printing Office]," 29 July 2011, http://www.sgg.gov.ma/Portals/1/lois/constitution_2011_Ar.pdf and http://www.sgg.gov.ma/Portals/0/constitution/constitution_2011_Fr.pdf. As Ahmed Benchemsi notes, the Arabic and French versions of the constitution are intentionally different and deserve critical comparison. Ahmed Benchemsi, "Morocco: Outfoxing the Opposition," *Journal of Democracy* 23 (2012): 57–69.

4. "Al-mamlaka al-maghribiyya, al-dustūr, ṭab'at 2011, al-Faṣl 5 [Kingdom of Morocco, The Constitution, Edition 2011, Articles 5]".

5. Ibid.

6. Abdelfattah Kilito, *Lan Tatakalama Lughatī* ["Thou Shalt Not Speak My Language"] (Beirut: Dar al-Talia, 2002).

7. Aiwa Ong, *Neoliberalism as Exception: Mutations in Citizenship and Sovereignty* (New York, NY: Cambridge University Press, 2006).

8. For details on the adoption of structural adjustment packages following the fiscal crisis of the 1980s, see Shana Cohen, *Searching for a Different Future: The Rise of a Global Middle Class in Morocco* (Durham, NC: Duke University Press, 2004). For details on the free trade agreements mentioned, see European Commission,

"Morocco," http://ec.europa.eu/trade/creating-opportunities/bilateral-relations/countries/morocco/; and Office of the United States Trade Representative, "Morocco Free Trade Agreement," Office of the United States Trade Representative, https://ustr.gov/trade-agreements/free-trade-agreements/morocco-fta/advisory-committee-reports-morocco-fta/.

9. For detailed elaborations of the colonial experience of language in the Maghreb, see Patricia Lorcin, *Imperial Identities: Stereotyping, Prejudice, and Race in Colonial Algeria* (London: IB Tauris, 1995); Pierre Vermeren, *École, élite, pouvoir au Maroc et en Tunisie au 20ème Siècle* [School, Elite, and Power in Morocco and Tunisia in the 20th Century] (Rabat, Morocco: Alizés, 2002); Spencer Segalla, *The Moroccan Soul: French Education, Colonial Ethnology, and Muslim Resistance, 1912–1956* (Lincoln, NE: University of Nebraska Press, 2009); and Katherine E. Hoffman, "Purity and Contamination: Language Ideologies in French Colonial Native Policy in Morocco," *Comparative Studies in Society and History* 50 (2008): 724–752. For studies that explore the legacy of colonial linguistic visions in nation-building agendas, see James McDougall, *History and the Culture of Nationalism in Algeria* (Cambridge: Cambridge University Press, 2006); Anne-Emmanuelle Berger, ed., *Algeria in Others' Languages* (Ithaca, NY: Cornell University Press, 2002); and Jocelyne Dakhlia, *Trames de langues: usages et métissages linguistiques dans l'histoire du Maghreb* [The Weaving of Languages: Linguistic Uses and Miscegenation in the History of the Maghreb] (Paris: Maisonneuve & Larose, 2004). For scholarship focused on the last decade, see Mohamed Benrabah, "Language Maintenance and Spread: French in Algeria," *International Journal of Francophone Studies* 10 (2007): 193–215; Khaoula Taleb Ibrahimi, "Algérie: l'Arabisation, lieu de conflits multiples [Algeria: Arabization, Site of Multiple Conflicts]", *Monde Arabe, Maghreb-Machrek*, 150 (1995): 57–71; and Mohamed Daoud, "The Sociolinguistic Situation in Tunisia: Language Rivalry or Accommodation?" *International Journal for the Sociology of Language* 211 (2011): 9–33. Due to lack of space, this sample of interdisciplinary work is highly selective.

10. For a constructionist perspective on language and identity, see Niloofar Haeri, "Form and Ideology: Arabic Sociolinguistics and Beyond," *Annual Review of Anthropology* 29 (2000): 61–87; and Yasir Suleiman, *Arabic Sociolinguistics: Issues and Perspectives*, 2nd ed. (London: Routledge, 2013).

11. For in depth reviews of such works, see Nicholas Harrison, *Postcolonial Criticism: History, Theory, and the Work of Fiction* (Cambridge: Polity Press, 2003), Réda Bensmaïa, *Experimental Nations: or, the Invention of the Maghrib* (Princeton, NJ: Princeton University Press, 2009); and Karima Laachir, "Contemporary Moroccan Cultural Production: between Dissent and Co-optation," *Journal of African Cultural Studies* 25 (2013): 257–260.

12. Jane E. Goodman, "Writing Empire, Underwriting Nation: Discursive Histories of Kabyle Berber Oral Texts," *American Ethnologist* 29 (2002): 86–122; Katherine

E. Hoffman, *We Share Walls: Language, Land, and Gender in Berber Morocco* (Malden, MA: John Wiley & Sons, 2008); Paul A. Silverstein, *Algeria in France: Transpolitics, Race, and Nation* (Bloomington, IN: Indiana University Press, 2004); and Charis Boutieri, "In Two Speeds (À Deux Vitesses): Linguistic Pluralism and Educational Anxiety in Contemporary Morocco," *International Journal of Middle East Studies* 44 (2012): 443–464.

13. Katherine A. Woolard and Bambi B. Schieffelin, "Language Ideology," *Annual Review of Anthropology* 23 (1994): 55–82; and Laura M. Ahearn, "Language and Agency," *Annual Review of Anthropology* (2001):109–137.

14. While a central pillar of the decolonizing agendas of Morocco, Tunisia, and Algeria, the policy of Arabization was implemented differently in the countries. For a thorough dissection of the three, see Gilbert Granguillaume, *Arabisation et linguistique politique au Maghreb* [Arabization and Language Policy in North Africa] (Paris: Maisonneuve & Larose, 1983).

15. Haeri, "Form and Ideology," 63–64.

16. Even though *tarifit*, *tashelḥit* and *tamazight* are regional classifications (subsuming further local difference), I label the wider group of these registers as *amazighi-yya*. However, I single out the standardized version of these vernaculars developed by IRCAM and transcribed in *tifinagh* alphabet as *Tamazight* (with a capital T).

17. The reflections of this chapter draw on ethnographic fieldwork on the urban public educational landscape from 2005 to 2011 with a sustained presence in Morocco between 2007 and 2009. The irony of formulating this argument in English while having conducted research in *dārija*, *fuṣḥā*, and French is certainly not lost on the author, who—while not Moroccan—is herself deeply implicated in the neoliberal landscape that makes *anglophonie* a hegemonic scholarly register and mode of access to academic and professional opportunity.

18. Irene Fernandez Molina, "The Monarchy vs. the 20 February Movement," 436.

19. For an analysis of the linguistic bifurcation of the Moroccan educational system, see Boutieri, "In Two Speeds."

20. Ibid.

21. The International Bank for Reconstruction and Development, *The Road Not Traveled: Education Reform in the Middle East and North Africa* (Washington, D.C.: World Bank, 2007); and Mohammed Bin Rashid al-Maktoum Foundation (MBRF), The United Nations Development Programme, and the Regional Bureau for Arab States (UNDP/RBAS), *Arab Knowledge Report 2010/2011: Preparing Future Generations for the Knowledge Society* (Washington, D.C: UNDP 2011).

22. *Wizārat al-tarbiya al-waṭaniyya wa-l-takwīn al-mihnī* [Ministry of National Education and Professional Training], 2008. *Malaf shāmil li-mashāriʿ al-barnāmaj al-istiʿjālī* 2009–2012 [Executive Summary of Projects for the Emergency Program 2009–2011], Al-mamlaka al-maghribiyya [Kingdom of Morocco]. http://portail.men.gov.ma/Prog_urgence_ar/default.aspx; accessed 10 September 2010.

23. For instance, French in Tunisia was an elite register in the late nineteenth century before the onslaught of French imperialism, evident in the founding of the first bilingual high school Lycée Sadiqi in 1875. Moreover, colonial administration in Algeria classified Arabic as a foreign language of instruction while in Morocco and Tunisia it preserved a bilingual model for mass education. For Tunisia, see Francis Manzano, "Le Français en Tunisie, enracinement, forces et fragilités systémiques: Rappels historiques, sociolinguistiques et brefs éléments de prospective [French in Tunisia: its Embeddedness and Systemic forces and Counterforces: Historical and Sociolinguistic Accounts and Brief Projections]" *International Journal for the Sociology of Language* 211 (2011): 53–81. For Algeria, see Mohamed Benrabah, "Language Maintenance and Spread: French in Algeria."

24. UNICEF, "At a Glance: Morocco," http://www.unicef.org/infobycountry/morocco_statistics.html.

25. MBRF, UNDP, RBAS, *Arab Knowledge Report 2010/2011*, 13–23.

26. The provision of the Francophone baccalaureate option was the product of an agreement signed between the French and the Moroccan Ministers of Education, Vincent Peillon, and Rachid Benmokhtar on 18 February 2014. See "Accords France/Maroc: Education et Baccalauréat International," *H24info*, http://www.h24info.ma/maroc/accords-france/.
maroc-education-et-baccalaureat-international/20224.

27. For a full transcript of the interview, see Driss Ksikes, "M. Chafik: Les dégâts de l'élite sont énormes," *Economia* [The Elite Has Caused Enormous Damage], http://economia.ma/fr/numero-10/e-revue/m-chafik-les-degats-de-l-elite-sont-enormes. Aldous Huxley, *Brave New World* (London: Vintage Classics, 2007 [1931]).

28. Ksikes, "M.Chafik".

29. Melani McAlister, "A Cultural History of the War without End," *The Journal of American History* 89 (2002): 439–455.

30. Shana Cohen, *Searching for a Different Future*; Mohamed Benrabah, "Language Maintenance and Spread: French in Algeria;" and Elizabeth Buckner, "The Seeds of Discontent: Examining Youth Perceptions of Higher Education in Syria," *Comparative Education* 49 (2013): 440–463.

31. Bonnie Urciuoli, "Skills and Selves in the New Workplace," *American Ethnologist* 35 (2008): 211–228. For a work that focuses on language, see Monica Heller, "The Commodification of Language," *Annual Review of Anthropology* 39 (2010): 101–114.

32. As research among students, parents, and teachers has suggested, school participants, even those who live in predominantly Amazighophone areas, view Tamazight as an addition to a weighty linguistic workload with limited professional potential. Mohamed Errihani, *Language Policy in Morocco: Implications of Recognizing and Teaching Berber* (Chicago, IL: University of Illinois at Chicago, 2007).

33. For the full speech see Assdae.com, "Khiṭāb al-malik Mohammed al-sādis

bi-munāsabat al-dhikrā al-sittūn li-thawrat al-malik wa-l-shaʿb" [The Speech of Mohammed the Sixth on the 60ᵗʰ Occasion of the Revolution of the King and the People," http://www.assdae.com/23943.

34. On the longevity of this skepticism, see Charis Boutieri, "The Abandoned Classroom and the Arab Spring," *Anthropology News* 53 (December 2012): 42.

35. Vijay Prashad, "Second-Hand Dreams," *Social Analysis* 49, no. 2 (2005): 191–198.

36. Emma C. Murphy, "Legitimacy and Economic Reform in the Arab world," *The Journal of North African Studies* 3 (1998): 71–92; Larbi Sadiki, "Political liberalization in Bin Ali's Tunisia: Façade Democracy," *Democratization* 9 (2002): 122–141; and Béatrice Hibou, *La force de l'obéissance; économie politique de la répression en Tunisie* [The Force of Obedience: The Political Economy of Repression in Tunisia] (Paris: Sciences Po—CNRS, 2006).

37. There is a sustained scholarly debate on the pedagogical dimensions of religious education in Morocco: Daniel A. Wagner, *Literacy, Culture and Development: Becoming Literate in Morocco* (Cambridge: Cambridge University Press, 1993); Helen N. Boyle, *Quranic Schooling* (New York, NY: Routledge, 2004); and Charis Boutieri, "Inheritance, Heritage, and the Disinherited: Ambiguities of Religious Pedagogy in the Moroccan Public School," *Anthropology & Education Quarterly* 44 (2013): 363–380.

38. "Mobachara Ma3Akom Nordine Ayouch et Abdel Aaroui," YouTube video, 28 November 2013, http://www.youtube.com/watch?v=_ad6bq5BbDs/.

39. For the Clean Art campaign, see Said Graiouid and Taieb Belghazi, "Cultural Production and Cultural Patronage in Morocco: the State, the Islamists, and the Field of Culture," *Journal of African Cultural Studies* 25 (2013): 261–274. For the Action Group Free Culture, see Karim Boukhari, "Tribune: pour une culture libre au Maroc [Tribute: For Free Culture in Morocco]," Slate Afrique, http://www.slateafrique.com/87035/-pour-une-culture-libre-au-maroc-%20mohammedvi.

40. For a review of some of these written works, see Alexander E. Elinson, "Dārija and Changing Writing Practices in Morocco," *International Journal of Middle East Studies* 45 (2013): 715–730. In the domain of music, see Cristina Moreno Almeida, "Unraveling Distinct Voices in Moroccan Rap: Evading Control, Weaving Solidarities, and Building New Spaces for Self-Expression," *Journal of African Cultural Studies* 25 (2013): 319–332.

41. The closing of Nichane, the Arabophone equivalent of the weekly magazine *Tel Quel* is the most publicized case in point. Launched in 2006, Nichane endured two lawsuits, one for publishing Moroccan popular jokes in *dārija* and one for addressing an open letter to King Mohamed VI in *dārija*. Supporters of Nichane have argued that its persecution and eventual closure, a result of the withdrawal of its advertisers, indicate that the Moroccan state prohibits the dissemination of critique in what is considered the most widely spoken register in the country. For

details, see Miller, "Observations concernant la présence de l'arabe marocain dans la presse marocaine arabophone des années 2009–2010."

42. For an exploration of the relationship between art and state in relation to the Moroccan Jewish minority, see Oren Kosansky and Aomar Boum, "The 'Jewish Question' in Postcolonial Moroccan Cinema," *International Journal of Middle East Studies* 44 (2012): 421–442.

43. For a critical reading of its operations, see Paul Silverstein and David Crawford, "Amazigh Activism and the Moroccan State," *Middle East Report* 233 (2004): 44–48.

44. Béatrice Hibou, "Le Mouvement du 20 Février, le Makhzen et l'antipolitique. L'impensé des réformes au Maroc [The February 20 Movement, the Makhzen and Anti-Politics: The Unthinkable Reforms in Morocco]," *Sciences Po-CNRS* (2011), http://www.ceri-sciences-po.org/.

45. Tellingly, the 20 February Movement refused to take part in the electoral campaign of June 2011. Their main slogan "mawsawtinch" (We will not vote) and other relevant statements disavowed the whole party system without being able to propose an alternative to it. Desrues, "Le Mouvement du 20 Février et le régime marocain," 22.

46. Fondation Zakoura Education, "Sabīl al-najāḥ, Le chemin de la réussite [Pathway to Success]," Colloque international sur l'éducation [International Conference on Education], Fondation du Roi Abdul-Aziz al-Saoud, Casablanca 4–5 October 2013, 2.

47. Yousef Ait Akdim, "Maroc: Fouad Ali el-Himma dans un cabinet royal XXL [Morocco: Fouad el-Himma in an extra extra large Royal Cabinet]" *Jeune Afrique*, 14 December 2012, http://www.jeuneafrique.com/Articleimp_ARTJAJA2657 p020.xml0_maroc-fouad-ali-el-himma-dans-un-cabinet-royal-xxl.html/.

48. www.assdae.com, "khitāb al-malik mohammed al-sādis".

49. Ibid.

50. Ibid.

51. Fondation Zakoura Education, "Sabīl al-najāḥ," 11.

52. Ibid., 7.

53. Aziz Allilou, "Morocco's Minister of Education: French is No Longer Valid, English is the Solution," *Morocco World News*, 29 March 2014, ttp://www.moroccoworld-news. com/2014/03/126856/moroccos-minister-of-education-french-is-no-longer-valid-english-is-the-solution/.

54. Burton Bollag, "Conversation with Tunisia's Higher Education Minister," *al-Fanar Media*, 9 April 2014, http://www.al-fanarmedia.org/2014/04/conversation-tunisias-new-higher-education-minister/.

55. Susan Slyomovics, "100 Days of the 2011 Moroccan Constitution," *Jadaliyya*, 30 June 2011, http://www.jadaliyya.com/pages/index/2023/100-days-of-the-2011-moroccan-constitution/.

7. THE POLITICS OF THE HARATIN SOCIAL MOVEMENT IN MAURITANIA, 1978–2014

1. See CNN report: www.cnn.com/.../mauritania.slaverys.last.stronghold/; see also Adam Nossiter, "Mauritania Confronts Long Legacy of Slavery," *New York Times*, 11 November 2013.
2. See Urs P. Ruf, *Ending Slavery: Hierarchy, Dependency and Gender in Central Mauritania* (Frankfurt: Transcript Verlag, 1999); Meskerrem Brhane, "Narrative of the Past, Politics of the Present. Hierarchy, Dependency and the Haratins of Mauritania" (PhD diss., University of Chicago, 1998).
3. Z. Ould Ahmed Salem, "Bare-foot activists: Transformations of the Haratin (*former slaves*) Movement in Mauritania," in *Movers and Shakers: Social Movements in Africa*, ed. Stephen Ellis and Ineke van Kessel (Leiden: J. Brill, 2009), 156–177.
4. See for example Alexis Okeowo, "Freedom Fighter: A slaving society and an abolitionist's crusade", *The New Yorker*, 8 September 2014.
5. N. Foster, *Mauritania: The struggle for Democracy* (Lynne Rienner Publishers, 2011), 2–3.
6. R. Botte, *Esclavages et abolitions en terres d'Islam* (Paris: André Versaille Editeur, 2010), 208; see also M. Bhrane, "Narrative of the Past, Politics of the Present: Identity, Subordination and the ḥaraṭines of Mauritania" (PhD diss., University of Chicago, 1998), 41, n. 1.
7. Urs P. Ruf, *Ending Slavery: Hierarchy, Dependency and Gender in Central Mauritania*, 93–105.
8. O. Kamara, "Les divisions statutaires des descendants d'esclaves au Fuuta Toora mauritanien," *Journal des Africanistes*, 70, 1–2 (2000): 265–289; Y. Sy, "L'esclavage chez les Soninkés: du village à Paris," *Journal des Africanistes*, 70, 1–2 (2000): 43–69; Olivier Leservoisier, "'Nous voulons notre part!' Les ambivalences du mouvement d'émancipation des Saafaalbe Hormankoobe de Djéol (Mauritanie)," *Cahiers d'études africaines*, no. 179–80 (2005): 987–1014.
9. Kamara, "Les divisions statutaires," 266, n. 2.
10. I have documented this process of former slaves becoming imams in Z. Ould Ahmed Salem, *Prêcher dans le désert. Islam politique et changement social en Mauritanie* (Paris: Karthala, 2013), chap. 5.
11. See E. Ann McDougall, "Living the Legacy of Slavery: Between Discourse and Reality," *Cahiers d'études africaines*, 179–180 (2005): 957–986.
12. For an excellent analysis of the situation, see the Amnesty International study, *Mauritania: A future free from slavery?*, London, 7 November 2002.
13. See her full report here: http://www2.ohchr.org/english/issues/slavery/rapporteur/docs/A.HRC.15.20.Add.2_en.pdf; see also Amadou Seck, "L'esclavage à la peau dure," *Courrier International*, November 2009.

14. See Walk Free: www.globalslaveryindex.org.

15. For an analysis of some cases brought before courts, see Z. Ould Ahmed Salem, *Prêcher dans le désert. Islam politique et changement social en Mauritanie*, chapter 6.

16. See Joel Quirk, "Ending Slavery in all its Forms: Legal Abolition and Effective Emancipation in Historical Perspective," *The International Journal of Human Rights*, 12:4 (2008), 529–55.

17. See Meskerrem Brhane, "Narrative of the Past, Politics of the Present. Hierarchy, Dependency and the Haratins of Mauritania").

18. Abdel Wedoud Ould Cheikh, "L'évolution de l'esclavage dans la société maure," in E. Bernus and P. Boilley (eds.), *Nomades et Commandants. Administration et sociétés nomades dans l'ancienne AOF* (Paris: Karthala, 1993), 181–193.

19. El-Hor, *Charte Constitutive*, Nouakchott, 5 March 1978, quoted in *L'Ouest saharien—Cahiers d'Etudes Pluridisciplinaires*, 4, Paris, L'Harmattan (2004): 183–188.

20. Ibid.

21. Ibid.

22. John Mercer, *Slavery in Mauritania Today*, Anti-Slavery International, London, 1981.

23. El Arby Ould Saleck, *Les Haratins: Le paysage politique mauritanien* (Paris: L'Harmattan, 2003).

24. El-Hor, "Les Haratins. Contribution à une compréhension juste de leur problématique," typescript, Nouakchott, 5 March 1993.

25. El Arby Ould Saleck, "Les Haratins comme enjeu pour les partis politiques en Mauritanie," *Journal des Africanistes*, 70, 1 (2000): 255–263.

26. Alice Bullard, "From Colonization to Globalization. The Vicissitudes of Slavery in Mauritania," *Cahiers d'études africaines*, 179–180 (2005): 751–769.

27. Some of these reports are available at: www.sosesclaves.org.

28. See the weekly *Mauritanie-Nouvelles*, 236 (28 January 1997): 12–13.

29. The Islamists of Tawasul who were part of the FNDD had decided to put up their own candidate. On the whole episode, see Noel Foster, *Mauritania: The Struggle for Democracy* (Boulder and London: Lynne Rienner Publishers, 2010).

30. Interview with the author, Nouakchott, May 2010.

31. Biram Ould Dah Ould Abeid, "*al-tashriu li al-riq khidmatan li-istimrarihi*" (legislation on slavery as a means of perpetuating it), *al-Raya*, 3 January 2006.

32. See the archives on the following sites: www.cridem.mr; see also, in Arabic, www.alakhbar.info, www.ani.mr, www.saharamedias.net.

33. Cheikh Ould Hassine was accused of enslaving two boys named respectively Said and Yarg aged 13 and 8 in 2011. For this and other stories, see: http://biramdahabeid.org/esclavage/.

34. On this case, please see: http://www.huffingtonpost.com/2011/01/17/middle-east-self-immolation_n_809935.html.

35. For example: El Hor movement, *Hartani, mon Frère* (Akhuk al-Hartani), a clandestine tract.
36. These refugees were repatriated to Mauritania between 2007 and 2012 as part of a government program supported by the UNHCR.
37. The document is still available, under the title "al-ba'th wa alharatin", "the Ba'ath and the Haratins", a typescript of some twenty pages.
38. "L'enjeu haratine," *Sud Magazine*, 4 (January 1987): 1.
39. Interview with *L'Autre-Afrique*, 57 (6 August 1997): 26.
40. Interview with the author, Nouakchott, May 2008.
41. Interview with the author, Jemal Ould Yessa, Dakar-Nouakchott, September 2008.
42. See Ahmed Salem, *Prêcher dans le desert*.
43. See Alexis Okeowo, "Freedom Fighter. *A slaving society and an abolitionist's crusade*".

8. KEEPING UP WITH THE TIMES: THE GROWTH OF SUPPORT FROM NON-STATE ACTORS FOR THE POLISARIO LIBERATION MOVEMENT

1. D.L.P. Byman, B. Chalk, B. Hoffman, W. Rosenau and D. Brannan, *Trends in outside support for insurgent movements* (Santa Monica: RAND's National Security Research Division, 2001).
2. Elizabeth Dickinson, "Playing with Fire: Why Private Gulf Financing for Syria's Extremist Rebels Risks Igniting Sectarian Conflict at Home," *The Brookings Institute* (2013): 1–27.
3. The four kinds of movements identified by Clapham were: anti-colonial liberation movements, separatist movements, reformist insurgencies and warlord insurgencies. Christopher Clapham, "Introduction: analysing African guerrillas," in *African Guerrillas*, ed. Christopher Clapham (Oxford: James Currey, 1998), 6–7.
4. Media reports can highlight Algerian support for Polisario e.g. http://www.bbc.co.uk/news/world-africa-14115273, last accessed 4 December 2017. Pro-Moroccan positions often frame Western Sahara as a conflict between Morocco and Algeria, as Anna Theofilopoulou has pointed out. See Anna Theofilopoulou, *Western Sahara: how to create a stalemate* (United States Institute of Peace, 2007). Available at http://www.usip.org/publications/western-sahara-how-create-stalemate, last accessed 4 December 2017.
5. See Jacques Roussellier and Anouar Boukhars, *Perspectives on Western Sahara: myths, nationalisms, and geopolitics* (Lanham, MD: Rowman & Littlefield, 2014), Stephen Zunes and Jacob Mundy, *Western Sahara: War, Nationalism and Conflict Irresolution* (Syracuse: Syracuse University Press, 2010).
6. Whilst Algeria's influence is at times transparent, e.g. in Polisario's acceptance of the second Baker plan for a referendum in Western Sahara, at other times Western Sahara is left off Algeria's public agenda. See Yahia Zoubir, "Tipping the balance

towards inter-Maghreb unity in light of the Arab Spring," *The International Spectator: Italian Journal of International Affairs* 47 (2012): 83–99.

7. In addition to shorter field trips in 2006, 2011, 2012 and 2014 in the refugee camps, and in 2012 in Moroccan-controlled areas of Western Sahara, I conducted two years of ethnographic fieldwork with Sahrawi refugees 2007–2009 with a geographical focus on the refugee camps. Living with local families, I studied sovereignty and revolutionary state power in exile. The main language of research was the Hassaniya dialect of Arabic, which I learnt.

8. On states' support for insurgency movements during the Cold War, see Cary Fraser, "Decolonization and the Cold War," in *The Oxford Handbook of the Cold War*, ed. Richard H Immerman and Petra Goedde (Oxford: Oxford University Press, 2013).

9. Byman, Chalk, Hoffman, Rosenau and Brannan, *Trends in outside support for insurgent movements*.

10. See ibid., 50.

11. Gyda Marås Sindre, "Rebels and Aid in the Context of Peacebuilding and Humanitarian Disaster: A Comparison of the Free Aceh Movement (GAM) and the Tamil Tigers (LTTE)," *Forum for Development Studies* 41 (2013): 1–21.

12. See e.g. Liisa H. Malkki, *Purity and Exile: Violence, Memory and National Cosmology Among Hutu Refugees in Tanzania* (Chicago: University of Chicago Press, 1995), Aihwa Ong, *Buddha is Hiding. Refugees, Citizenship, the New America* (Berkeley: University of California Press, 2003).

13. See Tony Hodges, *Western Sahara: Roots of a Desert War* (Beckenham: Croom Helm, 1983), 149–56. For wider discussion of Sahrawi nationalism, see Zunes and Mundy, *Western Sahara: War, Nationalism and Conflict Irresolution*, Pablo San Martín, *Western Sahara: The Refugee Nation* (Cardiff: University of Wales Press, 2010).

14. Hodges, *Western Sahara: Roots of a Desert War*: 149–56.

15. Julio Caro Baroja, *Estudios Saharianos* (Madrid: Consejo Superior de Investigaciones Científicas, Instituto de Estudios Africanos, 1955); Angel Domenech Lafuente, "Sáhara Español: del vivir nómada de las tribus," *Cuadreno de Estudios Africanos* 21 (1953): 31–43.

16. See Hodges, *Western Sahara: Roots of a Desert War*: 153–5.

17. Ibid., 159.

18. Ibid., 162.

19. Hodges, *Western Sahara: Roots of a Desert War*, 162.

20. Ibid.

21. Michael J Willis, *Politics and Power in the Maghreb: Algeria, Tunisia and Morocco from Independence to the Arab Spring* (London: Hurst, 2012), 273.

22. Ibid., 273–274.

23. Ibid., 277.

24. See ibid., 274–275.

25. Hodges, *Western Sahara: Roots of a Desert War*, 193.

26. Ibid.

27. On Algerian military support for Polisario, see Zunes and Mundy, *Western Sahara: War, Nationalism and Conflict Irresolution*, 42.

28. The UNHCR gave a figure of 165,010 in its yearbooks for 2002, 2003 and 2004. This figure is based on estimates, overlooks one refugee camp and overlooks population growth. See Dawn Chatty, Elena Fiddian-Qasmiyeh and Gina Crivello, "Identity with/out territory: Sahrawi refugee youth in transnational space" in *Deterritorialized youth: Sahrawi and Afghan refugees at the margins of the Middle East*, ed. Dawn Chatty (Oxford: Berghahn Books, 2010), 41. Using satellite images, the World Food Program estimated 100,000 refugees in 2005. See Zunes and Mundy, *Western Sahara: War, Nationalism and Conflict Irresolution*, 107.

29. See Carmen Gómez Martín, *La migración saharaui en España: Estrategias de visibilidad en el tercer tiempo del exilio* (Saarbrücken: Editorial Académica Española, 2011). SADR provides SADR passports, which are valid in countries which recognize SADR.

30. For a list of 80 recognitions of SADR by states as at 2006, including 22 cancellations or suspensions, see Anthony Pazzanita, *The Historical Dictionary of Western Sahara* (Lanham, Md; Oxford: The Scarecrow Press, 2006), 376–8. SADR has been a full member of the African Union since 1984.

31. E.g. James Firebrace and Jeremy Harding, *Exiles of the Sahara: the Sahrawi refugees shape their future* (London: War on Want, 1987), Christine Perregaux, *L'école sahrouie: de la caravane à la guerre de libération* (Paris: L'Harmattan, 1987).

32. Jacob Mundy, "Autonomy & Intifadah: New Horizons in Western Saharan Nationalism," *Review of African Political Economy* 108 (2006): 255–67.

33. See Alice Wilson, "On the margins of the Arab Spring," *Social Analysis* 57 (2013): 81–98.

34. For a discussion, see idem, *Sovereignty in Exile: a Saharan Liberation Movement Governs* (Philadelphia: University of Pennsylvania Press, 2016), 204–235.

35. Article 32 of the SADR 1991 constitution, available at http://porunsaharalibre.org/constitucion-de-la-rasd-19-de-junio-de-1991/, last accessed 4 December 2017. The constitution continues to be revised at Polisario General Congresses.

36. See Wilson, *Sovereignty in Exile: a Saharan Liberation Movement Governs*, 183–203.

37. On the political and practical dimensions of the different migratory trajectories of Sahrawi refugees, see Alice Wilson, "Cycles of crisis, migration and the formation of new political identities in Western Sahara," in *Crises et migrations dans les pays du sud*, ed. Marc-Antoine Pérouse de Montclos, Véronique Petit and Nelly Robin (Paris: Harmattan, 2014).

38. Carmen Gómez Martín and Cédric Omet, "Les 'dissedences non dissidentes' du Front Polisario dans les camps de réfugiés et la diaspora sahraouis," *L'annee du maghreb* V (2009): 205–222.

39. All names of interlocutors are pseudonyms.

40. Michael Bhatia, "Western Sahara under Polisario Control: Summary Report of Field Mission to the Saharawi Refugee," *Review of African Political Economy* 88 (2001): 293.

41. See http://www.unpo.org/members.php, last accessed 4 December 2017. Closer to home to Polisario, the Haratin movement in Mauritania (see Ould Ahmed Salem, this volume), for Mauritanians descended from former slaves (and for some of whom conditions of slavery are reported to continue), is a member of UNPO.

42. Gómez Martín, *La migración saharaui en España: Estrategias de visibilidad en el tercer tiempo del exilio.*

43. See Zunes and Mundy, *Western Sahara: War, Nationalism and Conflict Irresolution*, 128. There is ongoing controversy surrounding the number of refugees in the refugee camps, relating to the sensitivity of aid provision and the number of potential voters in a referendum.

44. Gómez Martín, *La migración saharaui en España: Estrategias de visibilidad en el tercer tiempo del exilio*, 121, note 208.

45. Ibid., 120.

46. On the role of diasporic communities as actors in conflicts in their homeland, see Hazel Smith and Paul Stares, *Diasporas in conflict: peace-makers or peace-wreckers?* (Tokyo, New York, Paris: United Nations University Press, 2007).

47. Gómez Martín, *La migración saharaui en España: Estrategias de visibilidad en el tercer tiempo del exilio*, 131.

48. Ibid., 37 note 57.

49. Ibid., 129.

50. Ibid., 129.

51. Ibid., 130.

52. Ibid., 58. All translations are mine unless otherwise stated.

53. Ibid., 130.

54. Gómez Martín, *La migración saharaui en España: Estrategias de visibilidad en el tercer tiempo del exilio*, 104, note 166.

55. Ibid., 104, note 166.

56. As my visits to other ministries at this time suggested, such facilities were something of a luxury in the refugee camps.

57. I knew one such judge myself who had migrated from the refugee camps to France in the hope of finding work there.

58. See Silverstein, this volume, Jane E Goodman, *Berber culture on the world stage: From village to video* (Bloomington: Indiana University Press, 2005).

59. On the annual cinema festival, see see http://fisahara.es/?lang=en last, accessed 4 December 2017. On the art festival, see http://www.artifariti.org/en/, last accessed 4 December 2017.

9. FILM AND CULTURAL DISSENT IN TUNISIA

1. El Général song "Rais Lebled" ("Head of State") inspired demonstrations throughout Tunisia and forced Ben Ali's regime to arrest the rapper on 6 January 2011, only to release him three days later following public and international pressure. For more on El Général and the role of Arab rap in the Arab uprisings, see Nouri Gana, "Rap and Revolt in the Arab World," *Social Text* 30.4 (2012): 25–53.

2. See Nouri Gana, "Introduction: Collaborative Revolutionism," in *The Making of the Tunisian Revolution: Contexts, Architects, Prospects*, ed. Nouri Gana (Edinburgh: Edinburgh University Press, 2013), 1–31; Nouri Gana, "Rapping and Remapping the Tunisian Revolution," in *Resistance in Contemporary Middle Eastern Cultures: Literature, Cinema and Music*, eds. Karima Laachir and Saeed Talajooy (Oxford: Routledge, 2013), 207–225; "Rap and Revolt in the Arab World," *Social Text* 30.4 (2012): 25–53. All of these writings, including this chapter, are part of a larger project, tentatively entitled *Ben Ali, Dégage: A History of Cultural Dissent in Tunisia (1934–2011)*.

3. I am partly inspired here by Michael Warner who complains about the fact that "the only way a public is able to act is through its imaginary coupling with the state" before he adds: "This is one of the things that happen when alternative politics are cast as social movements—they acquire agency in relation to the state. They enter the temporality of politics and adapt themselves to the performatives of rational-critical discourse. For many counterpublics, to do so is to cede the original hope of transforming, not just policy, but the space of public life itself," see Michael Warner, "Publics and Counterpublics," *Public Culture* 14.1 (2002): 89.

4. Arguably, the very creation of ERTT (Etablissement de la radiodiffusion télévision tunisienne) in 1961 and SATPEC (Société anonyme tunisienne de production et d'expansion cinématographique) in 1964 to facilitate the distribution of information and the production of local films came as a response to the refusal of a French laboratory to return the processed film of the massacre (of 1,300 Tunisians) committed by the French army in Bizerte in 1961. For more on the entanglements of cinema and state, see Florence Martin, "Cinema and State," in Josef Gugler, ed., *Film in the Middle East and North Africa: Creative Dissidence* (Austin: University of Texas Press, 2011), 271–83.

5. See Kmar Kchir-Bendana, "Ideologies of the Nation in Tunisian Cinema," *The Journal of North African Studies* (2003): 38. The article offers an elegant panoramic view of Tunisian cinema around the question of nation and national identity (*tunisianité*). Whether or not, though, Tunisian cinema, as Kchir-Bendana concludes, is "obliged to organise and present itself as 'national cinema' in a market where it has to face other national cinemas" (42) remains a debatable contention that, if tenable, risks homogenizing both the production and consumption of Tunisian cinema, which would not redound to anyone's benefit, except to that of the market industry.

6. Ferid Boughedir, "Malédictions des cinémas arabes," *CinémAction* 43 (1987): 10–15.

7. See Hédi Khelil, *Le parcours et la trace: Témoignages et documents sur le cinéma tunisien* (Salammbô: MediaCon, 2002), 387.

8. See Roy Armes, *Postcolonial Images: Studies in North African Film* (Bloomington: Indiana University Press, 2005), 48.

9. Nouri Bouzid, "New Realism in Arab Cinema: The Defeat-Conscious Cinema," *Alif: Journal of Comparative Poetics* 15 (1995): 249.

10. Laura Mulvey, "Moving Bodies: Interview with Moufida Tlatli," *Sight and Sound* (1995): 18. Note in passing that both Bourguiba and Ben Ali harped on the mantra of women's freedom as an alibi for holding on to power. See Monica Marks, "Women's Rights before and after the Revolution," in ed. Nouri Gana, *The Making of the Tunisian Revolution*, 224–251.

11. Roland Bleiker, *Popular Dissent, Human Agency and Global Politics* (Cambridge and New York: Cambridge University Press, 2000), 16.

12. Nouri Bouzid, "On Inspiration," in eds. Imruh Bakari and Mbye B. Cham, *African Experiences of Cinema* (London: British Film Institute, 1996), 49.

13. Nouri Bouzid, "New Realism in Arab Cinema: The Defeat-Conscious Cinema," *Alif: Journal of Comparative Poetics* 15 (1995): 249.

14. The Bey is the representative of the Sultan of the Ottoman Empire in Constantinople. Tunisia was technically a satellite state of the Ottoman Empire since the sixteenth century, but in reality it became an autonomous state ruled by the Hussein Dynasty of Beys (1705–1957). The Bardo Treaty (12 May 1881) established Tunisia as a French protectorate, a form of indirect governance, at once ending the Bey's rule yet retaining his reign. France wanted to preserve the façade of beylical sovereignty (under the principle of co-sovereignty) so as to spare itself the ugly work of empire (taxation and conscription).

15. See Peter Shabad, "The Most Intimate of Creations: Symptoms as Memorials to One's Lonely Suffering," in *Symbolic Loss: The Ambiguity of Mourning and Memory at Century's End*, ed. Peter Homans (Charlottesville and London: University of Virginia Press, 2000), 197–212.

16. In Viola Shafik, *Arab Cinema: History and Cultural Identity*, revised edition (Cairo: American University in Cairo Press, 2007), 194.

17. For more on this, see Nouri Gana, "Bourguiba's Sons: Melancholy Manhood in Modern Tunisian Cinema," *The Journal of North African Studies* 15.1 (2010): 105–126.

18. Nouri Bouzid, "On Inspiration," in eds. Imruh Bakari and Mbye B. Cham, *African Experiences of Cinema* (London: British Film Institute, 1996), 54.

19. Jeffrey Ruoff, "The Gulf War, the Iraq War, and Nouri Bouzid's Cinema of Defeat: *It's Scheherazade We're Killing* (1993) and *Making of*," *South Central Review* 28.1 (2011): 31.

20. For more on this, see Nouri Gana, "Bourguiba's Sons: Melancholy Manhood in

Modern Tunisian Cinema," *The Journal of North African Studies* 15.1 (2010): 105–126.

21. See Nouri Gana, ed. *The Making of the Tunisian Revolution.*
22. Ibid., 19.

10. "CURATING THE MELLAH": CULTURAL CONSERVATION, JEWISH HERITAGE TOURISM, AND NORMALIZATION DEBATES IN MOROCCO AND TUNISIA, 1960s–2017

1. Cnaan Liphshiz, "Moroccan King funding preservation of Cape Verde Jewish heritage—but to what end?" 13 May 2013, available at: http://www.jta.org/2013/05/13/news-opinion/world/moroccan-king-funding-preservation-of-cape-verde-jewish-heritage-but-to-what-end.
2. http://www.algemeiner.com/2014/01/16/tunisia's-next-tourism-minister-will-be-jewish/.
3. Aomar Boum, *Memories of Absence: How Muslims Remember Jews in Morocco* (Stanford: Stanford University Press, 2013).
4. Aomar Boum, "'Sacred Week': Re-Experiencing Jewish-Muslim Co-existence in Urban Moroccan Space" in Glenn Bowman, ed. *Sharing the Sacra: The Politics and Pragmatics of Inter-Communal Relations around Holy Places* (London: Berghahn Books, 2012), 139–55.
5. André Levy, "To Morocco and Back: Tourism and Pilgrimage among Moroccan-born Israelis" in *Grasping Land: Space and Place in Contemporary Israeli Discourse and Experience*, eds. Eyal Ben-Ari and Yoran Bilu (Albany, NY: State University of New York Press, 1997), 25–45; Oren Kosansky, *All dear unto God: Saints, Pilgrimage and Textual practice in Jewish Morocco*, Unpublished Ph.D. Dissertation (University of Michigan, 2003); Oren Kosansky, "Tourism, Charity, and Profit: The Movement of Money in Moroccan Jewish pilgrimage," *Cultural Anthropology* 17:3 (2002): 359–400.
6. Emily Gottreich, *The Mellah of Marrakesh: Jewish and Muslim Space in Morocco's Red City* (Bloomington, IN: Indiana University Press, 2006).
7. Susan Gilson Miller and Muaro Bertagnin, eds. *The Architecture and Memory of the Minority Quarter in the Muslim Mediterranean City* (Wilmington, MA: Kirkwood Printing, 2010).
8. Emily Gottreich, "Rethinking the Islamic City from the Perspective of the Jewish Space," *Jewish Social Studies* 11:1 (2004): 118–146.
9. Albert Memmi, *The Pillar of Salt* (Boston: Beacon Press, 1992), 7.
10. Aomar Boum, *Memories of Absence: How Muslims remember Jews in Morocco* (Stanford: Stanford University Press, 2013).
11. Said Ghallab, "Les Juifs vont en enfer," *Les Temps modernes* (April 1965): 2247–2251, 2249.
12. Barbara Kirshenblatt-Gimblett, *Destination Culture: Tourism, Museums, and Heritage* (Berkeley: University of California Press, 1998), 10.

13. http://www.strabotours.com/destinations/tours.php?tour=148 and http://www.tunisiatours.org/tours/jewish-heritage-tour/.

14. André Levy, "To Morocco and Back: Tourism and Pilgrimage among Moroccan-born Israelis", in *Grasping Land: Space and Place in Contemporary Israeli Discourse and Experience*, eds. Eyal Ben-Ari and Yoran Bilu (Albany, NY: State University of New York Press, 1997), 30–31. Also see Alex Weingrod and André Levy, "Paradoxes of Homecoming: The Jews and their Diaspora," *Anthropological Quarterly* 79:4 (2006): 691–716.

15. Frank Stern, *The Whitewashing of the Yellow Badge: Antisemitism and Philosemitism in Postwar Germany*, William Templer, trans. (Oxford, England: Pergamon Press, 1992).

16. Marion Kaplan, "Antisemitism in Postwar Germany," *New German Critique* 58 (1993): 97–108, 105.

17. Dimitri Ionnides and Mara Cohen Ioannides, "Jewish Past as a 'foreign country': The Travel Experiences of American Jews," in Tim Coles and Dallen Timothy, eds. *Tourism, Diasporas and Space* (New York: Routledge, 2004), 95–110.

18. Ruth Gruber, *Virtually Jewish: Reinventing Jewish Culture in Europe* (Berkeley: University of California Press, 2002), 5.

19. Ibid., 6.

20. Erica Lehrer, *Jewish Poland Revisited: Heritage Tourism in Unquiet Places* (Bloomington: Indiana University Press, 2013), 57.

21. Ibid., 56.

22. Jack Kugelmass, "The rites of the tribe: American Jewish Tourism in Poland," in *Museums and Communities: The Politics of Public Culture*, Ivan Karp, Christine Mullen Kreamer, and Steven D. Lavine, eds. (Washington D.C.: Smithsonian Institution Press, 1992), 382–427.

23. Michael Laskier, *Israel and the Maghreb: From Statehood to Oslo* (Gainesville, FL: University of Florida Press, 2004), 210–211.

24. Michel Abitbol, "From Coexistence to the Rise of Antagonisms," in *A History of Jewish-Muslim Relations: From the Origins to the Present Day*, eds. Abdelwahab Medeb, Benjamin Stora (Princeton, NJ: Princeton University Press, 2013), 298.

25. Laskier, *Israel and the Maghreb*, 187.

26. Ibid., 210–211.

27. "Interview with King Hassan II," *Al-Ahram* (24 December 1977).

28. Arlette Berdugo, *Juives et juifs dans le Maroc contemporain: Images d'un devenir* (Paris: Librairie Orientaliste Paul Geuthner S. A., 2002), 98.

29. Ibid.

30. Ibid.

31. Mark Tessler and Linda L. Hawkins, "The Political Culture of Jews in Tunisia and Morocco," *International Journal of Middle East Studies* 11:1 (1980): 59–86, 72.

32. http://www.jta.org/2014/02/21/news-opinion/world/moroccan-demonstrators-protest-exhibition-on-sephardic-jews.

INDEX

INDEX

Ali, Mouldi: leader of Jabhat al-Islah, 48
Alliance Israèlite Universelle: establishment of, 195
Almohad Caliphate (1121–1269 CE): 35
Almoravid (Al-Murabitun) Empire (1040–1147 CE): territory of, 34
Amar, David: 197–8
Amari, Raja: 171
Amazigh/Berbers (ethnic group): 74, 89, 94, 203; activism, 75–9, 81–8, 91, 162, 201–2; culture of, 79, 82, 90; diaspora of, 74, 88; language of (Tamazight), 74–7, 79–80, 82–3, 85–6, 89–91; militancy, 75, 89; poetry, 80; state efforts to appropriate movements, 81–2, 86; *Tafsut Imazighen* (Berber Spring), 80; Tifinagh (script), 79–80, 82, 90
Amazigh Association for Culture and Patrimony: 89–90
Amazigh Cultural Movement (MCA): 87; members of, 84
Amazigh Supreme Council: 90
American Association to Advance Collegiate Schools of Business (AACSB): 113
American exceptionalism: 107
American Institute of Research: 111
Amrouche, Taos: role in founding of ABERC, 79
Ansar al-Din: 47
Ansar al-Sharia (AST): 28–9; affiliates of, 30; founding of, 47; supporters of, 29
Anti-Slavery International: 125
Arab-Barometer: 21
Arab League: 196
Arab Maghreb Union: proposed creation of, 89
Arab Spring: 1–5, 8–11, 13–15, 25,

27–8, 46–7, 50, 73, 95, 98, 109, 133–4, 189; Algerian Protests (2011–12), 74; Bahraini Uprising (2011–14), 74; Egyptian Revolution (2011), 6, 22, 62–6, 74, 134; Libyan Civil War (2011), 48, 74–5; Morocco Protests (2011–12), 23, 55, 62–3, 74, 93; role of organized labor associations in, 51–4, 63, 71; Syrian Civil War (2011–), 29, 66, 74, 143; Tunisian Revolution (2010–11), 6, 9, 47, 62–6, 74–5, 89, 134, 165–7, 174, 181, 201; Yemeni Revolution (2011–12), 74
Arabic (language): 34, 42, 81, 86, 94, 104, 117, 119; *darija* (spoken Arabic), 7, 98, 103, 107, 109–10; *fusha* (Classical Arabic), 93, 97–8, 102, 105, 108–9; role in national identity, 42–3, 86
al-Arfaoui, Latifa: 166
Assaraf, Robert: 197–8
Assidon, Sion: 197
Association for Integration and Durable Development: members of, 85
Association of the Ulema (*Jam'ayyat al-ulema al-muslimin al-aljaza'iriyyin*): political influence of, 42–3; *al-Shihah* (The Meteor), 42
ibn Ata Allah, Taj al-Din: 35
Attia, Ahmed Baha Eddine: 170–1
Augustine, St: 80
Australia: Tamil diaspora of, 147
Ayouche, Noureddine: 'Sabil al-najah, le Chemin de la réussite' (Pathway to Success)(2013), 108, 111–13
Azoulay, André: 197, 202; nominated as economic advisor to Moroccan throne (1992), 199–200
Azoulay, Maxim: 197
Azzam, Abdullah Youssef: 43–4, 50

240

INDEX

121–3, 125; coup d'état (1978), 125; coup d'état (1979), 125; coup d'état (1984), 126; coup d'état (2005), 130–1; coup d'état (2008), 119, 131; economy of, 119; French Colony of (1904–60), 121; Haalpulaar population of, 119; Haratin population of, 117–18, 120; justice system of, 122; National Assembly, 126, 132; River, Senegal, 120; slavery in, 119–24; Soninke population of, 119, 121; Supreme Court of, 133; Wolof population of, 119, 121

M'bareck, Sghair Ould: administration of, 126

M'barek, Sonia: 166

McAlister, Melani: 104

Mehenni, Ferhat: founder of MAK, 84; Provisional Government of Kablia (Anavad Aqvalyi Usdil), 84

Meir, Golda: 196

Meijer, Roel: 30

Memmi, Albert: *Pillar of Salt, The*, 190–1

Messaoud, Boubacar Ould: 127–9; president of SOS-Slaves, 139; role in formation of El-Hor, 124

Mezouar, Salaheddine: Moroccan Minister of Finance, 64

Microsoft Corporation: personnel of, 111

Military Committee for Justice and Democracy (CMJD): role in Mauritanian coup d'état (2005), 130

Military Committee of National Salvation: passing of Abolition Act (1981), 125

Mimouna: members of, 202

al-Moqrani, Muhammad bin Ahmed: 34

Mohamed V, King: exile of (1953–5), 56

Mohamed VI, King: 49, 71, 94, 107, 112, 189, 200; address to nation (2013), 105–6; cultural strategy of, 44–5

Moroccan Association of Cultural Research and Exchange (AMREC): 82, 89; founding of (1967), 79

Moroccan Observatory Against Normalization with Israel: 202

Morocco: 5–6, 10–11, 14–17, 20–1, 27, 30–1, 34–5, 46, 61, 78, 80–1, 84–5, 87, 94–9, 104, 111, 136, 148–9, 152, 155, 187, 189, 191–2, 194, 197–8, 201; Agadir, 80, 86; agricultural sector of, 59–60; Bani Zarwal 35; Berkane, 40; Casablanca, 55–6, 65–7, 106, 202; Casablanca Bombings (2003), 44, 49; Casablanca Riots (1952), 56; Casablanca Riots (1981), 58; Ceuta, 35; Constitution of (1962), 58, 86; Constitution of (2011), 7–8, 16, 114–15; Draa, 201; economy of, 110; education sector of, 102–4, 108, 112–14; Educational Emergency Plan (2008), 102; Errachidia, 86; Fez, 35–8, 42, 46; French Protectorate of (1912–56), 42, 78, 115; government of, 82; High Atlas, 77, 81–2; al-Hoceima, 86; Independence of (1956), 56, 86, 188; Jewish heritage of, 9–10; Jewish population of, 188–9, 194–5, 197, 199–200, 202–3; Khouribga, 72; labor unions in, 52–4, 62–71; Larache, 66; *Majlis al-A'la li'l-Ta'lim* (High Council for Education), 102; Marrakesh, 201; Meknes, 88; Middle Atlas, 77, 82; Midelt, 77; Ministry of Education, 66, 104; Ministry of Finance, 65; Ministry of Health, 66; Ministry of Interior, 77; Mogador, 199; Nador,

INDEX